Preaching Well

Preaching Well

The Rhetoric and Delivery
of Sacred Discourse

Originally published in 1950

William R. Duffey
Former Professor of Speech
Marquette University

ROGER A. MCCAFFREY PUBLISHING
POST OFFICE BOX 1209 • RIDGEFIELD, CT 06877

ISBN 0-9661325-3-X

Even so we speak, not as pleasing men,
but God, who proveth our hearts.
St. Paul (1 Thess. 2:4)

Preface

This textbook presents principles of speech training for seminarians. It is not only a rhetoric of oratory but a manual concerned with the important matter of oral style in religious discourse, mechanics of speech, methods of presentation, and vocal and literary interpretation.

Quintilian has remarked that for the listener the importance is not in the thoughts as we conceive them so much "as it is in what manner we express them." People are moved only as they hear and see. Delivery, or the manner of speaking, is most important to a preacher who has a mission as a minister of Christ's Gospel to speak to man of his duties, and arouse him to his gravest interest — his salvation. A preacher, then, must not only put his thoughts clearly and effectively in symbols; he must have the speech ability to make himself agreeable to others and to persuade them to act as he wishes them to act. In other words, he must have skill in the manner of speaking as well as in the manner of composing. The purpose of this textbook is to help the preacher gain these skills.

The scope of the textbook is indicated in its subtitle, rhetoric and delivery. These two terms indicate a field broad enough to allow the author to discuss the structure, the division, and development of a speech and the kinds of pulpit address, as well as to analyze the advantages and disadvantages of the memoriter, extempore, and impromptu methods of presentation, the general notions of action in sacred oratory, visible speech, voice and diction, and the oral interpretation of Sacred Scripture. The problems of delivery are specifically attacked, for the author seeks to aid the seminarian or young priest in diagnosing his own difficulties, and he suggests for him means in the correction of his vocal faults, bodily mannerisms, and errors of diction. He would have him avoid artificialities and develop delivery as a response to thinking and feeling.

The author has not included here excerpts from speeches or literary selections inasmuch as works of extracts or abridged sermons are easily available. Although exercises and suggestions for practice are given in this textbook, the author has devised no set program, but has left this matter to the judgment of the individual teacher.

Much of the material for this volume the author collected during the past thirty years for his regular public speaking courses, certain special courses in preaching arranged for seminarians and young priests of the Milwaukee Archdiocese, and conference periods in remedial speech for groups of religious. In writing the present work in conformity with the suggestions made by certain teachers of sacred eloquence, he found it expedient to adapt material from his translation of *Manuel D'Éloquence Sacrée* written by L. Bellefroid, professor of Rhetoric and Sacred Eloquence in the Minor Seminary of St. Trond. This text has for years enjoyed great popularity among teachers of Sacred Eloquence in the European seminaries. Many teachers who used the translation in their classes were impressed with the ideas of Canon Bellefroid who wrote authoritatively on the nature of sacred oratory, the training of the preacher, and the advantages to be gained from knowing the specific characteristics of the forms of pulpit oratory.

For aid in the translation of *Manuel D'Éloquence Sacrée* the author of the following material on preaching expresses his thanks to Père Damase Caron of the Society of the Priests of the Sacred Heart, and to Mr. John F. Duehren, assistant professor of French, Marquette University. For help in copying and editing the manuscript, he is under obligation to Miss M. Phyllis Morris and Mrs. Anne Williamson. He acknowledges his indebtedness to his teachers, Dr. S. S. Curry and Anna Baright Curry of the School of Expression, Boston. Thanks is especially due to the Redemptorist Fathers of Oconomowoc, Wisconsin, for the use of their library in the collection of material.

W. R. D.

WHAT DISTINGUISHES THE PREACHER FROM THE SECULAR SPEAKER[1]

The Mission of the Preacher

The sacred orator is the depositary of that mission which God the Father gave to God the Son. Almighty God gave His Son to man not only to accomplish man's redemption, but also to endow man with the means whereby to profit by the adequate atonement. The Saviour was sent to earth to instruct man and establish truth. This mission came directly from God the Father (Luke 4:18; John 7:16; 8:26; 14:24; Matt. 17:5). In the councils of the three adorable persons of the Trinity, it was decided that not only must the Son of God take man's nature in order to satisfy God's justice, but He must live among men, creating in them by His word a new man, the new Adam, raising them from the slavery of senses to a new life (Matt. 4:4; John 10:10).

Awaiting the time when this double mission of the Son would be accomplished, God did not abandon His people. He spoke to the holy patriarchs, afterward to Moses, and to pious persons who transmitted His message to the people by living voice or writing. God raised up men who were the depositaries of the divine word and the interpreters of the truth (Matt. 23:2). Finally the Son of God, without leaving the bosom of His Father, appeared on earth (Hebr. 1:1; John 1:14).

After thirty years of seclusion, during which Christ prepared Himself for preaching, He was baptized by John, and fasted forty days. He then came into towns to announce the glad tidings of redemption, holding Himself rigorously within the limits of His mission (Matt. 15:24; Mark 10:18). He spoke with simplicity,

---

[1] This introductory material is chiefly a summary of Book I, Canon L. Bellefroid's *Manuel D'Éloquence Sacrée* (Liége, 1845).

placing His doctrine within the grasp of all men. He preached
to the poor and simple countryfolk, a fact which He offered to
John as a sign of His mission (Matt. 11:5). Although strict with
Himself, He was compassionate toward others whom He instructed, consoled, and in many instances cured of diseases. He
received sinners in His presence and ate with them. Having come
to save men, not to destroy them, He refused to strike with light-
ning the Samaritan village that had closed its doors against Him
(Luke 9:55). He spoke with authority, as a legislator and teacher
(Mark 1:22), and confirmed His doctrines by miracles. Finally
He bequeathed His mission to the ministers of His Gospel
(2 Cor. 5:20).

The Apostles whom Christ chose for the mission of evangelizing
the world learned from His divine lips both His doctrine and the
manner of teaching it (Rom. 10:17; Gal. 1:12). They accompanied
Him in His public life so that they might later serve as witnesses
to His words and deeds (Acts 1:8; John 15:27; Acts 1:21 f.).
That the Apostles might obtain greater results from their mission,
Christ gave them in private more perfect understanding of things
that had mystified them (Mark 4:34). Later He sent them the
Holy Ghost (John 16:7-14). He conferred upon them the power
of miracles and of preaching true doctrines (Matt. 10:1-8). After
His resurrection He appeared to His followers and, on a mountain
in Galilee, commissioned His Apostles to teach His truth to all
nations (John 20:22; Matt. 28:16-20; Mark 16:14-18). After
Pentecost, having received power and enlightenment, the Apostles dispersed throughout the world.

The successors of the Apostles have received from age to age
the heritage to preach the word of God. Christ remains incarnated,
hidden under the voice of the preacher who, like another John
the Baptist, procures for souls a new birth, forming Christ in
man and making him another Christ (Gal. 2:20; 4:19). As
each day the Son of God is given to man in the Holy Sacrifice
of the Mass, He obtains a new and mystical birth in the hearts
of men by the Holy Spirit who makes use of the words of
preachers to procure this action. There is a legitimate succession
of the holy word. The word of which the preacher is the minister

must be heard with great respect (Luke 10:16; Matt. 10:14 f.). It comes to him from Christ, who has perpetuated His word in the word of His envoy as His body is perpetuated under the sacramental species. Through Christ the word soars to the bosom of the Father where its birth is eternal.

Difference Between Preacher and Secular Speaker. Since the word of the preacher is truly the word of God (2 Cor. 5:20), there is an essential difference, of importance to the audience as well as to the preacher, between a preacher and any secular orator. The lay speaker and the preacher agree in their immediate purpose, persuasion; their use of the same general means, observance of proper formalities, enlightenment of the intellect, stimulation of the emotions, and penetration of the will; and they follow the same law of correct utterance drawn from nature and perfected by experience; but they differ in the nature of the matter each is called upon to treat. Sacred eloquence communicates to man the highest, most certain, and most essential truths dealing with his life and death, his eternal happiness or suffering; it reveals to him the existence of a Creator, a Redeemer, and a Rewarder; it directs him to his destiny; it speaks to him of duties; it fills his memory with images of events of lofty significance; it inflames his imagination with wonderful pictures of God's ways and works; it arouses not one emotion, but all emotions; it captivates man with its appeals, because it touches his gravest interests: salvation, heaven, hell, and eternity.

The preacher and the lay speaker speak under different circumstances. The priest delivers his sermons before an altar consecrated to religion. If he calls upon God, God is present upon the altar. If he talks of death, people remember funeral Masses in the same church. If he extends his hands, people recall that this day his fingers have touched the adorable body of Jesus Christ. People hear the preacher in religious silence. They do not presume freedom to question his opinions; they listen as disciples to a teacher who has authority to instruct them. Coming from all ranks, fortunes, and walks of life, they are assembled before the preacher to hear truth and follow doctrines.

The Preacher as an Instrument. The preacher who fails to understand his true position as a dispenser of God's word and as mediator between Creator and creature, will generally fail to make himself a useful instrument in the hands of God. The idea of the noble functions of preaching should inflame the zeal of anyone preparing himself for it. Who would dare to speak the divine word if God had not commanded it (John 20:21)? Keeping in mind that he is speaking in the name of the King of kings, he will not fear either wise men or rulers (1 Cor. 1:25; Jer. 1:17). Under the strong protection of Him whose holy will he discloses, he cannot become fainthearted. He will apply the words that the Almighty spoke to Moses, who excused himself because of slowness of tongue, "I will be in thy mouth: and I will teach thee what thou shalt speak" (Exod. 4:10–12). He will teach holy doctrine with the voice of authority (Mark 1:22).

No preacher who remembers that he is an instrument will have difficulty with purity of intention. He will not seek the praises of men or pervert the word (John 7:18). He will not profane it, making a holy thing an instrument of vanity (2 Cor. 2:17; 4:2). He will remember the glory of Him he represents and the salvation of souls, and he will count on the special assistance of grace to assure his success.

The Word of God. The preacher will look beyond created things for the origin of the holy word. God the Father knows His own infinite perfections, and from eternity this infinite intelligence of Himself is substantial, and constitutes a Second Person who is the expression of His thought, *Verbum*. This Second Person in created time, clothed in flesh, appeared to man in two manners: in the truth of His flesh; and in the truth of His word (Bossuet, *Sermon on the Word of God*). Christ lives among men in two forms. He has instituted ministers charged with the perpetuation of His mission as well as His real presence. In the Eucharist the species we see are signs. Beneath these appearances is the body of Christ. In preaching the words are signs. The thought that produces them and that the words carry into the mind of the hearer is the true doctrine of the word of God.

The word of God, then, is the channel of grace, and an important grace. Its qualities operate in the soul with gentleness but also with force (Wisd. 18:15). A marvelous strength in the mouth of Christ, it was also a power on the lips of Moses, Josue, Elias, and other holy men. It is especially admirable when it is exercised on the free will of man, and like beneficent rain gives life to the soil it waters (Isa. 55:10 f.); yet it may be a double-edged sword (Hebr. 4:12), or a hammer which breaks rock, or a living flame (Jer. 23:29; Luke 24:32). Christ Himself declared His word is spirit and life (John 6:64; 14:6). If the word does not bring life to the soul, it strikes it down to eternal death. As he who receives the body of Christ unworthily, receives it unto condemnation, so will he who with evil receives Christ's word have that word turned against him (John 12:48).

The virtue in the divine word is inherent and is independent of the talent, sanctity, and intention of the priest who speaks it. It has built the Christian Church; it has conquered a world. It is the word which helps to preserve in the world, faith, hope, and charity, the virtues, and the generous inclinations. It is efficacious in the mouth of the preacher who has done everything he can to become a useful instrument in the hands of God.

Few listeners are critical of Holy Scripture unless they lose sight of its divine character. If they do, they will not recognize the voice of God in the mouth of the preacher. St. John Chrysostom holds that man has an obligation to hear the holy word of God. No man fulfills this precept who feels that the power of God's word is dependent on the qualities of him who utters it. People who have faith in the word receive it submissively as the teaching of God Himself. People who have no faith in Holy Writ are like the Jews who would not receive the word of Christ as the word of God: "Is not this the carpenter's son?" (Matt. 13:55–57; John 6:42.) But the Jews were chastised for their disbelief (Matt. 10:15).

Contents

PART I. STRUCTURE

PART II. DIVISION AND DEVELOPMENT

PART III.   KINDS OF PULPIT ADDRESS

PART IV.   DELIVERY

PART V.   PRESENTATION AND INTERPRETATION

PART I

STRUCTURE

❧

Newman has said that if a preacher has a definite purpose in his preaching, and never wanders from his aim, or never allows his audience to drift away from it, he has accomplished most of his task. Once the aim of a sacred discourse is clear, it is not difficult to collect material to further this objective. To observe how this subject matter can best be arranged and developed to serve his purpose, the orator prepares a tentative plan to guide his preparation, and when necessary, an outline to direct him in the course of his speech. The principles of speech composition in relation to aims, collection of material, and plan for a sacred discourse furnish the content of Part I of this text.

CHAPTER I

Choosing a Subject

The preacher's first task is to study the nature and meaning of his subject, to learn what it is that he must accomplish, to know the limits of his efforts, and to decide what is necessary in order to convince others of his views or to persuade them to action.

1. *Determining a Subject in Light of the General Aims in Speaking*

The preacher must know the purpose of his speech before he can make a wise choice of subject. He must have in mind an objective for a particular audience, otherwise he may fail to select the right subject and may not use every proper means to attain his goal. Whether he should acquaint his audience with this purpose at the beginning of a speech depends upon the type of speech, the condition of the audience, and like considerations. In most deliberative and judicial discourses, the proposition expressing the speaker's general aim is well known. But whether or not the preacher explicitly states his purpose, he himself must always know it in order to determine the most effective means of gaining it.

A speaker may or may not have an ulterior purpose for speaking. He may wish to gain applause, to earn money, to hold a position, to demonstrate his ability, or merely to seek pleasure. These ulterior objectives influence the rhetorical purpose of speech in relation to audience reaction, but they are not the general ends in speaking.

Five General Aims. But what can a speaker have in mind as a general aim of a speech?

a) Instruction. He may decide to instruct an audience. If so, he can use the proved means which rhetoric offers him for promoting instruction, and he can avoid other means as waste of time or perhaps as actual hindrances to the gaining of his objective. His chief interest will be in exposition, although description and narration, even perhaps argumentation, may have some value.

b) *Conviction.* He may determine not to instruct only, but to convince his audience of some truth. He may use instruction in part as a means, but his aim is to prove some proposition. He wishes the audience to believe something. He puts into his speech only that which promotes his objective, and omits everything, no matter how good it may be of itself, that will not help to further his purpose. His chief means of conviction will be the rhetorical tools of argumentation.

c) *Action.* A speaker may wish to move his audience to undertake some particular action, *e.g.,* to go to church. It would be one aim to instruct this audience about the advantages of going to church; it would be another purpose to convince the audience intellectually that it should go to church; finally, it is entirely another objective to set out to get the audience to go to church. The end of this speech is not obtained until the action has resulted.

It is true, of course, that some people will undertake an action as soon as they have received an explanation of it. Others will begin with action once they are convinced of some truth. Yet others need to be motivated to action. They must be influenced and specifically directed. One man may give money to a missionary as soon as he hears his needs. Another understands the situation, but must be convinced that money will accomplish a definite purpose before he contributes. Yet another man not only must evaluate what is going on in the mission and be convinced that money will gain some objective, but he must be motivated by being assured of his own reward before he will make his donation. Generally that man needs to know the second collection has been designated for the missions, and not the first which will be for the church. To get him into action, he must not only be persuaded but given specific directions as to the manner of the action, and he must be told how to perform it with the least amount of effort. If the preacher decides that his purpose is to move his listeners to some overt action such as putting money in a collection box, he uses from among hundreds of rhetorical means those which will effect this aim.

d) *Feeling.* A speaker may not be especially interested in having an audience do any one thing in particular, such as going to Communion frequently; yet he is concerned with making his listeners feel deeply about some truth. He is aware the emotions will not act the same way or for the same end in each person, but he builds his talk with the hope of getting a general pattern of emotional action. Narration and description will be most helpful in building up the images which will incite emotions.

e) *Entertainment.* Amusement of an audience is a well recognized end of a speech. Entertainment varies in degree, of course, from intellectual enjoyment to downright physical laughter. It is inconsistent, if entertainment is to be the objective of a speech, to attempt to instruct, to create belief, or to promote action and feeling. It is especially absurd when the chief aim of a speech is instruction, conviction, action, or feeling to attempt to introduce entertainment as an end. True, an anecdote may be in place in a speech of instruction, but only as a means of instruction, or as one way to keep the attention of the audience.

Any one of the five general aims of speeches may serve any other, but one purpose must be the dominant or chief objective in speaking.

Restricting the general aims. The preacher, as a preacher, cannot have recourse to all the general aims of speaking. He is restricted in his religious work chiefly to instruction, conviction, action, and feeling. He can propose no other end than to edify people and to bring to the hearts of his listeners a useful persuasion for their salvation: nor can he have any ulterior purposes which would encourage him to parade his knowledge or brilliant style, to develop a reputation as a man of wit, cleverness, or erudition.

Specific Aims. The speaker wishes *someone* to believe *something*. He aims, likewise, not to teach *anything,* but to instruct an audience in some particular subject matter. In preparing a speech which aims at action, the speaker should have an idea of the precise action he wants, and often he should commit an audience to some overt act such as raising hands to express affirmation to some resolution, or to stand — any act will do which crystallizes the listeners' sentiments and sustains their resolution.

Within each of the general aims of speaking are potentially many particular ones. The speaker should know exactly what his specific aim is to be. To get a clear view of it, he should phrase it very carefully for himself. Putting an expression of purpose into a statement, theme, or proposition often sharpens and clarifies the idea for the speaker himself, and helps him to settle his mind as to what he is not to say as well as to what he will say. It will help him also to evaluate the necessary steps in taking his audience into his confidence in regard to his objective.

2. *Requirements of a Good Subject*

In choosing a subject, a preacher must give preference to the one which will bring the most benefits to his hearers, or the one most suitable and useful in the light of all the accompanying circumstances.

Practical. With this criterion in mind, he will find some subjects too delicate, some too intricate, and some too critical for the purposes of the general discourse. A sermon on the final condition of children dying without baptism or the chances for the salvation of heretics may call for erudition but may have little effect on the salvation of souls. Some subject matter is too puerile to lend itself to a pulpit discourse. Sermons dealing with the different kinds of luxury, the various vanities of women may get newspaper publicity, but they will bring few sinners to the confessional.

An important theme dealing with a beautiful and strong truth from which listeners can draw some conclusions against abuse is worth while. In choosing subjects like the obligation of baptism, the spirit of Christianity, contempt of the world, the dangers of an occasion of sin, there is a firm approach to battle against disorders.[1] The preacher not only traces rules of conduct but he applies them so that reason remains in the minds of the listeners, and persuasion endures. Sound subject matter does not

---

[1] *Manuel D'Éloquence Sacrée*, p. 115 f.

offend the petty affections of listeners as does a topic dealing with fashion or recreation. If the "sins of society" type of sermon is necessary, even then general moral truths should first be developed and proved so that the audience cannot so easily reject consequence of moral principles as mere dicta of some preacher. Doubtless, some subjects are more appropriate to a philosophy or theology class than to a pulpit, and likewise some matters of behavior are of more interest to the lecture hall than to the sacred rostrum.

Circumstances. In choosing a subject, a preacher must remember the circumstances under which his speech will be given. Consideration of time, place, conditions, and interests of the hearers and the capabilities of the preacher are important. Some subjects are for the city, some for the country; subjects agreeable to worldly people may be inappropriate for pious people. A poorly instructed congregation requires subjects not necessary for the well-educated group. For many church days no free choice for a sermon is allowed and certain liturgical periods, Lent and Advent, for example, do not permit a treatment of every kind of topic.

The degree of intelligence of the audience must be remembered and also the degree of authority on the part of the preacher which the audience will accept. The subject that the preacher can use to secure conviction and persuasion, and be of profit to listeners, is one that the listeners know has interested the preacher vitally, and upon which they feel he has reflected with much feeling.

Ordering of Subjects. There is naturally an advantage in arranging in some logical order a choice of subject matter.[2] The list must be adequate, and important matter must not be ignored. The chief truths of religion must be explained as well as vices common to the parish. Sometimes it is prudent to ask the advice of parishioners concerning the choice of subject matter, or, especially, the effect on the people of a particular kind of sermon. But the success of a discourse should not encourage a pastor to choose subjects at random. The truths of religion have

[2] *Ibid.*, p. 118 f.

great strength in their mutual dependence. Fénelon has well said, "There is no art or science that is not taught in consecutive order and methodically, and it is only religion that, by abuse, is taught otherwise."

Among the chief subjects which ought to find their way into any plan of presenting dogmatic and natural truths are: God; the Holy Trinity; the Attributes of God; Creation; the Fall of Man; Religion at the Time of Christ; the Person of Our Saviour; the Mysteries of Jesus Christ and of His Blessed Mother; the Descent of the Holy Ghost; the Foundation of the Church — its Character and Authority; the Word of God; the Sacraments (one or more sermons on each sacrament); the Obligations of Christians; the Christian Spirit; Detachment From the World; Mortal Sin; Venial Sin; Perseverance; Redemption; Occasions of Sin; the Holy Mass; Frequent Communion; Education; Vocation and the State in Life; the Last End; the Commandments of God and the Church; the Virtues; the Vices; Good Works; and Particular Devotions.

Although these general subjects are listed, the seminarian should remember that any specific discourse within a course of sermons cannot be a mere series of considerations, still less a group of thoughts and phrases on the particular topic. A speech tends to establish one objective by various means, and to persuade someone of an important truth. A sermon, for example, is more than a theme; it is a blend of parts into a whole, a combination of means, a perfect unity from which persuasion can result.

Determination of the Viewpoint. The preacher will find from experience the wisdom in determining a particular viewpoint and fixing in his mind the precise way in which he will treat the truth. If he visualizes his audience, and the circumstances of the speech, perhaps considering the audience as a single person in whom he has a vital interest, he will have a viewpoint that is not general and speculative, fitted only for a cold dissertation in the manner of a school exercise. He will have a definite viewpoint also, if he thinks of an audience as an adversary who must be overcome for his own interest and salvation. In his plan for the sermon, he imagines himself reasoning with his adversary.

The preacher sees what he is thinking, what he is objecting to, attacks him quickly with his arguments, and follows him to places where he cannot escape.

A viewpoint must be neither too comprehensive nor too narrow. Too wide in scope, a subject cannot be treated in its completeness; too confined, the matter is not sufficient for productive development, and the temptation then may come to fall into digressions or generalities. Take, for example, a discourse on a virtue; it is necessary not only to avoid treating its opposite vice (unless there is reason for a contrast being introduced) but to limit the instruction to the excellence of the virtue, its necessity, its results, or its practice. Again, it is impossible to cover adequately all phases of any sacrament in a single sermon; the subject should be limited to some of its aspects or to a summarized concise treatment of the sacraments as a whole. Such generalizing has a place in preaching.

But there is another type of generalization that is worthless. Macaulay (*Machiavelli*) has well observed that "Every man who has seen the world knows that nothing is so useless as a general maxim." Some preachers perhaps feel safe in treating a general social or religious theme when the audience has interest in the fate of an individual or a specific situation. Although it is less specific to urge people to go to church than to persuade them to attend Mass, both themes have their value. But to use generalities to clothe empty resolutions, cheap appeals, and popular abstractions, or to veil the disagreeable, will not gain the purpose of preaching. Sometimes general propositions on such subjects as Communism, the Russian influence, the Protestant belief, the Catholic notion of education — subjects that too often gain their strength from the interpretation given to them by each preacher — are not properly explained, and consequently the address strengthens prejudices rather than focuses the mind upon the details of the subject that must be known in the interest of truth.

According to Professor Hill of Harvard, a sermon cannot help people if it contains nothing but generalities. Even if a preacher decides to treat a matter broadly, he still must have in mind a definite proposition suitable to a particular audience. No discourse is good that does not fit the one audience present to the speaker. Dr. S. S. Curry of the School of Expression in Boston often remarked in his lectures to preachers, "A sermon equally good for any audience is assuredly a sermon good for no audience."

Professor Austin Phelps maintains the view that much of the clerical humdrum style comes from a mental attitude that glorifies a series of generalities (*Theory of Preaching*). Professor Hill finds a tendency in some preachers to cover a number of points while neglecting to press home any of them. They devise a strong development with little meaning, yet because they suggest many thoughts and images to people, they justify their wanderings as effective preaching. They feel that if a sermon has a definite point it may miss some sinner whereas by scattering the attack they gain a chance of hitting everybody. This view is not in accord with the opinions of rhetoricians and successful preachers. To these men a sermon must have unity to be effective.

The viewpoint must include the needs of the hearers. Abelly, a distinguished teacher of sacred eloquence, has said that "if there are few preachers who make converts . . . there are few who devise a practical plan . . . the salvation of the auditors was a thing about which they had never thought." Bellefroid feels that some preachers become so fascinated with the subject of religion that they forget to instruct or to help listeners with the means of fulfilling their duties.

Summary

In choosing a subject the general aims of speaking must be considered. The needs of the faithful come above everything else. Do the people ignore the truth of a dogma? Then the preacher must instruct them. Do they question a truth? Then he must prove it. Is there a disparity between their belief and their conduct? Then he must insist on the obligation which truth imposes upon them. The practice of morals must be stressed. Are passions in their hearts an obstacle to truth? He must oppose feeling with feeling, emotion with emotion. If necessary, certain of these viewpoints can be tied together in a discourse, each being modified according to the class of hearers and the means of examples and proof available.

In his treatment of any subject, the preacher must consider a Christian truth from a Christian viewpoint. He must have care, for example, not to confuse charity toward the poor with philanthropy, or humility with sweetness of character. The problem for the preacher is to have a clear purpose, use effective means to gain it, and thereby to answer the pressing needs of his audience with a Christian remedy.

CHAPTER II

THE MATERIAL OF SACRED DISCOURSE

1. *Collecting Material*

Every preacher has some ideas on the subject he has chosen and the viewpoint from which he will treat it, but these ideas, perhaps sufficient for his own direction, would not be adequate for the particular guidance of souls. More ideas, then, are needed; more content must be collected. Some five ways of getting material may be listed: observation, conversation, correspondence, reading, and reflection.

Observation. Personal investigation of any subject is worth while because it allows one to use his power of observation and utilize his experience. To use your senses, says a rhetorician, is to learn at firsthand how something feels to you; how it sounds, tastes, smells; and how it appears to your eyes. This experience gives life to all your subsequent images of the matter. The preacher will think more clearly and feel more deeply if he has direct experience with situations that will furnish him with material for his sermons. He has many opportunities through the confessional to hear about the problems of life. Through pictures, or perhaps by travel, he can gain a fair knowledge of the places known to Christ. He has other opportunities to make careful and full records of his experience, to undertake personal investigation, and to direct his observation.

Conversation. Talking a subject over with another interested person is a helpful way not only to get material but to strengthen one's opinion or to modify it in view of new information. A preacher generally has opportunity to "talk shop" with his co-workers; a seminarian, in particular, can discuss matters with his teachers and classmates. A person who is skilled in the technique of interviewing can gain much information, without seeming to impose upon the goodness of the informed person who is assisting him with his problem.

Correspondence. A common way to gain information is to write to those who are authorities on a subject. A preacher, generally busy with his duties as pastor or curate, has little time for correspondence. Yet there are times when a letter could be effective in getting information. If it does happen that the preacher seeks material by writing to someone, he should be sure before he writes that the information is not easily obtainable in books. He should address men, not general offices, and should ask for specific information.

Reading. This art is indispensable to the preacher who requires sure, precise understanding of some subject. For most speakers it is the chief means of getting material for speeches. Reading is also useful in making a matter better known, and perhaps of more importance to some people, it will stimulate the mind and often awaken the very ideas most needed.

On the other hand, reading may be a mere escape from thinking and personal observation, and may actually prevent a preacher from forming his own judgments and from collecting a variety of material. Some preachers need to learn that reading is not the only means of gathering material. Browsing in a library also is of value if it leads to an interest in keeping abreast of the material on a subject or guides one to knowledge of where material is found, but reading here and there in a library may be a waste of time for many people.

Specific reading calls for attention to material on a particular subject to the exclusion of interesting matter on other subjects. Even on one subject it is impossible to read everything. It is valuable to remember that selection of what is to be read is often more important to the speaker than what he has read. One book should be examined at a time until it has yielded everything possible for the development of certain points as indicated by a tentative outline. When searching for subject matter, it is well to look first for authoritative textbooks; then for reports, articles, and lectures; finally, current comments and criticisms should be examined. The reader should try to find material not only to support his case but to answer the strongest points against it. As the weight of an argument is important, he should read to get strong answers to objections; therefore he must use judgment in what to read, as well as in what to collect from reading. A discerning reader saves valuable time in his research.

"Read with pen in hand" is an old and valuable hint to speakers. They should record ideas, notions, proofs, authorities, images, even feelings. Good ideas not put on paper may be lost when the last idea received from reading drives out the earlier ones. Notes should be brief and they should be arranged in order as soon as possible.

The preacher generally will read for his speech material Holy Scripture, theological treatises, and ascetical works. These will furnish the strongest proofs and most moving considerations, and, perhaps for most preachers, more sure and precise notions and splendid action than any collection of sermons. In attempting to imitate the style, or to repeat the content of another preacher there is danger of copying his faults and a real threat to good thinking.

Reflection. No matter what means are used to collect material, reflection as a means of invention of thought should never be omitted. Reflection consists in placing matter under scrutiny, fixing thoughts in mind, and examining a subject in detail. If a preacher wishes to instruct, he must reflect upon all notions that contain the doctrine to be explained; if he wishes to convince, he reflects upon all the basic truths in the proofs which appear to him. He asks himself what is the most important thing to know about this point? What would make me admit this truth if I doubted it? Eventually, the preacher finds after consulting his intellect that it gives him intrinsic proofs, or proofs of reason, and after consulting his memory, it furnishes him extrinsic proofs or authorities.

When the preacher first reflects on his subject matter, some ideas may seem weak and insignificant. Deeper reflection, however, places ideas, proofs, and relationships in a clear light. Order, gradation, sequence, and unity are more exactly perceived after reflection, but what is of equal importance, the heart becomes vitally attached to certain thoughts, and, bringing warmth into the content, style, and action, it seeks its own share in establishing conviction and persuasion.

As the sacred orator must strive to persuade hearers, he should reflect on everything connected with his subject which can arouse feelings or awaken the emotions. The material for the Christian pulpit[1] is especially ample in its possibilities to incite every emotion, and the preacher is neglectful in preparation of his speech, who fails to discover the feeling value of ideas — some touching, others terrible, and others most consoling. All must be searched out and tested by the heart of the preacher. It is the warmth of an idea that is communicated to another idea, and subsequently gives warmth to a discourse. "Do you want to compose a speech?" asked de Besplas. "Then read a little, think more, feel much."

2. *Sources of Thought*[2]

When a preacher is seeking thought on a subject, he may find that certain topics will be helpful to him. It is often to his advantage to define a term, to enumerate facts, to consider a matter either from a general or a specific viewpoint, to search for causes or effects and antecedents or consequences, to draw comparisons, to establish differences, probabilities, and contraries, and to evaluate circumstances. In addition to thoughts which may be derived from within a subject matter, there are those extrinsic to it. The latter, topics of authority, are of particular value in furnishing thought to the preacher.

Definition. This topic gives an understanding of the nature and the principal qualities of a thing. It is either strict and philosophical or expanded and oratorical. In explaining a sacrament or a mystery, the preacher is obliged to give a strict definition. The same is true of some other subjects. For instance, when an audience understands that slander is an injury and a theft, the preacher can define an injury and apply the expression to a species of injury, slander.

---

[1] Consult *Manuel D'Éloquence Sacrée*, p. 127.

[2] Much of this matter has been abridged from the author's translation of Bellefroid's *Manuel D'Éloquence Sacrée*, pp. 128–160.

But the other kind of definition is more frequently used. This consists in an oratorical development suitable to set off a subject under a particular viewpoint by its nature and its principal qualities. Thus St. James defines human life: "For what is your life? It is a vapor which appeareth for a little while, and afterwards shall vanish away" (James 4:15), and in a previous chapter he defines the tongue (James 3:5–10). St. Paul gives a good definition of charity (1 Cor. 13:4–7). To define well is extremely useful in making a thing seem great, important, admirable, advantageous, praiseworthy, or, on the contrary, contemptible, dangerous, or dishonest. At times a preacher may begin by explaining what a thing is not in order to give a better understanding of what it is. Definition, then, can be by negation as well as by affirmation.

In a descriptive definition, one places an object vividly before the eyes, portrays it as if it were present, confines in its proper frame everything that is of a nature to characterize a vice, a virtue, a person. The definition by etymology sometimes gives proof, or at least is a way of presenting it cleverly and strikingly. "You are a monk," St. Jerome wrote to Heliodorus, "interpret the name that you carry. Why do you go then into worldly assemblies?"

The observation that in definition the sense of a term may seem to be clear, yet may have different meanings for different people, has value. Even the simplest terms have been subject to interpretations. Indeed, many legal, scientific, and literary terms require the opinion of experts for their interpretation.

The seminarian can gain practice in the use of this topic by giving a philosophical definition of life, a sacrament, hope, or a motive. In each case, he should state the genus he has used, and the specific difference. Let him check his definitions with authorities in particular fields. Let him give an oratorical definition of some religious subject: (*a*) by enumerating the parts of which it is composed; (*b*) by some effects; (*c*) by affirming some property; (*d*) by negation; (*e*) by some circumstance; (*f*) by figures of speech, principally comparisons and metaphors.

Enumeration. By lively enumeration of the parts of a thing, the whole becomes known. This topic of great charm and of importance is useful to the division, the subdivision, and the development of an idea. It may be employed in the introduction, refutation, and peroration, and is very necessary in amplification and in persuasion.

Genus and Species. The preacher may proceed from the part to the whole or from the whole to the part. If he starts from the fact that vice is odious, he may conclude that vanity, a species of vice, is odious. By going from the part to the whole, however, he cannot draw a rigorous conclusion unless he can affirm the same thing about all the species. He cannot affirm, for example, that virtue considered as a whole would be agreeable to God if he cannot affirm this fact of all the species belonging to virtue. Generally a speaker cites several examples which are concerned with the parts of a whole, and then leaves his auditors to conclude *a pari* the same thing of the other species.

The topic does not always serve as proof, but it can amplify or set off a subject. An audience is generally resentful when a preacher forgets the specific and delays too long upon a generality. There are times, however, when the preacher may use the topic of genus as a means to escape the boundaries of the text in order to treat a broad but useful principle. This device of oratory should be handled with caution.

Causes and Effects. There are four kinds of causes and consequently four kinds of effects that may be used in the development of the sacred discourse:

a) The Church often recalls to the mind of man his *material cause*. St. Basil remarks, "You glorify yourself in your beauty, in your riches, in the nobility of your grandparents . . . human pride . . . remember man that you are dust. . . . "

b) *Formal cause.* That which relates to its form characterizes a thing and makes it different from another thing. "Our soul is immortal, why seek pleasure in perishable things? It was created to the image of God, why disgrace it?"

c) *Efficient cause.* This is the producing cause: St. Paul proves the virtue of baptism by this reason that it was not instituted by man, but by Christ.

d) *Final cause.* This is the motive which makes us operate. Accordingly, as this cause exists or does not exist a thing is probable or not probable. This reason is used to demonstrate that a man is probably innocent of a crime of which he is accused; on the contrary, there is always a presumption against him if he had reasons of interest or passion.

Rhetoricians sometimes mention another cause termed *instrumental*. Medicine may be an instrumental cause of recovery from illness.

In controversy the preacher may deny the causes in order to attack the effects. Effects may be related to the inherent power in the cause. Frequently arguments are drawn from effect. We see order all about us and from this effect we can reason a cause. Many fallacies are related to the use of cause and effect.

Comparison. This act relates one thing to another, a different but analogous thing. There are three kinds of comparisons. One draws a conclusion from the more to the less: St. Paul remarks that if God has given us His own Son, if He has suffered to the death for us, would He still refuse us? Another comparison is from the less to the more: "Look at the birds of the air," says our Saviour, "your heavenly Father takes care to feed them: are you not worth much more to Him than many sparrows?" (Cf. Matt. 10:31.) In these two ways of reasoning a speaker concludes *a fortiori;* but in the first case, the first of the two objects compared is the more; in the second case, it is the less which is mentioned first. The third kind of comparison is equal to equal: "If what we know of the works of God is so divine and so admirable, why do we not conclude that what we do not know of these works is also divine and admirable?" (Massillon.) "If God inspires courage, He has not given less of the other great natural and supernatural qualities, both of heart and mind" (Bossuet).

A student will find it to his interest to develop arguments of probability. He might prepare a short speech based upon the principle that (*a*) if something more likely to happen did not happen, then something less likely is not likely to happen (negative conclusion); (*b*) if something less likely to happen has happened, what is more likely is more likely to happen (affirmative conclusion); (*c*) if something is likely to happen, then this is likewise likely to happen.

If a student wishes to gain an appreciation of the topic of likeness he might read a chapter from Isaias listing certain facts or ideas from it and then explain these by facts or ideas well known to the average audience. He should avoid, in going from the known to the unknown, the danger of descending to the too common or too vulgar likenesses. The known objects or thoughts can be expressed in pleasing, even noble, language. Let the student give a clear picture of the women of Jerusalem meeting Christ on the way to Calvary. He might explain why he has a good example of similitude. If a student chooses any of the parables of our Lord as examples of likeness, he might also show what elements of the comparison are no longer familiar to the average audience.

Differences and Contraries. This topic of difference sets up certain opposition between objects, or also between the different conditions of the same object. "The way of the just," said the sage, "is like to a brilliant light which moves forward and increases until the perfect day of eternity; the way of the wicked, on the contrary, is full of shadows. . . . " Jeremias gives a much more touching picture of evils of Jerusalem in opposing them with its ancient splendor. "How doth the city sit solitary that was full of people! how is the mistress of the Gentiles become as a widow: the princes of provinces made tributary!" (Lament. of Jer. 1:1.) Parallelism is related to this topic of difference.

A commonly used source of thought, contraries, consists in impressing a person that such or such a thing is so repugnant to another thing that the latter cannot subsist with the former. You pretend to be an exemplary character and your life is only disorder! Related to this topic is that of contrasts.

Use of the Intrinsic Topics. To impress upon the student the importance of the intrinsic topics, he might be directed to compose short speeches based upon definition, enumeration, genus, species, cause, effects, comparison, difference, or contraries. He might for example contrast St. Peter's impetuosity with his love of Christ, or show that if perverse men act in a certain manner, Catholics should conduct themselves thus and so. He might show the relation between events antecedent to Christ's action in quelling the stormy waters and the event itself. Inasmuch as the student may be in danger of fallacious reasoning while employing the intrinsic topics, particularly cause and effect, genus and species, antecedents and consequences (considerations similar in oratorical value to cause and effect), he should give his attention to textbooks on logic. Furthermore, he need not seek secular literature for illustration of these topics, for he will find them in Scripture.

Circumstances. This topic, although belonging to the sources of intrinsic proofs, is different from those previously discussed. It is not the same thing, for example, to consider a virtue in itself, independently of persons, and to treat it in a given individual. If a speaker deals with some person or cites some example, he draws very much from this topic. Every feature of Holy Scripture or of history could be treated in such a way that the topic of circumstances would be a source of instruction.

Circumstances can be distinguished into those of persons and those of facts. Among the first, we can place *name*. For example, a speaker can develop some beautiful paragraphs from the signification of the name of Jesus; by *birth,* for instance, a person can be shown unworthy in his conduct by giving the circumstances of illustrious grandparents and virtuous parents. A speaker can take into account the *sex;* for example, he can set forth firmness, grandeur of soul, courage of saints, especially of women martyrs, and treat the obstacles that the weakness of their sex placed against them.

A speaker can help his proof and amplification by treating *race, country, family, age,* and *all the qualities* of a person. Every circumstance may add a merit or a demerit; a person is, for example, from a civilized or barbarous race, from the city or the country, from high or low birth, in a tender or advanced age, of a weakened or strong constitution, endowed or deprived of natural gifts either of the body or of the mind, known or unknown in public or in private life. To *name* and *birth* may be added *education;* this man is well or badly trained; other circumstances are *fortune* — rich or poor; and *habits* — virtuous or vicious inclinations, tastes, knowledge, behavior, intentions, and speech.

The circumstances of things or of facts modify them in different ways, and often serve to establish and amplify them. *Who* refers entirely to the circumstances of the person. Who betrayed the Saviour? An Apostle, a friend, a confidant, a witness to many miracles, one destined to noble things? The other circumstances belong to things and actions. *What.* What is it? What did he do? What are the qualities of a thing? What is the object of that action? What was the reason for the treason of Judas? *Where* — in which place, public or private? Sacred or profane? Where did Judas begin the execution of his infamous plan? At the same table with Christ, after having Him wash his feet. Where did he conduct Christ's enemies? In that secluded place to which he had been given the secret; where he had been witness to the fervent prayers of the Saviour for the salvation of men; where he had received His wise instruction, a place washed by His blood. *By what means?* With what aids? What instruments? *Why?* By what motives? What viewpoints? *How* or in what manner? *When?* In what time? Day? Night? Feast day? Judas identified his Master to His enemies by the sign of friendship. He betrayed Him by a sentiment of infamous avarice, for thirty pieces of silver. He used, in order to seize the person of Christ, the time and the manner which one might use to arrest a dangerous robber; he came to get his God.

As an exercise in the topic of circumstance, the student might take the scene of our Lord preaching the Sermon on the Mount. He may gain thoughts from the following circumstances: Who? Where? What? By whom? How? When? How often? Why? Circumstances are listed by some rhetoricians as those of *person, things, places,* and *times.*

Authority.[3] This topic may refer to the person or to the subject matter of the person. The authorities particularly suited to sacred discourse may be considered in relation to extrinsic topics which present the witnesses on which one depends in order to establish truth. Authorities are divine or human. The latter ordinarily

---

[3] "Most of our opinions are based upon little else than authority, though we may have forgotten what authority. Men will have authority in one form or another. . . . Many things we must accept from those whose business it is to know" (Winans, James Albert, *Public Speaking* [The Century Co., N. Y.], p. 291).

give weaker proofs than those of reason drawn from the intrinsic topics. The former, on the contrary, are considered in themselves the strongest of all proofs, inasmuch as our holy religion is a revealed religion. The ancient orators scarcely called upon the authority of another, because those whom they could invoke as witnesses would hardly be better authorities than they themselves. But the sacred orator who is addressing himself to men on the part of a sovereign Master can and should unceasingly call upon Him who has sent him, and who has commanded him to speak in His name (Rom. 10:14).

Of the witnesses which the preacher can invoke, some are regarded by his hearers as infallible, the others are respectable. Relying on such authorities, the preacher can speak with assurance, taking an attitude and saying things that his hearers would not suffer perhaps from any other person. There are other advantages for the preacher: these same sources from which he draws proofs from authority furnish him at the same time the truths themselves, with the most beautiful thoughts, the best reasons, and every kind of intrinsic proofs.

Holy Scripture. The first source of authority, and likewise the first of all sources of proof, is Holy Scripture. The Sacred Writings will furnish the preacher with the very foundation of his address, with infallible proofs and the indestructible basis of the truth, and give him doctrine, eloquence, and impressiveness.

The preacher will draw from the historical books necessary proofs in order to establish facts concerning our holy religion. In them, besides, he will find a number of instructive and interesting treatises, as well as apt allusions and clever applications. The books of Wisdom will present him with wise maxims of value in directing morality. In the Psalms he will obtain sentiments of piety and exaltation, and subjects of the most beautiful paraphrases. He will find deep emotion in the prophets. Isaias is always sublime and magnificent in his imagery. Ezechiel is characterized by his intensity and somber vehemence; Jeremias is incomparable for feeling; Daniel, always noble and exalted. All the prophets supply us everything that can inspire eloquence, kindle enthusiasm, and touch the heart.

So far as the New Testament is concerned, frequent citation of the truths which it contains is so necessary to the sacred orator in order to give authority to his word that he should desire to know it by heart. He should remember the words of St. Jerome, "Ignorance of Scripture is ignorance of Christ."

The first step for the preacher, then, in preparing the matter for his sermon is to consult Holy Scripture for that which is directly concerned with the truth he proposes to develop. If he has been careful in his reading and in his habitual study of Holy Writ to take down items in the order of the most striking passages, he will begin by consulting his notes. In the absence of his own collection, he has the indices of the Bible, concordances, and other special works designed to help preachers in the composition of their speeches and to supply them with material on every kind of topic.

But a collection that a preacher has made for himself is always to be preferred, for, first of all, it stamps images in the memory, and, at the same time, by writing his notes the preacher gathers a number of important and beautiful truths. Besides, he profits by having many texts which he has chosen himself in pious and meditative reading, and he can retain much better the strength of truth which strikes him forcefully and enlightens him without the help of extraneous information. Finally, he avoids the danger common to many collections, of creating errors by false applications, or of taking away the full force of a passage by presenting it out of context.

From Holy Scripture the sacred orator should draw three things: (1) truths and their proofs; (2) the form under which they are presented, that is, the texts which are the basis of his sermon, given either as simple allusions or in exact quotation from the holy books; (3) the language itself of Holy Scripture, that is, the ideas, the images, the feeling, the spirit, the style, the action.

Tradition. In the eyes of the Catholic, the authority of divine tradition goes hand in hand with that of Holy Scripture. It is equally infallible because it is equally the word of God, equally transmitted from age to age, and proposed by the Church for the belief of her children. It is on the basis of tradition that we believe in the perpetual virginity of Mary, the number of sacraments, and in many other points of doctrine not explicitly stated in Holy Scripture. Besides the divine tradition, there is the apostolic tradition, such as the rule of observing Sunday, the Lenten fast, and the like; other ecclesiastical traditions have been established from the days of the Apostles, such as the observance of certain feasts. In offering proofs drawn from these last two kinds of tradition, the preacher should take care to establish their authority, one founded upon the sure authority of the Apostles, and the other on that of the Church.

The Church. The authority of the Church is infallible. Jesus Christ has made His Church the column and the foundation of truth, and the gates of hell shall not prevail against her. Thus she is, in the matter of faith and morals, infallible in her beliefs and in her teaching. But in order that proofs drawn from this infallible authority have their full force, it will be often necessary for the preacher to recall what the Church is and what is her divine mission. The preacher cannot insist too much on the obedience which is due her nor too often take the occasion to establish well this important dogma to which are attached so many particular points.

The Holy Father and General Councils. One holds as equally certain and infallible the decisions of the sovereign pontiff given as the supreme head of the Church in matters of faith and morals. He is the successor of St. Peter, and he continues the role of him for whom Jesus Christ prayed that his faith would not grow weak. The decision of the general councils establishes the rule of faith; the orator draws from them certain and infallible proofs. He will do well to have recourse also to the ordinances of particular councils, especially those of the country in which he speaks. Although this authority may not be in itself infallible, it is eminently respectable and weighty. "The *Catechism of the Council of Trent* with its notes and revisions contains an authentic collection of all the doctrines usually explained to the people and of the proofs chiefly to be urged in their support."[4]

---

[4] Coppens, *Oratorical Composition*, p. 284.

Fathers of the Church.   When the holy Fathers are unanimous, their authority forms infallible proofs, as when they give the understanding of the true sense of Holy Scripture, and the truths of faith. The Church, then, is expressing herself by the mouth of her doctors. The authority of a small number is likewise of great weight. Even the authority of a single one constitutes certain proof when the Church adopts and proposes his doctrine; for example, that of St. Athanasius on the Holy Trinity, or that of St. Augustine on grace. The benefit of the Fathers for the sacred orator is that he can give to his discourse their doctrine, their thoughts, their method, and their impressiveness.

Theologians and Canonists.   When theologians are in agreement on a point of religion, their opinion forms a proof of moral certainty. There is also this certainty for the opinion of canonists on matters which concern them. When theologians do not agree unanimously, the preacher must find on which side the greatest number leans, in order to judge their reasons and take notice of the degree of authority which the Church has accorded them. The sacred orator must leave out of his sermon all controversial points, and propose for belief only what is clear and certain. In bringing into his speech the doctrine of theologians, the preacher must strip it of technical terminology, and clothe it in attractive, even oratorical form.

Secular Authority.   Doctors of the Church have some particular right to be heard in corroboration of our belief. But can the same be said of secular writers, modern as well as ancient? The opinion of enlightened men, whatever the age in which they lived, on secular subjects may well impress an audience and incline it to think as they think, but hearers are never obligated to follow their opinions. There is, however, an advantage in an appeal to writers who can show that a particular doctrine or truth has been accepted by men over a long period of time. The topic of common consent has value in establishing a presumption in favor of the acceptance of a truth. Yet scientific theories must not be presented as facts. Preachers sometimes make the mistake of drawing examples from controversial theories rather than from exact science. As a general rule, it is rarely necessary to use secular writers as authorities. A preacher may sometimes, with reserve and without undue emphasis, ornament his speech with their beautiful thought. The preacher must also present their remarkable words, their beautiful traits of conduct as ornaments to his own thought or as proofs of reason, not citing them because of the authority of their name, much as St. Paul, himself, has quoted the Greek poets, but generally a preacher must accommodate the form or substance of their writing to his type of discourse.

Maxims. Among human authorities may be placed maxims and wise sayings of men whose names have authority in the world. They help at times to ornament, even perhaps to prove a point. When the speaker presumes that the wise saying which is cited is known to his audience, he only needs to allude to the remark. The auditors are flattered at this respect for their intelligence. The preacher must abstain generally from borrowing quotations from the enemies of religion. They cannot be quoted as authorities, unless to contradict themselves or to show the strength of the truth which draws from them such approbation or to confound them who procure for themselves admirers and partisans or to indicate the subject matter where they are truly authorities.

Examples. *Words convince; examples persuade.* Examples have been termed by Coppens "narratives of facts calculated to persuade." Among the proofs of sacred discourse, divine authorities rank first; the proofs of reason, second; and examples, third; yet examples have a superior strength from nature itself which inclines us to imitate it. Men are born with a certain sympathy which brings them to imitate easily the feelings of others and to accept what others do. One imitates willingly that which he wants to do or what he knows has been done, while the new and the unheard of can secure only with great difficulty a general credit and favor. Besides most persons have a certain natural curiosity about the affairs of others that causes them to follow with interest the telling of a story, and their attention is drawn to any picture which passes before the speaker's eyes. Examples, then, interest all of us and refresh us.

Besides this double advantage over proofs of reason, examples enter more easily into the mind, and are less suspected by the auditors. A reason is not always understood immediately, and it requires some effort on the part of the hearer; an example, on the other hand, is immediately understood as it is presented. The listener does not feel at once that an example may have been invented in order to illustrate a cause, whereas subtle reasoning not only may be beyond his range but may make him defiant. He believes that the speaker who is aiming to persuade him is deluding him with his superiority, setting some trap for him, and by an adroit argument taking advantage of his credulous simplicity. Before an audience made up of persons of average education, the sacred orator will do well to avoid all subtle reasoning, and give preference to proofs from authority, and especially from **example.**

As examples prove possibility, they are unanswerable for those who allege their impotence. St. Augustine encouraged himself by the example of the many virtuous Christians in breaking from the bonds which held him to vice. "Why can I not do," he asked himself, "what so many others have been able to do?" The example may be given also as an argument from comparison, or *a minori,* as when someone encourages us by an example of weaker persons or those less learned; the sage used this example of the ant in order to shame the lazy; God confounded the idolatrous Jews by the example of pagans faithful to their false gods, and the Saviour used as examples the queen of Sheba and the Ninevites. Or the argument of *a pari* can be used: There was a man; he could do this; you are a man; you can do this. Or the argument of *a majori* as when someone proposes to us an example of the Son of God.

A preacher may use example in order to insinuate certain delicate truths in the minds of his hearers, and indirectly place blame on those whom he might dislike to censure openly. Often a speaker uses an example without adding any words of exhortation. He finds that the example has opened all the avenues of the heart, and he is master of it, even before his auditors are aware of it. Finally, the sacred orator will employ examples when he praises and when he censures people. Thus he can make Christians feel ashamed by contrasting the falling off of their ardor with the fervor of the first Christians. He can, likewise, contrast the understanding of an animal that attaches himself to the man who feeds him, with the ingratitude of a man who turns against his Creator. The priest should borrow examples from the life of Christ and the lives of the saints. The inclinations of their lives are very useful in applying the rules of morality and piety. Their examples show an audience the possibility of an action and inspire courage; they captivate the attention; they clothe precepts with authority; and they give much impressiveness and variety to an address.

Assignment.

1. Prepare a ten-minute speech dealing with St. Paul. Some of these moral topics may help you with your invention: justice; honor; ease and pleasure of accomplishment; use and necessity. Use advantageously some of these topics of person: birth; race; country; sex; age; intellectual training; adjustments; mental, bodily, and emotional habits; conditions of life; inclinations; social characteristics; power; and reputation.

2. Prepare a ten-minute speech dealing with *Baptism*. Apply the topics of definition, enumeration, cause, examples of benefits and consequences.

3. Develop a few paragraphs on some subject by the use of authority.

4. Develop a few paragraphs on some subject by the use of example.

5. Develop a short speech on the subject of *Family Prayers* by means of analogy.

CHAPTER III

The Plan of a Pulpit Oration

1. *Why a Plan?*

Assume that the speech material is assembled, and that the preacher has taken notes on everything that his reading and meditation can give him on the subject he proposes to treat. Before him are his texts from Holy Scripture and the Fathers, ideas and proofs from theology or other sources. Lastly, he has everything that reason and feeling have suggested to him on the subject matter. He has likewise his tentative outline, which has helped him in the collection of material. Now it remains for him to bring this more or less confused mass into order, to make "a deposition of parts suited to obtain a certain effect."[1] For this purpose, he must set up a good plan or outline of his speech.

2. *Advantages of a General Campaign Plan*

Wise planning will allow the speaker to avoid repetitions and digressions which tire and worry an audience, and it will hold him to his purpose. It is an aid to clear, precise thinking and strong instruction, and to disregarding vague and common expressions, particularly in the introduction of the speech, where, because the mind is not yet warmed, the expression tends to be feeble, languid, or cold.

3. *Symbols for a Plan*

An outline is generally helped by the consistent use of symbols; for example:

I.

  A.

    1.

      a.

---

[1] Coppens, *Art of Oratorical Composition,* p. 92.

4. *Types of Outlines*

These vary with the nature of the material and the ordering of material to suit the purpose of the speech.

a) Many outlines are simply an enumeration of points; of value, however, only if the speaker can keep in mind the order of their importance and their relationship. If all the points seem to be of equal value, he would have no subordinate points or, in other words, subheads. Generally a proposition is capable of a division into two or three points, each with a few subheads.

b) The natural order (often a time order) is an effective way of organizing narrative or expository material: a story, a lecture, or the explanation of a process. The listeners easily understand a subject presented from this time to that time, this period to that period, the general to the particular, the anterior in time before what is posterior, the known to the unknown, the simple to the complex, the near to the far, and the cause to the effect. Sometimes in the establishing of a truth, some one part should be treated before some other, inasmuch as the last point proves nothing if the first point is not well founded, or because at least it will borrow some strength from it.

c) The logical outline is necessary when a speech depends for its strength upon closely knit reasoning. Generally four or five statements express the reasons why something should be done or, in other words, when proved, they prove the proposition. Under each subhead are reasons and evidence for its proof. Usually a logical outline is arranged to present the stronger reason first, then the strong, and lastly the strongest.

d) The most widely used outline is topical. Main divisions and subheads are arranged usually in an oratorical order, or order of importance. The order best for one audience may not have climactic value for another; consequently the topical outline should be arranged to suit the need of a specific audience.

5. *Qualities Required for a Good Outline*

Unity. Any plan, to be good, must have unity for its fundamental quality. It must be a plan of action set forth to accomplish some precise aim. As a plan of campaign, an outline settles the speaker's mind about what belongs to the speech and what is to be excluded. It establishes in a single proposition the whole multitude of thoughts, and it centers the particular propositions which the speech contains in the development of this one truth.

What does the speaker wish to show? Which truth? On this truth everything should revolve; it furnishes what is called the proposition of the speech which can be viewed in different ways; or perhaps demonstrated by two or three important proofs. In attentively running through his mass of material, the preacher will observe that it can be arranged under two or three main headings; these will form the chief members of the outline. A plan need not be developed extensively, yet a few subheads are generally placed under each main heading. The examples, illustrations, and principal topics of amplification are placed with their points. There is then a clear pathway with signposts which should guide the speaker to his destination.

The outline must be designed for a definite period of time, and must be suited to an occasion and a particular audience. In this it differs from a legal brief and a tentative outline. A brief is an orderly arrangement of all the evidence and argument that can be gathered to present a given side of a question. A tentative outline lists a proposition, main heads, subheads, evidence, reasoning, illustration, scriptural citations on some subject, let us say, the sacrament of matrimony. Both the legal brief and the tentative outline contain total material out of which many particular speeches might be made. Neither, however, is the complete form needed for a particular speech, before a particular audience, and on a particular occasion. That outline for a specific speech is guided by the purpose of the speaker, and is characterized by logical division, proportion, viewpoint, and logical sequence.

Coherence in the Speech Outline. In any type of plan, subheads may be considered general propositions fertile enough to furnish a convenient series of reasons and their oratorical supports, but are, at the same time, rightly unified among themselves. When subheads are taken together, they themselves may be summarized in a single, but more general, proposition which is that of the speech. In the disposition of his material, therefore, the orator follows a path precisely the opposite of what he will follow in his speaking. He instructs himself by analysis; he will instruct others by a synthesis. From particular ideas he comes to general propositions in preparing his speech. In his speech, however, he will place these general propositions as headings: first the main proposition of the speech; then the general subordinate headings; then the subdivisions of each of these subordinate headings in turn; each subdivision will have its own proofs, and each proof its own development, and each development its own thoughts.

This combination ought to be brought together so well and executed so perfectly that the hearers can always understand the relationship of the thought to the proof which it seeks to develop, of this proof to the next member of the subdivision, to the subdivision, to the member of the corresponding division, and to the general proposition of the speech. Thus by each point of development a speaker can, as by a ladder, climb to the general proposition of the speech.

Since the disposition of the matter is made in a way of forming a single unity for the purpose of establishing a single truth, the preacher must begin by looking for the proposition of the speech when he establishes the outline. Next he selects from the texts of Holy Scripture that he has collected the one which seems best placed at the beginning of the introduction. He determines at the same time the idea or the matter most suitable for the opening and closing of the speech.

The preacher cannot go into these details until he has a general idea of what material will be suitable for the body of the speech. But before he settles his mind regarding the completed form of the body, we must remember that, before writing anything, he must reserve and place aside something for the peroration, which forms an important part of the speech. He should remember that, if he has used all he has in a strong and striking confirmation, he will have only the weak and common thoughts, with which to carry the final points.

6. *Regular Partition*[2] *of Ideas*

The general proposition, the main heads, the text, the idea for the introduction, and the idea for the peroration enter into the plan of a sacred discourse. Is it necessary to make main heads of equal value? The ancients did not have regular partitions; we find no traces of them in the Fathers. Equal division has two important difficulties: one is that speaking first of everything that should be said takes away the pleasure of surprise and deprives the speaker of that advantage which is often necessary to cover his advance in order to arrive more surely at his destination; the other is that, when each member is subdivided into three or four equal subheads, the spirit of eloquence is hampered.

On the other hand, regular partitions of ideas help order, clarity, and the understanding of the speech. They make attention easy. The hearer knows where and how the speaker is leading him; he sees on his route proper pauses that give him rest. As a consequence he listens with pleasure and retains what he hears.

Characteristics of a Good Partition of Thoughts. Each main heading should be (1) ample in itself so that it may be given a well rounded development; (2) entire, so that the main heads grouped together cover the breadth of the subject comprehended in the proposition, and no one part is too comprehensive or too meager, consequently the two or three heads exhaust the whole subject; (3) exclusive and inclusive so that one point is not contained within another; and (4) a progression graded from one member to another. Growth of interest in a speech is one of its chief merits, and contributes particularly to persuasion by maintaining attention and laying hold of minds. Frequently there is in the progression of main heads a natural order that should not be changed. When this is lacking, the speaker must look for what is most likely to interest the hearer and place it at the end, as has been indicated, building up the speech on the principle of stronger, strong, strongest.

---

[2] The subject matter of partition and examples of its use are taken chiefly from an abridged translation of the same content in Bellefroid's *Manuel D'Éloquence Sacré* pp. 150–161.

We hardly need to remark that the parts of an outline should be simple and natural. If the subject itself seems to favor a partition into two or three parts, the orator should formulate two or three general propositions. He should avoid any division that appears forced, affected, or too subtle. Particularly in a moral discourse he should watch the divisions, which are sometimes forced and in bad taste.

Bourdaloue's first sermon for the feast of All Saints offers to the preacher a model of exact, natural, progressive, even beautiful, division of a text. Note the divisions:

Rejoice and exult for behold your full reward is in heaven.

1. The reward of the saints is sure, whereas the recompenses of the world are uncertain and doubtful. *Behold your reward.*

2. The reward of the saints is an abundant recompense, whereas the recompense of the world is empty and defective. *Full reward.*

3. The recompense of the saints is eternal, whereas the recompense of the world decays and perishes. *In heaven.*

The preacher could, as in this example, get partitions from the text of the discourse, even in a moral address, but they should present themselves naturally.

Ordinary subject matter for preaching can be divided into: (*a*) instruction, (*b*) proof, and (*c*) moral application or practice; or sometimes into only two of these headings. If the speech deals only with instruction, all explication and all the development will be related to certain main headings. These are the natural divisions. In questions of formal proof, the preacher must decide whether different proofs are required: for example, proofs from reason, from authority, from Scripture, from the Fathers; or whether to use proofs and their consequences; or whether to employ the same proof presented in several ways. Partitions follow; then the kind of proof. Some preachers put the major premise of a syllogism in the first part of the speech, and the minor in the second. Some prefer to make the entire body of a discourse the development of the minor premise while the major premise is treated, or at least proposed, in the introduction.

If the sacred orator notices also the attitude of his audience in regard to a certain truth, vice, virtue, duty, or point of doctrine, he will be able to reduce these views to two or three headings. If he attempts to combat different prejudices affecting some dogma or sacrament or precept or usage, he will notice why and how people fail in certain religious practices and devotions. The parts of his sermon will fall into the points he wishes most to apply to correction. Thus Massillon in a great number of his speeches seeks to combat the various difficulties of men and the pretexts that the world adduces in opposition to the truths of Christian morals. This is what we notice in the division of his sermons on *The Evidence of the Divine Law, The Immutability of the Laws of God, Slander, Afflictions,* and others.

In treating a moral matter, the preacher will naturally point out to his audience why something is right, why it is useful, why a certain obligation ought to be satisfied or a practice adopted. He will treat a moral matter in relation to duty and practice. He will say one should do it, one can do it. He will sometimes set forth the motives that should bring a man to take a resolution, and he will help him in his practice by suggesting the means of executing this resolution. The different motives and the different means will form the subdivisions of the sermon. If the preacher limits himself in his treatment to one of these two things, motives and means, he will still have excellent main heads for his outline. For example, there are means of acquiring such a virtue, and here is the way to avoid such a vice; here are the qualities of this virtue, its beauties, its utility, and the like; here are the deformities of its opposing vice.

7. *Examples of Partition*

To understand better the manner of forming good main heads for an outline, some examples drawn from the great orators are here set down.

Main ideas: (*a*) *God;* (*b*) *ourselves;* (*c*) *our neighbor*

Bourdaloue, *Sermon on the Nativity of Our Lord,* makes the following use of these ideas. Glory to God in the highest, and on earth peace to men of good will: (*a*) peace with God; (*b*) peace with ourselves; (*c*) peace with our neighbor.

Bossuet in his *Sermon for Passion Sunday,* employs the same thoughts. To love the truth wherever it is found: (*a*) in God, it rules us; (*b*) in ourselves, it stirs and enlightens us; (*c*) in our neighbor, it takes hold of and corrects us.

Bourdaloue's *Sermon on Respect* applies the partition of ideas to the unworthiness of human respect: (*a*) to ourselves; (*b*) to God; (*c*) to our neighbor.

Bourdaloue, in the second part of the *All Souls' Day Sermon*, again uses this division. Not to work in helping the souls in purgatory is an unkindness which offends the interest (*a*) of God; (*b*) of our brothers; (*c*) of ourselves.

Bourdaloue, *Exhortation for Religious Communities,* finds these main ideas advantageous to his purpose. We shall not be able without observing rules to have peace (*a*) with God; (*b*) or with ourselves; (*c*) or with our neighbor.

A final example of the application of this partition of thoughts is from Bourdaloue in a sermon on *Obligation*. The obligation to exert oneself for the salvation of servants is to the interest of (*a*) the servants; (*b*) God; (*c*) the employers.

Main ideas: (*a*) *God;* (*b*) *ourselves*

Bourdaloue used these ideas in two of his sermons. (1) Two great interests hold us to satisfactory work: (*a*) the interests of God that we have to satisfy; (*b*) our own interest that we must procure. (2) Mortal sin: (*a*) sovereign evil to God; (*b*) sovereign evil to man.

Main ideas: (*a*) *Christ;* (*b*) *ourselves*

Bourdaloue in a discourse used this separation: (*a*) how Christ speaks to us in the Holy Sacrament; (*b*) how we should speak to Christ.

In a sermon on the divine perfections the same author has these main ideas. The mystery of the Passion shows forth: (*a*) power; (*b*) wisdom.

Bossuet, taking these ideas of the divine perfections, uses the following main heads in three of his sermons. (1) The mystery of the Passion shows forth: (*a*) power; (*b*) mercy. (2) In the conversion of sinners the glory of God appears (*a*) by mercy in the remission of sins; (*b*) by the justice in penitence. (3) The three bases of divine justice are (*a*) the misunderstanding of power; (b) the goodness embittered by ingratitude; (c) the majesty and sovereignty violated.

Bourdaloue grouping his thoughts under the main heads of (a) the mind and (b) the heart, for his sermon *On Christian Peace,* takes the topic with the following subheads: Peace be with you: (a) the peace of mind in submitting to faith; (b) the peace of the heart in submitting to the law of God.

Bourdaloue, using the same partition as before, now makes use of this topic. We owe the Church a double obedience: (a) the obedience of the mind in order to believe the truths which she proposes; (b) the obedience of the heart in order to follow the law which she imposes upon us.

Bourdaloue uses these two main notions for two of his sermons: (a) the body; (b) the soul. (1) The conformity of the religious state which Jesus Christ resurrected: (a) by the relation of the body; (b) by relation to the soul. (2) The Christian penitence is a double sacrifice which God demands of us: (a) sacrifice of the body; (b) sacrifice of the soul.

Main ideas: (a) *reason;* (b) *faith*

Bourdaloue uses traditional divisions in this sermon: At the last judgment God will produce against us two things: (a) our faith, in order to judge us as Christians; and (b) our reason, in order to judge us as men.

Main ideas: (a) *the rich;* (b) *the poor*

Bourdaloue in his sermon on *Alms-giving* finds two natural partitions: By establishing the precept of almsgiving, Divine Providence shows His blessing toward (a) the poor; (b) the rich.

In his *Sermon on Hell* and the one on *Penitence* he uses these ideas for each sermon: (a) the present; (b) the past; (c) the future. (1) Unhappiness of the wicked: (a) the past is filled with the cruelest regrets; (b) the present gives the most mortal sorrows; (c) the future will bring the most frightful despair. (2) Frequent falling into sin stamped by (a) false penitence in regard to the past; (b) obstacles for the true penitence in the future.

Bourdaloue used the following partition successfully: (a) crime; (b) folly; (c) unhappiness. Effects of behavior: (a) his crime who does not want to submit to Providence; (*b*) his unhappiness who does not want to conform to the conduct of Providence.

Massillon employing the same ideas apportions the matter of his outline as follows: False confidence; (*a*) foolishness; (*b*) consequence.

A sacred orator can get good notions for a sermon by considering the following points: the three divine Persons; faith, hope, and charity; nature, grace, glory; heaven, earth, purgatory, hell; the three states of the Church; before, during, after; time, eternity; in itself, causes, effects; duty, motive, example; to think, to speak, to do; persons, words, actions; birth, life, death; glory, riches, pleasures; humiliation, poverty, suffering; nature, end, means; end, motives, means; remedy, preservation; circumstances, who, what, where, etc.; grace in God, joy in life, increase in salvation; different ages of life; individual, society; society, family, individual; political society, religious society, domestic society; the three ways, purgative, illuminative, unitive; penitent, novice, perfection; sinner, righteousness, perfection; general reasons, particular reasons, etc.

An orator sometimes separates his matter by contrasts. Thus Bourdaloue in his sermon, *Unhappy Eternity,* gets this partition: faith should confirm us in the belief of an unhappy eternity; and the belief in an unhappy eternity should excite us to the practice of the works of faith. Again in his *Sermon on the Passion,* he follows the same principle of division: Jesus Christ judged by the world; the world judged by Jesus Christ. In another sermon *On the Passion,* he employs these subheads effectively: Sin caused the death of Jesus Christ; Jesus Christ caused the death of sin.

Massillon in his discourse on *Mixture of Good and Evil* used this contrast: Good people should serve either for the salvation or for the condemnation of the wicked; the wicked are suffering on account of instruction or because of the merits of justice.

PART II

DIVISION AND DEVELOPMENT

❧

This section of four chapters considers first the introduction and the conclusion of a discourse. Since the speaker has an obligation to himself and to his composition, he must remove obstacles to his success, explain his purpose, and prepare the audience for the development of his subject. Likewise, he must arrange a worthy conclusion to his speech, for it is in this part where important decisions are often made regarding the matter presented in the body of the address.

The body of the discourse, making use of the material which develops the proposition of the speech, is treated in a separate chapter. It explains the details of a subject and sets forth the arguments, facts, and examples that support the theme of the address.

The important duty of a preacher to persuade people to face the truth and overcome the habit of deceiving themselves is treated in Chapter VI. If agreeable feeling can be aroused in connection with a discussion presented by the preacher, agreement to his purpose is likely. The last chapter of Part II relates to the problem of style in religious discourse. Style must be appropriate to the dignity of the pulpit, the nature of the preacher's mission, and the type of content.

CHAPTER IV

Introduction and Conclusion

Division. The term *division* has had two meanings in the rhetoric of oratory. The first relates to the proposition and its sub-heads, or the divisions of the outline; the second more accurately refers to the different parts of a speech. There has not been much change in the suggested division of a speech from the days of Corax (466 B.C.). Aristotle's four divisions and Cicero's six amount to an introduction, a discussion, and a conclusion. The term *discussion* generally means the proof and its refutation. *Peroration* is today a more exclusive term than conclusion; it refers now more to an emotional climax or ending. In this chapter, the two parts of a speech — introduction and conclusion — will be treated.

1. *Introduction*

The opening remarks should prepare the minds of the hearers for the speech to follow. They are a means of getting contact with the listeners, and of preparing the way for the main event. Cicero has said that the purpose of the introductory remarks is to get the attention of the audience, excite good feeling, and open its mind to conviction (submission). The more prejudiced the audience, the more the speaker, with a modest and a persuasive manner, must try in the introduction to remove these prejudices; the less knowledge an audience has of a case, the more explanation of the problems is required.

When the interests and feelings of a congregation are practically identical, the preacher who finds words to keynote an expression of this harmony will have the favor of the group. But if the preacher must oppose this feeling, he has a most difficult task. He must find some common ground for his approach to the problem. Generally speaking, an audience at the start of a speech, being more heterogeneous, has no member who has an ax to grind. Most of the generally used factors for the securing of attention and interest will prepare the ground for the ideas and images of the body of the speech. Often, a clearing away of extraneous matter, an explanation of the subject, or a history of the controversy under its different viewpoints will bring the listeners up to date with the subject. At times it will be necessary to define terms or enumerate the divisions of a problem. Frequently an outline of the issues may clarify the purpose of the speaker.

a) Common faults to be avoided. Some preachers in preparing an instruction fail to keep in mind the audience, its size and age, or perhaps the occasion and the general setting. Often the occasion and the purpose of the speaker himself must be of chief concern in adapting remarks to a group. In every case, an introduction should be as brief as circumstances will permit, and usually should be in proportion to the length of the address. If there are no prejudices in the audience, to attempt a motivation against some assumed prejudice as an antagonist is stage play or mere talk. If an audience understands the situation of the speech or has a good grasp of the matter, the preacher should not talk merely to have an introduction. If satisfactory feelings are already aroused, the speaker need not labor to incite what is already a reality.

There is seldom an occasion for an excuse or an apology from any speaker, and most rarely from a preacher. The preacher's office does not call for him to speak of himself as humble, abject, or lacking talent. He can avoid pomp, false humility, or boldness, persecution complex or pretensions. An apology is often simply a cheap way of attracting attention. Firmness is not antagonistic to modesty or warmth. An attempt at humor on the assumption that an audience must be aroused, is often thought to be a routine necessity for any speaker, even a preacher. Humor indeed may have a place in the introduction but only (*a*) when it is required by the circumstances, and (*b*) when it is humor.

The most common fault of speakers, and particularly preachers, is concerned with false leads. They vary from flattering an audience regarding its intelligence, and then saying little that requires such intelligence to the condition of misleading listeners as to what actually will be said in the discussion. Some preachers make the mistake of wandering around, opening up the possibilities of many fields, or bringing in irrelevant material on the assumption that an audience must be warmed up, or toned down, as the case may be. Other faults might be mentioned, but a further enumeration is unnecessary if the prospective preacher will remember that *any introduction is good that leaves the audience attentive to the speaker, interested in his subject matter, and willing to help him fulfill the purpose that he proposes to accomplish.*

b) Types of introduction. Some type of introduction is necessary in sacred oratory, but one type rarely has a place: an abrupt introduction with emotional vehemence. The occasion may call for a very short introduction similar to that used by St. John Chrysostom in his sermon for Eutropius whom the people wanted put to death. The emotional picture of the fallen foe, Eutropius, was enough to make the audience willing to listen to the discussions of the vanities of life, the power of God over His enemies, and Christ's example of forgiveness. Obviously, then, the short introduction need not be either abrupt or bold.

The bald-statement-of-purpose type of introduction is quite common. The preacher states his purpose, and often points out specially the road he will travel. The comparison kind is based on the principle that something about the audience, place, time, or speaker is in relationship to something well known to the audience. The introduction which furnishes a text or a quotation is, of course, common to all types of sacred orations. Another, and perhaps the most used introduction, is the common-ground type. The speaker sets out to find a common bond with his audience in his subject matter, attitudes, backgrounds, interests, or loyalties. He does not overgeneralize any one of these bonds, but seeks to make it exclusive. He talks to any audience as Catholic rather than Christian, and members of St. John's Church rather than Catholics. The more intimate he can make the bond, the more effective is the common-ground type of introduction.

c) Some factors of a good exordium in sacred discourse. The opening phrases are important in stimulating the minds of the hearers. They should be beautiful and impressive. But the initial remarks should not be inconsistent with what will follow; they can be clear, concise, and brief, and if one speaks to children and simple people, within their comprehension.

The style of the introduction in general should be simple, natural, and interesting.[1] To that part of his speech the orator must give particular care, for the success of the whole speech depends upon first impressions, and no part of it is heard with greater mental poise, curiosity, and attention than the introduction.

The introduction of a sacred discourse is divided into four parts: (1) the text; (2) the introduction of matter; (3) the explanation; and (4) the invocation.

1. *The text.* This theme drawn from Holy Scripture or the Creed, placed at the beginning of a discourse, is a relic, a vestige of the methods used in the early years of the Church when the preacher was ordinarily limited to the explanation of a more or less lengthy passage from Holy Scripture. The quotation with which the address is opened is not only a monument of antiquity but a reminder to him who utters the word of God that everything that he says should be founded upon Holy Scripture. At the same time, the language of the preacher commands more respect if it is presented as a development of the words of the Holy Scripture. For these reasons, and for the latter particularly, the text incites the attention of the average audience which always looks for a succinct expression of the thought of the preacher. He, knowing the importance of the text to the speech, must choose it with care and discernment.

Since there must be some natural relation between the text and the subject, a preacher should not force the sense of the text in

---

[1] Rhetoricians generally distinguish two kinds of introduction: the calm and the abrupt. The calm may be subdivided into the simple, the solemn, and the insinuating. The simple is ordinarily heard in instruction; the solemn is heard in sermons for special occasions (cf. Bossuet's funeral orations, Cicero's *Manilian Law*); the insinuating is frequently found in controversy. Examples will be found in *British Eloquence*. (See also Cicero, *Speech Against Rullus*.) Credit for many ideas in this section must be given to Bellefroid. Consult *Manuel D'Éloquence Sacrée*, pp. 173–181.

adapting it to the matter. Fénelon finds fault with the preacher who on Ash Wednesday had taken for his text a verse from Psalm 101: *For I did eat ashes like bread*. There is no relation between this text and the ceremony of the day other than the childish relation of a word. For stronger reasons, a sacred orator must avoid altering the sense of the text either by assigning to it a literal meaning or by giving it a mystical one that does not belong to it. This observation applies to every passage of Scripture which the preacher uses, but particularly to the fundamental text of the speech, for this should contain in germ the entire discourse. At least, the introduction should show its intimate relationship with the subject.

The orator should also, as often as possible, use a text that will naturally make an impression on the audience by the beauty of its thought, its strength, the energy of its expression, or by the fact that it contains a beautiful phrase, a wise instruction, a living sentiment, a warning, or a strong apostrophe. He should avoid the text which places an interpretation on the subject which he intends to treat, such as this example placed at the head of a sermon on death: "And as it is appointed unto man once to die and after this the judgment" (Hebr. 9:27).

The text ought to be more or less general, or more or less particular, according to the subject matter. If the preacher wishes to speak in the same discourse of knowledge of Christ and faith in the Saviour, here is a text: "Thou art the Christ, the Son of the living God" (Matt. 16:16). If he intends to speak only of knowledge of our Lord, this text will serve him: "Now this is eternal life, that they may know thee, the only true God, and him whom thou hast sent: Jesus Christ" (John 17:3). If belief in the Saviour is the subject of his speech, he may take, for example, this text: "You believe in God, believe also in me" (John 14:1).

The preacher should guard against allegorical texts the explanation of which is obscure and needs, in order to be well understood, a lengthy unfoldment. He must avoid also in sermons for special occasions texts that mention the names of heroes. Using these texts is quite childish and in bad taste. Although, in general, it is the literal sense that is to be preferred, a preacher may in special sermons, and even in moral discourses, use the accommodated sense. But he must apply it so very naturally that it seems to come from the text itself, or at least that there is enough connection to justify this sense. Some texts contain a happy allusion to place, time, or presence, but they should be wisely applied in relation to present-day circumstances.

The orator must interpret the text simply and faithfully and never run risks of erroneous analysis. Seminarians can, as a matter of practice in choosing and developing texts, decide on a text; consult a commentary; quote interpretations by the Church Fathers; explain the meaning of each word; use comparison and contrast with other texts of Holy Writ; give circumstances involved in the creation of the saying; state what caused the assertion; draw conclusions; and find examples which indicate the truth of the text.

2. *The introduction of matter.* Formerly there were two exordiums, one for the introduction and the other for the explanation of the subject. The present-day speaker makes an intimate connection between the two. He will search in his general explanation for an idea or a principle which will introduce, or upon which can be based, the proposition and division of the speech. For this he should not go back to the creation of the world or the fall of man, but rather should select the truth that gets down to the subject immediately. The subject or the circumstances, or the two together, will often themselves suggest to him a principle or an idea. If he wishes to preach on the goodness that procures for man the practice of humility, he can devote his exordium to establishing how the practice of humility, in general, contributes to man's happiness in this world. He can do this by a developed definition or an enumeration of virtues considered in relation to the part that each of them plays in dealing with the goodness of man.

Sometimes a preacher will use a proof of a different order from that developed in the discourse. If, for example, he should limit himself in the discussion to the use of the proofs of authority, he may in presenting the introduction draw his proofs from reason, yet he may give them under the form of considerations rather than as argumentation which does not belong to the exordium.

If the preacher wishes to instruct and explain a Christian truth, he will have to make his audience see that this truth is interesting, little known or well known, important, sublime, that it must be understood, or must be known to produce this or that happy effect. If he wishes to prove, to demonstrate, a truth, he may insist on the importance of this truth, its relation to the constant faith of the Church, how it was attacked only in this or that epoch, or the reasons which prevent it from being known. This last idea very naturally establishes a division which would be formed according to the different classes of adversaries, or the different objections which have been urged against the truth in question.

Often a speaker can limit himself in his introduction to explanation of a parable, a historical treatise, or a passage from Holy Scripture from which the text is borrowed. In general, a historical introduction gains much attention and interest. The preacher may get ideas for an introduction from the circumstances in which he finds the hearers, or from the circumstances in which he finds himself. The place in which he is speaking, the happy or unhappy events, the feast days, the sanctity of the times, the nearness to a solemn feast, the needs and dispositions of the hearers, may all offer ideas. In a sermon that forms part of a series of discourses as, for example, in Advent or Lent, it would be natural, and very useful, to recall in the introduction the conclusions of the previous sermons and then to show, without too much extension, the sequence of the matter.

3. *Explanation of the subject.* The proposition or an announcement of the subject under consideration may or may not be formally presented to an audience. When the subject tells enough about itself, especially in a short speech, this proposition is not necessary. In general, however, it is useful, and often even indispensable to good explanation, to state the formal proposition so that the preacher fixes on this single point the whole attention of his audience.

The preacher must carefully relate the proposition to what precedes it, and see that it is not so enmeshed in reasoning or verbiage that the audience has difficulty in distinguishing it. It should be expressed simply, exactly, and precisely. A direct proposition is more striking and also more apostolic. In place of saying: "The Christian should pardon his enemies," the preacher might better say: "You must pardon your enemies." There is more direct appeal in *you* than *it* or *he*.

In almost every kind of sacred discourse, and above all in that which treats of practices and duties, the preacher ought to state his main headings as well as his proposition, clearly, simply, and concisely. The audience will better understand the strength of his reasoning, the force of his proof, the sequence of the speech, and the exactness of his conclusions if it is forewarned of the pathway it will take. A brief outline of the truths that will be presented, proved, and developed is of help to cultivated persons as well as to those who only by chance know the isolated truths. The latter class loses the significance of a truth unless it has an understanding of the place of the truth in the sequence of a discourse. No long phrases, no periods, no useless repetition, no synonyms are necessary to tell an audience of the essential ideas that will be treated.

The speaker may sometimes clarify the division with different viewpoints, but it is childish to repeat the main heads of a sermon in three or four different ways with rich developments. The orator must use in the proposition and statements of the division concise and rigorous terms, and avoid a too marked antithesis as well as an affected symmetry, quibbles, rhymes, and play on words. He does not ordinarily present the subdivisions of his outline in the introduction: this might confuse the mind of the hearers and, in any case, is unnecessary.

4. *Invocation.* From time immemorial in the life of the Church the preacher, before beginning the development of his subject, has invited the audience to join him in calling down the assistance of the Holy Ghost through the intercession of the Blessed Virgin.

The preacher may use the invocation simply, without showing

its relation to the subject, but, when it has a natural connection with it, he may well use it with profit. He may also bring into the invocation a prayer addressed either to God the Father, to the Saviour, to the Holy Ghost, or to the Blessed Virgin herself. In the United States the invocation is often restricted to the more formal type of discourse.

2. *Conclusion*

The end of a speech is its decisive moment. In a sermon, it is the time when listeners are determining their acceptance or their resistance to the impressions of grace. This part, like the introduction, depends for its form on the purpose of the speech, the type of audience, and the circumstances of the occasion. The ideas of the conclusion must be prepared when the material is being collected for the address. "Whatever is excellent, save for the peroration," said Cicero. If the speaker has a good notion of the points of the discussion, he will have little difficulty in choosing effective matter for the conclusion as well as for the introduction. But since the peroration is certainly the most difficult part of the discourse, the speaker ought to meditate on his selection of material, and work over it with care. He should remember in choosing matter the remark of Socrates as quoted by Plato in *Phaedrus*. "I boldly assert that mere knowledge of the truth will not give you the art of persuasion."

a) How to gain good form. Aristotle pointed out that the end of the speech should leave the audience well disposed to the speaker. He suggested in controversy the need of amplifying the values gained from the conclusions of arguments and of diminishing the effects of the opposing reasons and evidence. He stressed the importance of leaving an audience with their emotions toned to the speaker's views and of giving their minds a clear view of a case by summarizing the points presented in defense or in explanation of the proposition of the speech.

Some conclusions are merely abrupt endings which perhaps startle an audience; in preaching, they are distasteful even shocking, and at times accepted humorously. Although no conclusion to a sermon should be abrupt, any conclusion should be brief for a long, involved summary is worse than none. From the viewpoint of the listeners the two worst faults in preaching are a new sermon started in the conclusion of another sermon, and the repetition of the matter of the body of the sermon.

There is hardly place in pulpit oratory for the conclusion that is a condensed view of the speech as a whole, or for the type that points out merely the high lights of the speech. These conclusions have some value in instruction, but even in instruction there is a reason for an appeal for specific application. A recapitulation is for the head, not for the heart. Persuasion once started in a conclusion does not leave the heart for the head. A substantial résumé of a doctrine, reassembling under a single viewpoint the principal notions, generally in themselves summaries of other points, is dry even in a speech of instruction. If some animated remarks will encourage and stimulate love for the truths which have enlightened the intellect, they belong in the conclusion. Sometimes, after a highly emotional appeal, a preacher may end with a decided contrast by stating calmly and coldly, but briefly, a sequence of strong and evident conclusions. Even one strong, incisive remark may be then very impressive.

Is there a place in preaching for that impassioned personal appeal to certain emotions common to judicial, demonstrative, and deliberate oratory? In any sermon, the emotional appeal by a dispenser of the word of God is for man's own salvation. The preacher must seek the most suitable emotions for strong motivation and arouse in the conclusion the emotions which prevailed in the body of the speech. Often the appeal starts with the remarks addressed to God and ends with an exhortation for the audience to do something of value to itself. The device of addressing God and fashioning an action in the name of the listeners is extremely useful, even in the course of the sermon if it does not interfere with the sequence of ideas. Ejaculation, resolutions, and concise prayers used in a sermon, particularly in the conclusion, often teach an audience how to pray, and how to take resolutions for a better way of life.

The storytelling type of conclusion has been used by preachers with good effect when the story illustrates the whole point of a sermon. Sometimes a quotation from the Fathers or from Holy Scripture has persuasive appeal. Often a single example which drives home the chief purpose of the speech is effective. If the preacher takes the same text to close his conclusion as he used in his introduction, he may gain striking results, or he may suggest some pious practice which contains the richest fruit to be obtained from the application of the principles enunciated in the sermon.

A number of subjects might be fittingly closed by a conclusion beginning with a proposition which summarizes the view of the entire sermon. The preacher then gives a rapid and concise enumeration of the principal reasons advanced for the proof. He proceeds to an animated exhortation and an urgent prayer. In the appeal, he has recourse to ideas and images that give lasting impressions: the glory of heaven, the hour of death, the comforts of peace, the love of God, the providence of the Father, or remorse of conscience. Such impressions placed before the listeners help them to carry away from the sermon not a mere speculative proposition but an efficacious resolution of amendment.

The preacher generally finishes his sermon by blessing his audience and wishing it eternal life. He may, likewise, direct his listener's needs to God. If the sermon has revolved about matters of painful obligations and terrifying truths, the preacher may well end with some consoling ideas. In giving comfort to people, he is following the spirit of the Church which, filled with the love of its divine Leader, never ceases to show mercy to the sinner, and cries out to him that he must never fall into despair.

b) Common faults to be avoided. Generally it is in the conclusion of the speech that an audience is settling its mind as to the qualities of both the preacher and the sermon. Of course, if the preacher is already well known to the audience, it has made certain judgments regarding him. Perhaps it is aware of the same faults that appear in his preaching week after week. He, of course, is the last person to hear the criticisms that make the rounds of the parish and then they come to him in denatured or greatly modified form. But whatever his own estimate of himself or his preaching, people will make judgments of him and his work. He may be termed confident, worldly, bold, good-natured, serious, humble, boastful, holy, careless, and the like.

Yet so far as a particular speech is concerned, if an audience finds agreeable qualities in either the preacher or his sermon, it will forget some of the disagreeable impressions it might have previously held. On the other hand, if it detects qualities in the concluding remarks that it dislikes, it generally will react against the purpose which the speaker has advanced or remain indifferent to his appeal. The combination of current disapproval or approval and favorable or unfavorable past impressions is always heightened by audience reactions during a conclusion of a speech, and either is much more marked in any member of an audience than it would be if he were an isolated individual.

The preacher who habitually writes the "erudite passionless spiritual essay," to use a phrase of William Allen White, will not compose a conclusion that appeals to people. He will have a summary that smells of the oil of preparation. The peroration must appear to listeners as a spontaneous outcome of a situation, or as remarks growing out of the occasion. It must leave the impression that the emotional feelings of the preacher are aroused by the audience and inspired by its welfare. It should bear no marks of having been framed in advance, and have no semblance of being practiced until each sound has been tested by the critical ear. "To be always sublime," according to Fénelon, "would be wearisome." To overwork a conclusion makes a preacher wearisome.

A certain John Foster complained that one of the sermons of the famous Dr. Blair "was chilled through in standing so long to be dressed." A work apparently literary may lack the human appeal. The tendency that is found in some seminaries of making preaching a literary exercise impairs its value as an agent of persuasion. The student often becomes indifferent to the needs of a real audience and builds a dull bookish sermon with an ostentatious peroration or disputatious instruction. The type of summaries sometimes used by seminarians often indicate that they are not aware of the limits to an audience's power of assimilating ideas.

CHAPTER V

Discussion

In modern usage the term *discussion* covers the confirmation and the refutation of the older rhetoricians. It is divided into its main heads generally of two or three chief considerations. When these points are amplified, they compose the body of the speech which is long or short according to the development of the matter. In the body of the speech, it will be remembered, the subject matter is presented in such a way as to accomplish the end that the speaker has in mind.

1. *The Ways of Gaining the Preacher's Purpose*

We have seen in Chapter I that a preacher must adapt his matter to further his own purpose which will be one of the five general ends of speaking. He aims usually not only to gain the assent of the intelligence of his hearers but also to move their wills to accept what he has in mind. Are the persons whom the preacher will address ignorant of the relation of the points that he will treat? Then he clarifies the matter by instruction. Do they doubt? He is determined to convince them. Are they still hesitating, enchained by evil passions and bad habits that prevent them from following their own light? He tries to move them, to arouse them, to oppose passion with passion, to reawaken feeling, and to make conviction efficacious.

2. *Importance of Instruction*[1]

The first duty of a preacher is to instruct. The instructive part of the discourse is the part devoted to defining, explaining, and transferring to the minds religious notions, the understanding of

---

[1] Most of the matter of this section is a free translation greatly abridged from Belle-froid's *Manuel D'Éloquence Sacrée*, pp. 187–213.

principles, the facts of Christianity, the dogmas, morals, discipline, and liturgy. The commission for this has been given to the preacher from on high: "Going therefore teach ye all nations" (Matt. 23:19). Before everything, he must give people an understanding of the mysteries, commandments, and sacraments; he must teach them what they must believe and practice in order to be saved. But before undertaking to prove to people a dogma or a point of morals, the preacher should make his listeners understand the importance of instruction.

The ancients gave instruction in their speeches only when it was necessary to make people understand the state of a question, to explain facts or political and judicial circumstances. In Christian eloquence, however, the occasion for instruction presents itself very frequently because the first need of religion is to enlighten. "To teach is a matter of necessity," said St. Augustine.

The number of people who are solidly instructed in their obligations and in their belief is generally much smaller than is commonly believed. As a consequence, the preacher should sometimes limit himself to simple teaching. At least part of his discourse should be devoted to instruction, and often the entire speech. The preacher should present again and again the elementary religious truths, the commandments of God, the duties of a state in life, the proper obligations of particular positions. He should avoid lofty subjects which his hearers would scarcely understand even though they might recognize his discourse as brilliant.

It would be helpful for clergymen to consider their daily work as a preparation for the function of instructing men by means of preaching. Every part of their experience contributes to the wealth of their sermons. True, a preacher must take time to outline and organize his material; and because of his labors he may have less time to gather ideas from books. Yet he still has many sources for his invention, and he must learn to arrange his subject matter quickly and efficiently.

The duties and obligations of the clerical state must not absorb the time of the preacher to the extent that he begins to lose interest in instruction. If they do, he will put aside preparation for instruction until such times as he feels it will not interfere with his other duties. This evaluation of instruction as of lesser worth than other services weakens the view that preparation for instruction is necessary. It finally favors the notion of some pastors that instruction itself can be left mainly to subordinates. Eminent moralists have opposed this view and have held that teaching men the way to salvation is the chief concern of preachers.

Instruction does not require as much talent in the preacher as the argumentative or emotional discourse. Yet clear instruction pierces minds like a ray of sun penetrating pure crystal. Since religion corresponds so well to the needs of men and accommodates itself to the different situations in which Providence has placed them, it possesses a special charm and grace for winning hearts when it is simply explained. Even heretics are touched by a clear explanation of doctrine and sinners feel a need for virtue when the love of religion is presented as a reasonable act.

3. *Method of Instruction*

Ideas are placed in the mind in two ways: by succession and by development. The first mode brings into use the memory; the second, the reason. The aim of the first is retention; that of the second is understanding. If a preacher presents a historical fact, or one of nature, in the way it was offered to him, there will be a natural succession of ideas. When he explains a commandment or a sacrament in relation to the dispositions of his hearers, he amplifies a number of ideas and then summarizes what he has said on the subject. Instruction, then, is a way of giving facts to a person whose reason accepts them and whose memory retains them.

What must the preacher do in telling an audience about dogma? The preacher can teach only what our faith teaches about it. He speaks of its history, heresies, the opposing errors, their condemnation by the Church, and the moral consequences. What about a sacrament? He teaches its nature, history, motives of its institution, its matter, its form, its effects, the ministry of it — when, where, how it is necessary to administer it, and conditions required to receive it. About a virtue? A vice? He teaches their nature — kinds, causes, effects, practice, and details of morality.

The great rule in instruction is to go from the known to the unknown; consequently, the speaker must know perfectly the condition of the people he is evangelizing in relation to their knowledge of religion and their understanding of their duties. Besides the well-informed people in his audience, there will always be some who are less intelligent. For them, some simple notions should be placed even in the more difficult sermons. The preacher can present simple ideas as if by chance, and make them the basis of a development of much interest even to a well-informed audience.

The preacher can associate the notions which he wishes to give with those his people already possess. Before less educated audiences, instruction should be started from a catechetical basis. The Creed, the Lord's Prayer, the Hail Mary, and the Commandments might also be the theme of most of the instructions. To simplify is an important rule in instruction. In order that people might profit from the usual understanding of matter and by it proceed to the knowledge of the things of God, our Saviour always used familiar material — allegories, parables, and comparisons. He never forgot, however, the dignity of the pulpit.

4. *Amplification in Instruction*

To amplify matter in a speech of instruction is to give an idea all possible clarity, to identify unknown things with the known, to explain details, and to make the development naturally, with order, giving to comparisons and to allegories simplicity, truthfulness, and naturalness. A speaker cannot presume that any truth is so well known to his listeners that he can present it too simply, or that he can stress too much the same idea or important points. Yet the preacher, who is relatively limited in his choice of subject, must have variety in treating the same matter so that his hearers will have no cause to complain that he is continually repeating the same truth. Ideas must be presented, as St. Augustine suggests, in such a way that the reason can grasp them easily; it should be given nothing too difficult to believe nor be exposed to anything which is repugnant to it.

The preacher must place the diversified notions in sequence and relationship in order that they may lend themselves to persuasion. The simplest points should come first; next, those which are less simple; finally those more complicated. General principles should be expounded before conclusions are drawn and applications made. Finally, it is well to give, at times, as preliminary observations, all the implications which later will enter into the plan of instruction.

5. *Refutation in Instruction*

Refutation enters in instruction in resolving errors and prejudices which might prevent the understanding and retaining of notions which the preacher wishes to impart. It often happens that an explanation is not understood because the listener does not appreciate the fundamental point to which it is attached. The preacher who is alive to the needs of his listeners generally knows the difficulties that prevent instruction from penetrating into their mind. He can refute objections as he proceeds with the instruction, and he can bring forth notions appropriate to the needs of his flock.

6. *Conviction*[2]

To convince, in the opinion of rhetoricians, is to compel someone by reasoning or by sensible proofs and evidence to live in accordance with a truth or a fact; to persuade is to bring one to believe or to decide to do something. Conviction is a matter more of the intellect; persuasion more of the will. To convince is a purpose of philosophy, but for the orator, it is only a means. A preacher does not accomplish much if he fails to move the will. Consequently he seeks to enlighten the intellect by proofs, to arouse affection for the truth, and to stimulate a desire to possess it in some efficacious and practical way.

Conviction is generally a prerequisite to persuasion. Persuasion,

---

[2] Although rearranged, most of this matter has been taken from Bellefroid's *Manuel D'Éloquence Sacrée*, pp. 199–251.

then, is the end which a preacher intends, an effect which he wants to produce. If an audience is thirsty for truth, the preacher will be able to accomplish his purpose simply and easily by instruction. But the task of the sacred orator is not always so easy. In general, men like to give homage to their reason and ask its assent. They appeal to a preacher to give them an understanding of cause, to present motives, to devise considerations capable of satisfying a reasonable mind. They want everything placed first on a solid foundation by good proofs. As a rule, only after satisfying the intellect by sound reasons and forceful arguments can the orator excite the hearts of men to open to him their confidence. Although formal proofs are not rigorously necessary, they are often used to advantage in leaving in the mind a good basis for a doctrine, and in giving to truth a solid understructure. Generally a person attaches himself more to religion and practices it with greater pleasure when he is convinced of the certain foundation of the truths which it teaches.

Method in Conviction. In order to instruct, a speaker goes from the *known* to the *unknown;* to convince he proceeds from the *certain* to the *uncertain* in making clear that the truth in question is contained in one or many truths already known by him or in those he grants. This method operates in two ways: the one, positive, and the other, negative. The first consists in concluding from a truth known by the hearer, the truth which is taken in the thesis; the second consists in showing that if the supposed truth taken in the thesis is false, it is necessary to reject also the truth admitted to be unquestioned. Each of the two methods has its advantages: the latter is more piquant, the first is more logical, and in a sense, more dignified and more rational.

There is no historical or dogmatic truth which a speaker cannot prove in the negative way. If this truth is uncertain, there is nothing certain. If you must, for example, renounce a belief in some truth, you are obliged to admit an absurdity, e.g.: If Jesus Christ is not God, the religion of Mahomet is the true religion; or: Either Christ is in the Eucharist or there is no God. Finally a moral truth can equally be proved by the argument of absurdity;

if such an obligation can be regarded as doubtful, the same judgment can be brought against other obligations. This method, however, must be used with prudence and circumspection.

A speaker can go from the certain to the uncertain either by *analysis* or by *synthesis.*

Analysis consists in pulling apart for the hearers the plan of the speech and leading them unconsciously by a series of reasons, which they do not understand immediately, until they are forced to admit a conclusion. If, for example, a preacher wishes to prove the existence of God, he may begin with the observation that everything which we see in the world has necessarily had a beginning; he continues to reason that everything that had a beginning must have an anterior cause; he remarks that in going from a cause to another cause, a listener must arrive at a first and supreme Cause, the only source of order and the plan which a person perceives is working in the world. This method of *analytic* reasoning can be adapted only to few subjects, and it is not the method to be used for a discourse before a cultured audience.

The ordinary progress of sacred oratory is by *synthesis,* in which a speaker proposes first the subject under discussion, then indicates the purpose to be attained, and follows this proposal with arguments until he has convinced his audience.

To use the method of going from the certain to the uncertain, there must actually be some uncertainty in the proposed question. Proof must be directed only against what the auditor doubts or what exposes him to doubt. When anyone raises opposition to a dogma, his conviction in relation to that truth really upsets his mind. Generally, however, the preacher must take for granted that everyone of his audience accepts the chief truths — the existence of God, the immortality of the soul, the divinity of Jesus Christ, the existence of hell, and some others — these he must not stop to establish or defend. To search for proofs for these important truths and to spend considerable time expounding them may suggest to the audience that these truths can be seriously questioned. Yet, if the speaker incidentally mentions the proofs, he should avoid any suggestion that these truths can be seriously doubted. Some truths are so *constant* that they need no proof, but if they are proposed, they can be explained without prejudice to their validity.

There are the principles which carry their proofs with them, and these are so evident that one cannot deny them with any appearance of reason; there are also other principles which may not be so clear to the mind and these must be sustained by evidence. The general rule might be stated thus: everything that can be contested ought to be proved or at least defended. Sometimes an incidental reflection or a word will be sufficient; often a speaker must offer proof, or even many proofs. If the mind, in order to be convinced, should be led from the certain to the uncertain, it follows then that the preacher should seek to understand what the hearer admits as well as to discover that which he will not admit.

7. *Choice of Proofs*[3]

There are two characteristics by which the sacred orator will know a good proof, and which will direct him in his choice of the means of conviction.

1. *Definiteness*. A proof must definitely prove a proposed point. The following propositions, for example, are very different and require separate proof: (*a*) *one must restore the goods of others;* and (*b*) *one must restore the goods of others immediately.* If the preacher intends to prove the second proposition, whereas his arguments only establish the first, it is evident that he will not achieve his end. Thus, if the speaker confounds close ideas, either he takes a part of the proposition or he proves the subject in place of the attribute, and as a result all his reasoning becomes false, and all the consequences which can be drawn from the premises are false. The isolated truths may, it is true, produce some very uncertain effects. But the principal end of the speech will not be attained, and the general effects will be lacking. Obviously, it is a good rule to prove the proposed proposition.

2. *Capacity for audience acceptance*. The antecedent truth

---

[3] This and the following section of this chapter are practically a free and an abridged translation of Bellefroid's *Manuel D'Éloquence Sacrée*, Chapitre VIII, Seconde Partie.

ought to be granted by the audience. If it is not approved, the conclusion can never have more strength than the principle of which it is the consequence. For example, the speaker may regard the authority of Holy Scripture as infallible, whereas the hearers may not have the same idea. Sometimes the preacher is obliged to multiply his proofs, since the different classes of persons who make up his audience do not apply entirely the same arguments with the same force.

Circumstances Influencing Choice. Since proofs should be disposed, combined, and assembled so as to form a single whole, a perfect ensemble will bring about the establishment of one and the same truth. As the order of proofs does not depend entirely on matter but on a number of circumstances, a few suggestions may be helpful:

Nature of Subject Matter. The sequence is sometimes entirely dependent upon the nature of the things which should be treated. Although causes are generally placed before effects, and moral principles before their consequences, it may be that the subject can be better handled by speaking first of the effects, and then of the causes, or by explaining morality, then relating applications to principles. Thus, in a sermon on a saint, the preacher may establish the topic of necessity; he gives the characteristics of virtue, then he makes an application of the matter to the saint; or he may first give examples of good works, and then follow this by treating of the virtue which has inspired these works.

Order Influences Choice. The natural disposition of proofs means that all those belonging to the same order are grouped together. It is contrary to good sense to go from one order of proofs to another, then back to the first; for example, from proofs of authority to proofs of reason, and then back to proofs of authority.

Choice According to Benefits. Proofs must be considered in relation to motives. These may be classified according to the different benefits brought to the listeners as follows: honesty, utility, certainty, agreeableness, ease, and necessity. This subject of motivation will be discussed in the next chapter.

Choice Influenced by Strength of Proof. When there is freedom of choice regarding the class and the distribution of proofs, a speaker should follow the order indicated by Quintilian and other rhetoricians: *Stronger, strong, and strongest* (Quintilian b. 5, C12; Cicero, *De Oratore*, 2:77). The right premise predisposes hearers in favor of a thesis. A speaker may then place in the middle of his speech those considerations which, taken all together, will aid the proofs which precede them and those which are to follow them. The very strongest proof is reserved for last, because ordinarily the last impressions of a speech are those which remain. The old maxim has it "that the speech should ever grow and swell."

Sometimes a speaker places at the beginning of the subdivisions a proof more brilliant than *really* strong, but then he understands that people do not attach too much importance to it. The speaker must remember that usually he is dealing not with the objective strength of proofs but rather with their relative strength, for their force varies infinitely, and with circumstances. The use of an opponent's actions or words as an argument against him is certainly not in itself always the most sound argument, yet is ordinarily placed at the end of the speech, because relatively it has great strength.

Objectively, the strongest of all proofs of religious truths are those of divine authority; following these are the proofs of reason; and then in third place are examples. Yet a preacher cannot base his arrangement on this estimate of comparative strength because actually the strength of any proof has a subjective element. In a thousand cases a proof from authority — from Holy Scripture or from the Fathers — will be more demonstrable than a proof from reason, but often a proof from reason will have more force. A convenient enough order for the preacher is first to use the proofs from reason as they are understood by everybody; usually they prepare the way for authorities. If the preacher follows the rational proofs with texts from Holy Scripture, they will give support to reason and submit it to divine authority.

As there may be some obscurity in a quoted text, the preacher will clarify it for the hearer by placing along with the quotation the authority of the Fathers, who are regarded as its natural interpreters. Finally, the speaker will add some examples which will confirm the established doctrine, show the practice, and encourage his hearers by giving some striking and appropriate models. There is the natural order; but the art consists in knowing how to vary it to advantage and agreeably, in diversifying it in each subject according to the circumstances and the choice and arrangement of the proofs.

Reasoning. In eloquence, conviction is the result of exact reasoning, of exact consequences flowing from true principles. In a logic class, reasoning takes on the driest and most rigorous forms, but in speaking they are avoided in favor of amplification and ornamentation. Yet the preacher who fails to leave clear and precise notions in the minds of his hearers does not advance his cause. Hence an audience must be led by a chain of syllogisms more or less marked, more or less developed, to understand that a certain conclusion is evident or a certain proposition true.

Matter. Matter of the argument has its source in the topics; they often enter into proof of a point by definition. The speaker may explain a term by demonstrating its parts, its species, or its genus, its causes or its effects, its relation or its opposition to other things by its circumstances, and, finally, by the number of authorities.

Form. The form of an argument consists in the structure, in the arrangement of terms. The principal form from which all others can be reduced is that of the *syllogism*. *We must love what procures for us eternal happiness. But the virtue of mortification procures for us eternal happiness. Therefore, we must love this virtue.* Ordinarily the preacher avoids the use of this orderly and concise method. Rather he presents his argument under this form: *mortification procures for us eternal happiness; therefore, it is necessary to love mortification;* or better still, under the form of enthymeme, itself an abridged syllogism: *it is necessary to love mortification which procures for us an eternal happiness.*

The *dilemma*, another form of argumentation, consists in forcing an adversary to choose between two propositions, either of which defeats him. If the dilemma is to be valid, the propositions must be related and opposed in a sensible and striking manner. For example, in order to prove that the circumstance of a man in office who cannot fill the duties of his position is inexcusable, one will say: *either this man is capable of filling his functions, or he is incapable of it: if he is capable of it, he is not excused from not doing his work. If he is incapable of it, he is not excused for having accepted this position.*

The *sorites* is a sequence or series of propositions with one so depending upon another that the predicate of the first proposition becomes the subject of the second, and the chain follows in this manner until the subject of the first proposition becomes joined in the conclusion to the attribute of the final one. Thus Bossuet wished to direct his listeners to a special consideration of the last words of our Saviour on the cross: "It is consummated." He follows this proposition by this sorites: "There is nothing nobler in the universe than Jesus Christ; there is nothing nobler in Jesus Christ than His Sacrifice; there is nothing nobler in His Sacrifice than His last breath, and then the precious moment when His very holy soul separated from His adorable body." The conclusion ought to be naturally: "Therefore, nothing is more sublime in the universe than the last breath, than this last word: 'All is consummated.'" Bossuet, however, avoids the scholastic form, and substitutes for the formal conclusion a magnificent development which makes the truth more evident.

Sources of False Reasoning.   Among these may be listed:

Wrong relationship. In a chain of thought that develops one of the propositions of a syllogism, as well as in the sequence of the proof, any preacher is in danger of becoming unconsciously mixed by the affinity of thoughts. He must not lose for an instant the general purpose of the speech nor his point.

Overamplification. Even a good mind, because of its understanding and skill, may be seduced by the pleasure of adding thought to thought, ornament to ornament; then it will give little proof, yet weaken the speech by overelaboration. Sometimes some young preacher with a desire to enrich his sermons with beautiful thoughts will sacrifice soundness for cleverness. He wishes to escape the commonplace and to find the new and startling. He attempts to clarify the truth by a great number of citations, allusions, and comparisons, but if he examines his matter he will find that instead of making the truth clearer, he has obscured it, or entangled it in the explanations.

Injudicious Use of Figures of Speech. Farfetched comparisons and enigmas, said St. Jerome, can never have great weight in explaining a doctrine. Once engaged in an allegory, the sacred orator may wish to continue with it. He finds between the two subjects taken in the parallelism a crowd of relationships more ingenious than real, and often he draws from such matter a false conclusion or no conclusion at all.

Problems Created by the Use of Two Unproved Premises. Sometimes also the preacher is obliged to develop two premises in succession, both of which need proof. When two propositions must be proved, hearers often follow the reasoning with difficulty. Hence there should be one premise that does not require proof.

Uninteresting General Proofs. Some preachers find it attractive to develop general principles with magnificent descriptions. But the audience gains a great deal more from the treatment of particular propositions. The audience waits particularly for a demonstration and grows impatient when it is not presented.

Overstressing or Understressing the Conclusion of a Syllogism. Although the preacher must not allow his hearers to draw just any conclusion from what he has said, he need not, on the other hand, repeat his conclusion constantly, but he must formulate it correctly for them. Good proofs sometimes remain ineffective because the speaker is content to slide over conclusions as if they were only for himself and not for his hearers.

8. *Amplification in Argumentation*

Reason and amplification are rightly linked together, one being the development of the other, and the both together serve conjointly to set forth the truth which the speaker has in mind.

Reason addresses itself only to the intelligence, and it has no other end than conviction; amplification, however, tends to deal with the will in exciting feeling. Amplification gives strength to argumentation and to emotional appeal so that no preacher can move an audience efficaciously without its help. "The one and suitable gift to oratory — the highest gift of eloquence is to amplify the subject matter," said Cicero.

Instruction explains an obligation; argumentation gives its proof; amplification unfolds its nature and its grandeur. If the preacher presents simply a long sequence of brief, well-ordered reasons, he may have a very beautiful dissertation but he will not have a good sermon. The dryness of plain reasoning drives away the well-disposed listener, for it is impossible for him to understand proofs when presented rapidly and in a concise and rigorous form. The force of any argument escapes an audience if proof is not developed. Amplification gives to each of the propositions all its evidence, and shows the connection among them. It is especially necessary when an argument would leave doubt in the mind of a hearer, or when even though understood, its strength would not be felt.

"Amplification begins with an oratorical definition," said Cicero. It likewise employs the topic of enumeration. Pure reasoning and amplification both draw their matter from topics, but reason reduces itself to a syllogism, while amplification enumerates, lists, and goes into detail. In order that the amplification be good, the thought must be amplified. If the purpose of amplification is to bring out the real value of a proposition, the preacher should not amplify what is weak, or the audience will quickly sense its weakness. The speaker must delay on strong proofs, treating them as separate units, even separating them to demonstrate them and to bring out their special values. At the same time he will do well to remember that nothing worries an audience more than his stubborn insistence upon explaining the force of a point which it already understands. He must not exaggerate the importance of every subdivision simply because he has his heart set on convincing others of its importance.

9. *Amplification of the Consequences in Moral Matters*

Bellefroid maintains that in preaching the sacred orator cannot content himself with a conclusion dealing with some general practice. He must present details of obligations and deficiencies. The pagan orators generalized their moral conclusions, and gave no specific instruction on duties toward their gods. The prophets of the Old Law however, as well as the prophets of the New, the preachers, have a special mission: "Cry, cease not, lift up thy voice like a trumpet, and show my people their wicked doings and the house of Jacob their sins" (Isa. 58:1).

When the preacher speaks only of vices and virtues in general, it is impossible to make a practical application of his words. He must come down to particular cases which his hearers will understand. He must present some type of conduct by means of striking illustrations which will force the hearer to recognize his own conduct no matter how he may try to deceive himself. The hearer then feels an obligation, or recognizes clearly the effects of a vice, and he will regard them as personally applying to himself. Seeing these things in relation to himself, he profits from the sermon.

An auditor never takes much interest in sermons unless the preacher makes him believe he is reading his heart, that he is conscious of his most intimate thoughts and his most secret actions. In so doing the orator touches a sensitive chord; he has discovered the way to a heart and has become master of it. Not only has he proved that an obligation exists, but he has explained the moral consequences in such detail that each of his hearers, seeing his own deficiencies, can say to himself in the words of the prophet Nathan: "You are that man." Father Louis of Grenada has summed up the matter well: "Personal appeal is the essential part of a speech."

Although moral conclusions would naturally follow the explanation of a duty, the opportunity to bring out a point of moral principle should not be missed, no matter where it occurs. Christ in His reproaches to the Pharisees particularizes and goes into detail; He likewise enumerates some of the works of mercy for which He promises a reward on the last day.

The Acts of the Apostles, and the Epistles furnish us with many proofs that such was also the method of the Apostles.

If the preacher has demonstrated, for example, that a person should have limitless confidence in Divine Providence, he concludes with some moral applications. He shows in detail how few men have confidence in this wise economy: one man fears for his health, another for his fortune; or the mother trembles for her child. Again, if he has proved the grievousness of the sin of slander, and has shown how easily people fall into this sin, he has shown the different species of it by a chain of examples. He could even take one or another of the different professions, and show in a survey of it how one could by slander rob a man of his reputation, his ability, or his integrity, and take away his means of existence. He then can explain the duty of restoring what has been ruined, and the extreme difficulty, the almost impossibility, of such reparation.

The preacher must guard against the use of childish details; for example, those touching on manners, finery of dress, or feminine foibles. For stronger reasons, he must avoid anything that could at least alarm chaste ears, and everything that the gravity of the pulpit, the sanctity of the altar, and the edification of the auditors would not warrant. He should avoid, for example, the dramatic representation of the behavior of sinners or of the conditions of vices, and even the slovenly appearance or indecencies of some Christians in church. The decorum of the pulpit must be respected, and the preacher ought not indulge in too much dramatic detail.

10. *Proofs From Holy Scripture and the Fathers*

The sources of amplification and of reasoning are the different topics which have been explained in Chapter II. It may be well to offer here some observations on the use of texts from Sacred Scripture. Texts, although decisive authority for a proof, must be used in moderation. The more excellent the texts, the more likely they are to be multiplied needlessly, even ostentatiously, as pure ornament. Quotations from Holy Scripture are to be respectfully cited and not pompously declaimed. Three or four texts rightly presented will give a more solid basis to a sermon than twenty of them used simply as a show of learning.

No preacher need force the sense of a text in adapting it to his subject. If the sense is obscure, he can call to his aid a good interpreter of the Holy Scripture. He can escape grave errors by not making false application of a text. He must avoid altering its sense or making any arbitrary interpretation.

St. John Chrysostom holds that to treat Scripture in its *literal* sense (sometimes called the historical or the traditional interpretation given by the Church) is of great value to the preacher. Among the Latin Fathers, even those of the first order, the bad taste of their times is sometimes evident, when they give to a sacred text a weak or improbable sense. The preacher must be aware of this fact, and must avoid such interpretations. At the same time, he need not adhere only to the literal sense; use of the *mystical* sense also is justifiable. This is often related to faith (allegorical sense); to hope (anagogical sense); and to the conduct of morals (tropological sense). Thus the word *Jerusalem,* which in a literal sense is a village in Judea, is often found used in one or the other of these three mystical connotations, for the Church, for heaven, and for a Christian soul. It should be noted, of course, that every text has a literal sense, but not every text has a mystical sense.

No one may interpret freely the Holy Scripture. When one is in doubt whether a text should receive a mystical interpretation, St. Francis said, it is better to cite a text in the form of a comparison or an application. It is then that Holy Scripture is given a third sense called the accommodated sense, of great use to preachers. This is a simple application of the words of Scripture to a new subject. Of these three senses the *literal*, the *mystical*, and the *accommodated*, the first two alone form certain proof, the Holy Ghost having them always under His direction.

A preacher does not explain a text in the manner of a theologian giving a dissertation, or in the way of argumentation. He may employ the different interpretations when they are favorable to the thesis, provided, however, they do not scandalize the weak or bring doubts into minds. He can also very often have recourse to the sense of the Greek or Hebrew texts when the Vulgate appears less energetic. In any case, the texts, as means of conviction, ought to be applied according to the general rules of proof. They must be suitable to the subject, yet make an impression on the audience.

Any text should be avoided if it offends the delicacy of the audience, or if it prevents the listeners from getting an understanding of the principles to be proved. The preacher may use a text without amplification as a proof in itself, or he may begin with a citation of a text, develop it, explain each term, use comparisons, or call upon other texts for explanation or emphasis. He, likewise, may paraphrase a text, or he may present the sense of the text under different developments, yet always concluding with a repetition of the text. Generally speaking, he will seldom find it necessary to quote a text in Latin unless perhaps to indicate a literal translation of it.

The sacred orator can use the works of the Fathers for a solid foundation of doctrines, for examples of good reasoning, for striking thoughts, and for eloquent action, yet in a sermon he should not give many or lengthy quotations from their works. A small number of impressive texts are, however, generally valuable for proof, especially on certain points of doctrine. Often it is necessary to choose between the thoughts of the Fathers in order to borrow from one a particularly forceful or vital expression, for example, an expression from St. Augustine: "God created you without your help; He cannot save you without your help." Sometimes a speaker develops his own thought, then summarizes it in some forceful and profound patristic passage.

11. *Example*

Example is used in a speech on the assumption that new points will be admitted by the listeners when they realize that there is a similarity in the example to what is known. When analogy is used, however, the similarity is in the relationship, and not in the things themselves. Examples have a definite place in the body of a sermon. They should be of a nature, not to arouse doubts, but to bring confidence to the listeners concerning religion itself. The speaker should choose appropriate examples and not too many of them. He should select those which apply precisely to the particular proof being illustrated. He should present examples naturally and interestingly, and he should deduce consequences from them that are suitable to the audience and that refute some of its wrong conclusions.

Examples should, likewise, be accommodated to the age, the conditions, the situation, the intelligence, the prejudices, and the weaknesses of the audience. Certain miraculous stories found in the lives of the saints, for example, must be used only with caution, if they are likely to arouse antagonism on the part of men in the matter of their faith. A speaker who can cite very strong proofs in favor of the truths of our religion does not need examples that will undermine the confidence of his hearers. He will find that the examples which come from his long experience as a preacher have a particular persuasive force.

12. *Forms of Expression of Help to the Proof*

When an orator wishes to use certain matter that he cannot present as proof, he may speak about it as if he were intent on omitting it; actually, of course, he is insisting on its value. He appears to be employing caution and perhaps standing on middle ground. He recalls to the listeners certain facts, opinions, or situations, which it is not opportune to bring fully before them, but of which the remembrance is important to his case.

The preacher sometimes concedes one point to insist more strongly on another. He may, after establishing certain premises, draw a conclusion contrary to the one that his hearers expect: "I wish," said Massillon speaking on slander, "that the faults of your brother would be slight; and the slighter they are, the more unjust you are in noticing them. . . ." When the preacher dramatizes the weak and oppressed as making concessions, he can incite a particular emphasis of pity toward these unfortunates and indignation toward their oppressor.

A preacher may retract, modify, or explain a thought which he has presented when it appears to be badly accepted. "Worthy of a better fortune," said Bossuet in speaking of the Queen of

England, but he added immediately a corrective: "if the fortunes of the earth were such a thing!" Sometimes a correction is only an adroit turn on the part of the orator to give the appearance of omitting something essential or of presenting at random some proposition to arouse attention while he insists upon it more strongly as he passes to a stronger point. This manner of expression gives variety, transition, and gradation to a speech.

A preacher may appear to depend upon the judgment of his hearers and to give up his attempt to win them over to his views. He appeals only to their good faith and common sense. He leaves the issues to their decision. This persuasive oratorical form, with its free and easy style, suggests confidence. It has frequent usage in the Christian pulpit as the preacher may leave to a congregation a decision regarding a cause which is their own. Massillon, in exhorting his hearers to keep the Lenten fast, exclaims: "Will you, while the Church moans, while she covers herself with the vestments of mourning, as her ministers . . . as your brothers . . . as all announce the sorrowful mysteries of a suffering God, and everywhere is the covering of suffering, will you alone fall into an unworthy flabbiness?" The orator here appeals to the heart of his hearers, and he makes them the judges of their duty, the practice of which he has recommended to them.

The preacher may give a preview of a situation, setting forth the difficulties of his hearers who are opposing him interiorly so that they may look at their problem objectively. He may also ask himself or his hearers a question and immediately add an answer. He may engage in a kind of dialogue which gives the discourse warmth and variety. This form of expression, often stronger than simple interrogation, is a very adroit way of impressing people, of destroying doubts, and of refuting pretexts. He may likewise suppose a thing possible or impossible and then draw some consequences that will become powerful means of conviction.

Digressions are generally avoided as tending to take an orator away from his purpose. They may, in circumstances, rest the mind of the hearers, and in turning it briefly from its particular objective, arouse its curiosity on a new subject. They serve sometimes not only as an ornament but as a support to a theme that an orator feels touches certain points better than his prepared subject matter. Sometimes, a preacher may digress to a useful moral point which is not the principal object of his discourse, but he should return to the more important matter as soon as possible. Digressions may be used, for example, as reference to means of obtaining the removal of a disorder, extirpation of a vice, perseverance in a practice, utility of a devotion, or a taking of a good resolution. In a long sequence of homilies, St. John Chrysostom so arranges certain digressions as to return to, and emphasize the necessity of stamping out the vice of swearing.

Digressions, if they are to be good, ought to be, above all, necessary, very useful, interesting, and vivid. If they lead far away from the subject, they are entirely out of place. One that is particularly wearisome is the bringing into a discourse of material from other sermons, particularly from those that had been previously successful. Repetition, indeed, is needed in teaching and preaching, but when repetition increases the length of a lesson or a sermon, the audience considers it a consequence of a lack of preparation, a stressing of some pet point, or an expression of some idiosyncrasy.

13. *Refutation*[4]

In sacred oratory, refutation is not a special part of a speech as in forensic or deliberative oratory, inasmuch as there is no advocate for the opposing party whose argument a preacher must be prepared to anticipate or elude. He has only to refute the objections which are forming in the mind of his auditors while he is establishing a truth and explaining a conclusion drawn from a truth. Refutation goes hand in hand with argumentation in the treatment of a proof, and is its complement. If a speaker neglects it, he will leave in the minds of his hearers ideas opposed to the truth and doubts of his reasons, even his words.

---

[4] This section is a translation of Bellefroid's *Manuel D'Éloquence Sacrée*, p. 246 f.

Quintilian and other rhetoricians agree that defense is more difficult than offense. Special training in refutation is important to the sacred orator in order that he may avoid three major faults of refutation: namely, (*a*) answering everything but the essential issue; (*b*) weakly answering the issue; (*c*) putting an argument in the mouth of an adversary and answering it, instead of stating fairly, and answering definitely an opponent's argument.

The preacher must realize that refutation requires a penetrating, discerning mind, and a certain disposition to controversy, along with a large understanding of the human heart. It further demands a sense of wise reserve and a cautious respectful style, for a preacher must fight without irritation, triumph without humiliating his opponent, and succeed without embittering any adversary. A preacher with a sure insight knows when souls are attempting to run away from repentance, to make excuses, to embrace false principles, or to draw false consequences from good principles in order to evade a correction suggested to them. He brings forth objections in all their strength, and in the way that the hearers have formulated them interiorly. He speaks them exactly so that he can say to his listeners: "Here are your thoughts," and each hearer could reply, "That is precisely what embarrasses me." Hearers will be interested that he has so clearly read the depths of their hearts, and that, far from despising their argument, he considers it at least plausible and sees reasons for leaving or **accepting it.**

Manner of Refutation. When a preacher in his refutation gives the appearance of justifying his hearers under certain conditions, he spares them embarrassment and humiliation. Then he will later show the reasons or the prejudices which perhaps have for a long time ruled them. Above all, he must avoid any appearance of insulting the weakness of a hearer's reason, and after having won an argument, of humiliating anyone by even a suggestion of boastful triumph.

Refutation, although cautiously and discreetly presented, should be categorical and decisive. A feeble, vague, or random response is much worse than the objection itself, for it may scandalize the auditor who is in good faith, while to one in bad faith it will give a feeling of interior triumph at the lack of skill in the speaker. Sometimes a short response will weaken a difficulty until the preacher finds among his proofs something which has the nature of diminishing the effects of objection. Often in an audience there are persons who have sentiments and ideas on which a frontal assault would be dangerous. If a preacher undertakes an indirect yet not weak way of fighting these notions without giving the appearance of combating them, he may be more successful with his persuasion.

In confronting objections, a preacher can determine if he is dealing with a bad principle or a bad consequence of a good principle. Most prejudices will be found to be false applications of good principles. Thus a woman inclined to suicide may pretend to justify her viewpoint by a good principle; namely, that a Christian should carefully guard her honor and her reputation. "Take care of a good name" (Ecclus. 41:15). Sometimes a preacher finds his proof attacked in both principle and application. He may refute the opposing principle, or he may assume it to be true but then deny entirely the application which favors his opponent or turn it against him. He may also make a double refutation of the same error — in principle and in consequence.

At times the sacred orator may propose an objection which he grants entirely so that he will have occasion later to insist very strongly on some point or on some consequence which seems to him to offer difficulty. Thus, for example, after having shown the dangers of riches, he may assume that people have made this objection to his argument: "But, if it be as you have said, then it is very difficult for the rich to be saved." The orator will grant the entire objection and insist on this truth in presenting the words of the Saviour. "And again I say to you, it is easier for a camel to pass through the eye of a needle than for a rich man to enter the kingdom of heaven" (Matt. 19:24). This manner of handling an objection has some advantages over the ordinary steps of refutation. The hearer is struck by the concession which he did not expect. His entire attention was on the response which he expected to be given to the objection.

In the example cited, after having given a rebuke to the selfish heart of certain rich, the preacher may console them and encourage them to charity and then cite the subsequent part of the text: "With men this is impossible, but with God all things are possible" (Matt. 19:26).

A preacher must always determine if an objection comes from an error of the mind or from the corruption of the heart. If from the first, refutation must be clear; in the second, the speaker must not only advance strong argument but he must use effective means of arousing emotions, particularly by employing strong figures of speech. Speaking to man of his last end often will still the murmuring of his passion.

Use of Intrinsic and Extrinsic Topics. The pulpit orator should remember that sources of thought which serve proof serve equally well for refutation. For example, to enumerate the objections quickly in the order which one has proposed them, produces always an excellent effect upon an audience. "You complain," said Father Neuville in a sermon for the feast of All Saints, "of the tyranny of your emotions: but the Church shows you a Paul — a Jerome . . . you bring the excuse of the corruption of your time, or you hold that your difficulties are with your state in life: but the Church shows you men who under the tempestuous weather of the century have saved the flower of their delicate and fragile innocence. . . ."

Practice. As a matter of preparing for effective refutation, seminarians can give answers to objections directed against supposed facts or false reasoning. They could bring to class five examples of erroneous facts brought against some religious dogma or some religious practice. For another class exercise, they might present examples of false reasoning against faith or morals. They might for drill: (*a*) deny a proposition, question the supporting evidence, or support their own propositions; (*b*) distinguish truth from falsity; and (*c*) retort an argument. Another class exercise of value is pointing out the following fallacies in some current religious discussion: (1) missing the issue; (2) begging the question; *post hoc, ergo propter hoc;* false analogy; incomplete or faulty induction; false assumption;

ambiguity of terms; and other faults of syllogistic reasoning. Classroom practice may likewise be devoted to methods a preacher should use in meeting the average objections against religious practices and devotions, for example, against frequent Communion, forming a Holy Name society, and the like.

Assignment.

1. Prepare a ten-minute speech using the chronological order.
   - *a*) The life of St. Paul previous to his conversion
   - *b*) The facts of his conversion
   - *c*) The life of St. Paul after his conversion
2. Prepare a ten-minute speech using the logical order.
   - *a*) Any great activity in life needs a leadership; but living a Christian life is a great activity; therefore it needs a great leader; but Christ is a great leader, consequently we should choose Christ as our leader.
   - *b*) If some men reject the doctrine of original sin, they can see little value in the facts of redemption. But some men reject this doctrine; therefore they see little value in the facts of redemption.
   - *c*) "Now the sting of death is sin, and the power of sin is the Law. But thanks be to God who has given us the victory through our Lord Jesus Christ. Therefore, my beloved brethren, be steadfast and immoveable, always abounding in the work of the Lord, knowing that your labor is not in vain in the Lord" (1 Cor. 15:56–58).
3. Prepare a ten-minute speech using the oratorical order, or the order which departs from the natural order for the purpose of gaining emphasis or some advantage.
   - *a*) Effects of sin
   - *b*) Causes of sin
   - *c*) Remedies of sin
4. Develop a proof from reason; substantiate your views with scriptural citation; show your interpretation of a doctrine is approved by quoting from the Fathers.

CHAPTER VI

1. *Misconceptions Regarding Persuasion*

Affective States Indispensable. Persuasion is not always well understood, especially as to its nature and purpose. Many preachers, reacting against exaggerated "revivalist" emotionalism, declare that not being emotional themselves they cannot bring emotional values into their preaching. Actually, however, no matter how proper the opposition to excessive sentimentality, one could not remain human without emotions. No Christian preacher can even accept the Stoic conception of them and remain consistent with his Christian principles. But even were it possible for him to destroy his own emotional life, he still would be faced with listeners who possess an emotional nature that brings much happiness or unhappiness to them. They will be the first to admit that many of their beliefs have deep roots in their emotional life. Sometimes they believe what they feel like believing; and they may wish others to believe also on the basis of feeling.

Man's Nature Must Be Known. The problem of the sacred orator in directing conduct makes it necessary for him to know human behavior, to interpret action, and to be well acquainted with the workings of the mind and the forces of impelling motives. He must, in a word, understand the psychological nature of man. In fact, the more he considers the various forces which act upon man in the light of their psychological influence, the better he will interpret man's behavior. Since it is the business of a preacher to get listeners to want to do what he knows they should do, he must realize also the

possibilities of using his own emotional life as a means to
obtain the proper ends of his preaching.[1]

The Fear of Being Emotional. Some preachers who readily
admit that emotionless speaking must be actionless speaking try
to avoid this catastrophe by imitating the external manifestations
of the emotional life of others, while keeping their own emotional
life in a straight jacket. This despite the fact that an audience
feels sincerity, rather than judges it. Such men will admit that
general bodily activity, with more or less indeterminate reflexes
and sensory experiences, is of great importance in the audience
for the creation of beliefs. Adopting Shakespeare's principle to
"assume a virtue if you have it not," they build up for the sake
of a better speaking technique, an external pattern of emotional
representation. These preachers unwittingly become actors; and
the more successful they are, the more likely they are to become
demagogues. Or, on the other hand, if the role of moral agitator
becomes sickening to them, they will finally maintain that true
preaching is merely the presentation of a case to the intelligence,
and they will decry motivation as a process of manipulating minds.

Aristotle in his *Rhetoric* has an answer for those who feel
that the art of persuasion is the art of insincerity, and who try to
find in all motivation the speaker's concealed desire to secure
by perfidious measure some personal gain. The Philosopher knew
that emotions could be aroused by false facts and fallacious
reasoning. But this fact did not tempt him to the conclusion that
all persuasion is tainted and hence not to be used. Aristotle
knew, moreover, that the Sophists had made persuasion an evil
art, but he had experience to guide him in the remark that
persuasive speech could come from the mouth of one who was
honest, had an understanding of another's problem, and was
attempting to move a person for his own good to accept a
course of action.

Some clergymen, realizing that clerical power has been used
at times for personal or class benefit, or knowing that many
persons are jealous of the prerogatives of the clergy and accuse

---

[1] St. Paul may be studied for his technique of persuasion. He was a master of
motivation.

priests of domination, try to avoid the responsibility of leadership by presenting religious truths simply as facts, leaving the persuasion to God. These preachers not only fear the art of motivation but distrust their own good judgment of their feelings. They forget that both reason and authority prove a virtue should be not alone known but also practiced. They fail to face the fact that moving souls to practice virtue is their obligation.

What Is Required in Persuasion? The actor, of course, is out of place in the pulpit, but so is the man of pure intellect. Preaching demands a human being who understands that the art of persuasion requires two important gifts of nature and of grace — *a feeling soul* and *true piety*. One gift without the other could only defeat the ends of good preaching.

Psychologists, as well as rhetoricians, have declared that sympathy is a most important asset to a speaker. The sympathetic speaker has a feeling soul by which he realizes that the responses of his audience are of much concern to him, and he is quick to sense audience reactions and to adjust himself to situations. His sympathy for people is the key to his understanding of the intellectual views of others as well as to his appreciation of their emotional manifestations. He knows, for example, that everyday habits can successfully mask the loathsomeness of sin. The views he has gained from reflection upon this fact he does not expect will be acquired by others without motivation. He, therefore, seeks to have people loathe sin rather than accept some philosophical expression of its loathsomeness.

The sympathetic preacher, knowing his own emotional life, can vicariously enter into the emotional life of others, and if he is a pious soul (a necessary condition in Christian motivation), he does not take advantage of this emotional life. The preacher, realizing that situation and circumstances may incite emotions in the soul of each of his hearers, presents it with what can attract it, and what can drive away from it that which it can dislike. He places the things of God before each hearer so that they are the magnets of attraction, and he displays evil in its true light so that it is avoided as a detestable thing. The pious soul who has feeling for others can motivate others, morally certain that his objectives are good, and his means not only effective, but worthy.

2. *The Nature of Emotions*

Feeling is not a sensation but a reaction to it; consequently there are various feelings as effects of agreeable or disagreeable sensations. The active objective intelligence obeys a different law than does subjective blind feeling. Emotions, like feelings, are elements of the affective state. They are related, on one hand, to physiological functions, and on the other, to psychological states of thinking and willing. Emotions produce a full complement of bodily resonances, but they themselves are reactions to meaning, and they come about from an intellectual insight into a situation. They remain in their glow while their cause is present, but generally when the cause disappears, their flame goes out. Pleasure, like sorrow, cannot be without limits. When either reaches its maximum intensity, it tends to recede very quickly to more or less indifferent responses.

Some emotions, like love and hate, are slow to develop; some like envy and pride must be constantly fed, but they usually enjoy a long life. Any emotion may create a state of mind conducive or nonconducive to reason. Some are most infectious, yet some of the more turbulent may arouse opposing emotions and feelings.

Although an emotion cannot be decreased or increased by resolution, it can be indirectly controlled. It may be intensified, for instance, by directing attention to the meaning behind the emotion; or it may be weakened to the point of disappearing by changing the focus of attention to other matters.

In directing the behavior of any group, a preacher will need to apply his knowledge of the passions. He will recall that man is inclined to respond to what his imagination holds out to him as good and to avoid that which it presents as evil. Man is, therefore, subject to the concupiscible passions, or those dominated by desire, consequently conditioned by the absence or presence of an object. From his grasp of the good comes love; of evil comes hatred; apprehending a present good gives joy;

a present evil gives sadness; apprehending a future good gives desire; a future evil gives aversion. But man finds obstacles in his path in attaining good and rejecting evil. He is subject to the irascible passions. Apprehending some good which is attainable gives rise to hope; unattainable good produces despair; apprehension of evil that seemingly cannot be avoided excites fear; evil that can be avoided with a successful struggle arouses courage. Anger rises from an apprehension of present evil. Other names applied to these eleven passions indicate more or less the intensity of the emotion, or the application to another's good or evil, as envy or pity (St. Thomas, *Summa,* Part I, Ques. 81, Art. 2).

3. *The Emotional Element in Sacred Discourse*[2]

Emotions are part of man's natural equipment and are designed to help him find enjoyment in life in the pursuit of good and the avoidance of evil. As a consequence of man's fall, emotions do not always bring happiness to him but instead often weight him down, pressing him at times so heavily that they make him oblivious of the severe prescriptions of reason. The seductive voice of strong emotion may still so captivate and ensnare a man that he mistakes evil for good or a merely apparent good for some real good. At each instant of his life, man is receiving impressions that he accepts as good or evil, either present or absent, real or fancied, and any instant he may accept them blindly (Aristotle, *Rhetoric,* Bk. 2; Quintilian, *Institutes,* 6:2; Cicero, *De Oratore,* 2:51).

Power of emotions. Emotions, as Aristotle pointed out, exercise on man such a power for good or evil that the sacred orator who fails to call them to his aid neglects one of the most powerful means to success. If the preacher will reflect for a moment, he will see that all the disorders, all the vices — all, in short, that he intends to reform in his hearers — have their single cause in the disordered actions of the heart. Even unbelief itself is almost always the fruit of bad passions. When the unbeliever is stripped

---

[2] Sections 3 and 4 are based upon the translation of Bellefroid's *Manuel DÉloquence Sacrée,* p. 252 f.

of his fatal servitude, his unbelief is generally cured. According to many great saints who have studied the cause of sin, certain disorders arising from emotions should be treated in their causes. If the preacher knows how to oppose the culpable emotions with contrary emotions, he can triumph over the evil. "Depraved emotions, like a key in the lock, are turned by contrary emotions," said Grenade.

Bad Passions, the Enemy of the Preacher.[3] When the preacher has given instruction and explained duties, when he has proved his points, and even convinced his auditors, they still hesitate to change their conduct. Why? Because passion resists interiorly. The hearers are convinced but not persuaded; their will is not won over. Their intelligence is not sick, but the heart is dominated by the passions, and arguments have little power over the heart. Feelings, inclinations, emotions are the true adversaries of the preacher. They are the enemies which he must fight, and he must use as weapons in order to save man the same means which were powerful enough to have served souls that were lost. These means, which are certainly in nature, strongly affect man as his mistakes themselves show, and these means have at least equal value in effecting his reformation.

Emotions, the Friend of the Preacher. The means of combating and destroying the effect of a passion which is opposing the reclamation of the soul of a hearer, is the use of the same passion which removes the virtue. If the preacher knows the passions which exercise on his hearers the greatest domination, he can give them the saving remedy. If he knows, for example, that shame is keeping some people away from confession or forcing them to be silent in the confessional regarding certain sins, he knows that to overcome this obstacle he must picture clearly for this group the universal assembly of all humankind at the Last Judgment, and make them understand how much more terrible then will be their shame and disgrace before this multitude if they do not overcome the shame which is now restraining their tongues.

---

[3] "Men, no matter what their training, are governed by their passions, and the most we can hope to accomplish is to keep the handsome passions in the majority" (from speech by Woodrow Wilson before the New York Southern Society in 1910).

Although the Catholic preacher aims to help his listeners form intelligent convictions, he need not expect that these judgments will always be made on the basis of reason. But he can look for his listeners to use reason guided, and even dominated by, the authority of God Himself. Yet even with reason and divine authority on his side, the preacher must appeal to the emotional nature of man. Even realizing that man's emotions are frequently the strongest tool in the hands of Satan for man's own destruction, no preacher should even suggest as an aim the destruction of emotions on the assumption that they are intrinsically evil. His aim is to get people to guide passions into proper channels. The realistic preacher presents an adequate program for the development of emotions, a plan that directs man to a right attitude toward his social obligations and offers him a fulfillment of his nature while leading him to his proper end.

Few Catholics really doubt the existence of hell, but some live as if there were no hell! These persons do not lack instruction; rather their hearts obey their disorganized inclinations despite the cry of conscience. Preachers who convert men affect the heart which in turn speaks to the mind. The more a preacher appeals to the intellect, the more he must address the heart also if he is to bring his hearers to manage their lives effectively. The preacher who can arouse feeling for his cause and discourage feeling against it is, in truth, helping his listeners get thoughts, images, and feeling. If they have an interest in reacting to meaning, they get more meaning when they respond to some situation with emotion.

Persuasion, Chief End of Preaching. "Who moves the most preaches the best" was the rule given by Fénelon to aspiring preachers. All the masters of sacred oratory have continually advised students to remember that the prime end of preaching is persuasion. "All the force of the word," said Fénelon, "ought to tap the hidden resources which nature has placed in the heart of man." The words of St. Francis de Sales on meditation — "It is not necessary to spend too long a time with the reasoning of the mind, but one should give himself up principally to the affections of the heart" — can be applied no less to

preaching. God Himself, in fact, is not content with bringing
light into the mind; He draws out, He moves, He wins the
will. The spirit of God even turns us from speculation to
practice. "I am the Lord thy God that teach thee profitable
things" (Isa. 48:17). Grenade, who had such influence on
preachers of the past century, has remarked, "To move minds is
the principal function of a preacher." St. Alphonsus Liguori,
who took deep interest in studying oratorical advantages, has
stated that "what is most important in preaching is moving the
will of an audience."

4. *Determining the Bad Passion*

Human nature would not be complete without the seed of
every emotion. Yet each seed is not equally fertilized in every
person. What is weak in one person is precisely what dominates
another. Each person has a passion which tends to master him.
Some people, for example, have a very strong belief that their
lives are guided solely by reason — an indication that they are
actually slaves to a belief based upon emotion and feeling. Attitudes of people toward emotions change. In one age love, for
example, may be viewed in relation to protection and devotion;
in another period have a voluptuous quality; at still another
time, it may be associated with fancy and idealized loveliness.
The nature of the vices likewise may seem to change. Although
seldom have they been free from a superstitious veneration in
any age, they have been glossed over with shades of gray in
one period and made ink black in another. Nothing is more
helpful to a preacher than to know exactly how a particular
vice is regarded in a particular parish and what blessings have
been imparted to a vice by local custom and the sanction of
accepted leaders.

5. *Prevailing Emotions*

In view of the importance of audience reactions, it is wise
for the preacher to test his views on prevailing emotions in
certain more or less fixed groups, for example, in the congregation at an earlier Mass as compared to one at a later Mass.

The Catholic priest generally accepts his audiences as believers, and prepares his sermons, as he should, in view of the beliefs of his hearers. Sometimes it is well for the preacher to test his sermons for sentiments and thoughts that are acceptable to him and his listeners, yet may be producing little practical results. He may even, for the moment, regard himself or his listeners as unbelievers and, from this viewpoint, criticize his own sermons. He may find that he will have to add explanations, or perhaps to change the whole plan of his discourse in order to make his presentation clearer and more persuasive, even for those who agree in his conclusions. Again, he may find that many of his presumptions regarding his audience need to be reconsidered.

If the preacher would understand the difference in people, particularly at different social levels, he should consider the complexion of emotions as found in types of persons or under certain circumstances. He will find some advantage in studying classifications of groups according to general personality traits, or as they react to the conflicts of living.

6. *Classification of Emotional Types*

Psychologists have many ways of classifying personality types. It is to the interest of the preacher to learn the characteristics of such reaction types as the sanguine, the bilious, the phlegmatic, and the melancholic. He will find that some people fall into a type that seems to be governed by fears, fixations, and depression. Others may be classified as oversensitive, the ascendants, the seekers after attention and sympathy, the anxious class, the overactive, the lethargic, the suspicious and reclusive type, the deterioration class, the extroverts, the introverts, the highly suggestibles, and the nonsuggestibles, the compensators, and the sublimators.

Classifications should not be applied too rigorously. Few people have all the characteristics of any one type. There is, however, an advantage in knowing the general reactions of a type as an aid to the study of the group mind, and the crowd, after all, is the chief textbook for the preacher in his psychological study of human nature. The more he knows the crowd-mind, the more he will understand the controlling incentives which make people think as they think and act as they act.

7. Choice of Emotions in Persuasion

Sacred eloquence calls upon all the emotions, because all can be used as powerful aids in moving man to value his highest interests in life. As to the choice of emotions which a preacher ought to make, he may be guided by the progression of interior action, by which, according to the Council of Trent, a man arrives at his justification. Before speaking to the heart and inciting feeling there, a preacher must remember that the mind must be illuminated by the light of faith, the foundation, the indispensable base of the entire edifice of preaching.[4] The pulpit orator should strive first to give birth to, or to reawaken, faith by his instruction and his reasoning. Intelligence illuminated by faith will dispose the heart to feeling, and it will open it to the sentiments of fear, hope, and love.[5]

Fear. Fear exerts a great dominion on man since it affects what is very strong in him — love of happiness. When fear has God for its object, the beginning of all wisdom and the principle of all perfection, it has power to rule man. It will prevent him from committing certain acts, even such as are known only to himself, and which the world would never know. Men often check their criminal desires because of the thought that God sees them and because of the dread of punishment. The fear of hell is a powerful incentive for banishing the tyranny of evil habits and for disrupting illicit attachments. The preacher ought, then, to hold himself ready to incite in his hearers a salutary feeling of fear by continually recalling the judgment of God and man's last end. This is particularly true when the preacher wishes to incite his hearers to a difficult renunciation of something very dear to them. One thing must be borne in mind,

---

[4] "The beginning, the foundation, and the root of all our justification is faith" (Council of Trent). "God does not ask of you blood, but faith" (St. Cyprian).

[5] This treatment of the emotions is based chiefly upon a free and abridged translation of Bellefroid's *Manuel D'Éloquence Sacrée*, pp. 256–263.

however: a sermon should not be concluded by an appeal based upon fear.

Despite the fact that many modern educational psychologists maintain that reward is the only effective agent of motivation, and that fear only defeats itself when used as a basis to obtain some action, fear remains a factor that determines conduct, and a good legitimate means to obtain a proper end. It is true, of course, that the appeal to fear can be wrongly exaggerated, badly placed, or overused. There is evidence to support the view that the fear of the devil or of hell is not such a strong impelling force as always to sustain belief in God, or unfailingly to draw sinners away from the alluring vices. Some men have an almost pathological fear of the devil and yet continue a life of sin — lapsing eventually into either presumption or despair.

Fear regarding a future state may be sidetracked by various reactions such as anxiety and compensatory or defensive tactics concerning other affairs. Yet despite this temporary submergence, fear still remains a painful emotion excited by the apprehension of impending danger. If the danger involved in the loss of a soul is properly presented, the emotion of fear will naturally follow and such an emotion is not agreeable.

Hope. The noble sentiment of hope brings the soul close to God. A pulpit speaker does a great service when he arouses in a man confidence in the infinite mercy of God. Since more sinners are probably lost through despair than through presumption, the preacher must build up the courage of the sinner. He must open his heart to him, and constantly show him the possibility of his return to God, the grandeur in the mercies of our Saviour, and the ease of conversion for one who sincerely desires it.

An old missionary was constantly advising young preachers to "put something in a sermon to let people dream about." Just as people are interested in the success stories of other people because they are stimulated to enjoy vicariously the hopes and fears of other human beings, hope in God's mercy may arouse a crusader's belief in some positive action. Often it arouses discontent for a sinful life which may increase day by day. Reform is seldom a spontaneous affair, but comes from a long-time disgust for the supposed pleasures of sin.

In preaching on the more difficult commandments, the pulpit orator must constantly proclaim the efficacy of grace, the infallibility of prayer, the merits and the results of confidence in God. When he has spoken emphatically against the disorders of man, he must inspire a lively fear of God's judgment and the punishments of the future life; but he should not fail to give courage to his hearers, presenting to them some consoling consideration which makes easy the sacrifice that fear alone would never bring about.[6] If he wishes to console those who suffer, to raise those who have fallen into anxiety and other distresses, he will find no more efficacious means than to give people Christian hope.

Love. Through hope, we arrive at love of God as the sovereign Good of our souls. This love of God for Himself, and for His infinite perfections, is the ultimate goal of the preacher. To love God above everything and to love one's neighbor as oneself for the love of God is the fullness of the law. This proposition the speaker should unceasingly repeat to his audience. The flame of charity, kindled by him, should warm every heart.

Subsidiary Feelings. These three feelings of *fear*, *hope*, and *love*, which can lead men to the most intimate union with God, encompass a great number of other emotions, such as hatred of vice, desire of eternal reward, compassion for the unfortunate, sorrow for sin, and the like. Any of these may be chosen to excite hearts depending upon circumstances, particularly circumstances of taste, inclination, affection, interest, and virtue of the hearers. "I apply all my energy to try to discover the most secret thoughts of my hearers," said Cicero, "so that I may discover what they feel, what they have, and what they wish," for he adds, "it is easier to incite action than to overcome indifference." The preacher can determine what emotions generally accompany the matter he is treating. It would be ridiculous, for example, for him to have recourse to a strong passion in a peaceful subject. The

---

[6] It has been said that the following thought from Edmund Burke has helped many people over difficult situations: "Never despair. But if you do, work on in despair." If such thoughts can wield such influence over people that they arise to new tasks with courage, Christian hope should have so much more value.

nature of the subject, then, as well as the personal disposition of the hearers, greatly determines the technique to be used in persuasion.

8. *Place and Order of Emotions*

There is a proper place in any speech for persuasion; but it can likewise be used inopportunely. People distrust a preacher who makes known from the beginning his intention of being carried away by his emotions. They believe that one who fails to appeal first to the understanding must be weak in good reasons. On the contrary, when the speaker begins by instructing his hearers and proving the truth, they judge his proposition to be well established and worthy of assent. They will then derive satisfaction and enjoyment from his later emotional appeal.

Feeling must be used fittingly; it is essential to give the emotional factor time to work. The blustering vehemence to which some speakers give way before they have sufficiently prepared their listeners for persuasion leaves the hearers cold, astonishes them, and very often makes the orator appear ridiculous to them. The preacher should follow the progress of nature. Feeling grows in hearts gradually through meditation on some strong truth or through consideration of some striking image. This same gradual process should be followed in persuasion. The preacher must prepare minds for oratorical action, which, when used, must appear to be spontaneous. He should appear to be inspired by the situation, and say or do nothing that would allow his listeners to infer that he proposes to excite their feelings.

In general, a speaker must abstain from intense emotion at the beginning of a speech. A soul in passion is in a violent state which cannot last a long time; hence too great tension of mind will soon exhaust an audience. A preacher should in general grade a sermon to high feeling and stop or make a transition to milder feelings, perhaps to mount later to the *highest* emotional appeal of all. But he should avoid anticlimax or a vain attempt at a second climax. Sometimes a speech raised to an emotional climax may be effectively finished with a few calm but impressive sentences.

The natural place for emotional action is at the end of the main heads of a speech or at their subdivisions. The speaker must give forceful conclusions to strong proofs in order to change simple summaries into those of action. He may also present certain proofs with greater feeling than others. With the intellect won over, the will bows easily and accepts the action impressed upon it. When it admits a conclusion, it will react quickly to the fear of evil, the desire of good, or other emotions. If, on the contrary, after a preacher has presented his proof and the audience is ready to respond emotionally, he proceeds to enter immediately into a new order of ideas or new proofs, the effect of the awakening emotion is lost. The minds of listeners may be enlightened, but their hearts are not changed. When an audience is emotionally incited, the preacher must press his advantage quickly and wholeheartedly. An emotional awakening in the audience must be treated as the signal, for attack, and the sacred orator cannot give the audience a breathing spell. The natural wave of feeling is a God-given means to bring souls to their salvation.

Emotional appeal may be placed in a certain order.[7] When the preacher wishes to incline the will by the means of certain emotions, he uses first whatever emotion does not depend upon another emotion. His final appeal is with the strongest motivating agent he possesses. For example: he wishes to help a person avoid sin. He searches for the feeling which should remove the desire to sin. He awakens in his listeners the love of God or the fear of hell. He must decide generally between these two feelings to determine the stronger, the more proper to incite — not every audience, but the one he is addressing. To use another example: he wishes to arouse an aversion for sin. Should he awaken the love of a person's welfare, in that sin deprives man of heaven, or

---

[7] If some basic condition be established, for instance, reverence for the body as a temple of the Holy Ghost, then other desired qualities similar in nature — respect, purity, or love can be sought after in some proper order.

should he incite a fear of hell? The speaker will choose one of these sentiments according to the circumstances of the audience. If he appeals to the same emotion by different considerations, he will grade them in a way to strengthen impressions. He will place the first impressive one in the introduction where its flame will increase and be developed in the body of the speech, while in the peroration he will use the one best adapted to incite the highest degree of action.

9. *The Use of Emotions in Relation to Motivation*

The motives most suitable to arouse the will are divided into two orders: the interests of the supernatural order — heaven, grace, and the like; and those of the temporal order — fortune, honor, health. Although heaven, hell, and eternity are the important interests which should take a hold upon the soul, actually they do not always make the impression that they ought. For various reasons they are often regarded as something far removed from man's immediate concern.

For this reason the preacher will often find it useful to appeal to motives which are attached to more immediate interests. Persons who are steeped in vice are less sensitive to a supernatural motive than to the loss of health, honor, reputation, or life. The desire for wealth, fame, fortune, or possession is found in many, if not most, men. If any of these desires can be aroused in listeners, they will be impelled to action.

Those who do not wish to believe can find fifty reasons for not doing so; on the other hand, if the right motives are presented the will-to-believe can be aroused. Let the preacher consider such motives as arise from social pressure, interests, justification of a course of action, trustworthy evidences, credible testimony, sound reasoning, long-standing desires, and the something-behind-the-drive to get something done. Then, too, men by nature wish to be happy and to keep out of trouble, to avoid worry, and to get rid of discomforts. They can be motivated, if they feel that they will be rewarded. The preacher's problem is to choose the right impelling motive.

Practical Values Related to Benefits. Different benefits have motivating values.

a) Easy and attainable. To get some people to believe in religious truths, a proposition must be placed before them which will arouse no resistance. It may be received with no noticeable pleasure, but it is agreed to chiefly because there is no difficulty involved in its acceptance. "This commandment that I command thee this day is not above thee, nor far off from thee" (Deut. 30:11).

Some people allow their religious affairs to continue as they are, because to accept a new view or course of action would involve a degree of unpleasantness, difficulty, or trouble. If a preacher stresses the difficulty of gaining belief or of living decently, he will drive people to maintain at least their present status. The advertising man knows that interest is aroused when a person feels he can do something without expending too much effort, or if he will find certain zest, perhaps adventure, in overcoming obstacles. The preacher can demonstrate the adjustments people must make in everyday living to gain temporary rewards, and then show how, with at least equal industry and effort, they can adjust themselves easily to situations that will benefit their eternal future. He can illustrate his point with concrete and specific examples based on human experiences.

b) The decent thing to do. Men are greatly influenced by what is socially "the thing to do." In some the social motive may be so strong as actually to engender sinful pride in their religious behavior. Such persons avoid sin chiefly because they feel that as models they should set an example to the weaker brethren. *"My dignity"* or *"my honor"* are factors behind certain beliefs.

Yet honor is a particularly strong motivating force especially when related to a moral ideal and when considered as a perfection of a reasonable nature (*l'honnête, honestum*). This is the motive that our Saviour advanced in responding to the young man who had questioned Him: "If thou wilt be perfect, go, sell what thou hast, and give to the poor, and thou shalt have treasure in heaven: and come, follow me" (Matt. 19:21). To *honor* is related

the *praiseworthy* and the *glorious,* both of which speak of the
grandeur of the soul, of its generosity, and of its magnificence.
It is by these motives that Judas Machabeus encourages his
warriors from running away before a battle. "God forbid we
should do this thing, and flee away from them: but if our time
be come, let us die manfully for our brethren, and let us not
stain our glory" (1 Mach. 9:10).

Likewise to correct or to turn someone away from a certain
action, a speaker may proceed to show that the action is shameful,
vile, and dishonest. Thus a very powerful means of warning young
people against the dangers that menace their innocence is to
strengthen and augment their natural modesty by inspiring them
with a great horror and disgust for vice as a hideous thing and
dishonorable even in the sight of reason. This motive will often
be more effective in a critical occasion than even the fear of hell
or the judgment of God.

c) *Utility.* Gain and advantage are the motives that our
Saviour used in the text previously cited: "And thou shalt have
treasure in heaven." A speaker cannot too often show the advantages of a thing in order that people will accept it, or its disadvantages in order that they will turn away from it. People like
power and influence. How can religion give these values? Self-
interest is in general the most powerful motive instigating human
actions. Some classes of society are very susceptible to praise and
glory, and are easily persuaded by motives drawn from upright-
ness; but for most men the less noble motive of utility has the
greater attraction. "What will I get out of it?" is a common
enough question. The pulpit orator may speak to worldly young
men whom he wishes to restore to grace so that they see themselves rewarded for good conduct and gaining particular blessing
from heaven on their endeavors.

d) *Other good motives* relate to the *safe* way of doing something. To those who felt themselves too weak to protect their
continence, St. Paul advises marriage as the better way for them.
"But if they do not contain themselves let them marry, for it is
better to marry than to be burnt" (1 Cor. 7:9). The *agreeable,* too,
is a common motive: "For my yoke is easy and my burden light"

(Matt. 11:30). *Necessary:* "Now I say to you: but except you do penance, you shall all likewise perish" (Luke 13:5). *Contraries:* to dissuade someone from evil a speaker may set forth the opposing evils in contrast with the benefits derived from a good life.

10. *Feeling Related to Knowing*

In order to excite the emotions of his audience, the preacher must pay attention not only to its age, education, habits, and customs but also to its intelligence. Feeling is not so blind as always to be illogical; it does not always act independently of intelligence. In fact, "what we do not know we do not desire." A person perceives an object. He dwells on it by reflection, he knows it, he appreciates it, either hating or loving it, desiring it or having an aversion to it. That every person is not moved in the same manner is due not always to more or less feeling, but to a more or less developed intelligence which does not know equally well all force of the truths and therefore presents these truths to the affective states with varying emphasis. Moreover, the same truths, motives, or purposes, when presented too often, fail to incite the emotions and have less stimulation and interest value.

The controlling incentive is found in some good. The chief concern of the preacher is to find and utilize the controlling incentive behind actions. He figuratively throws a switch when he effectively transfers to his audience the information that it is a good thing to do this or that. The will of each person in the audience is then inclined to be moved by what has been presented as good or valuable. The assent usually brings into play an entire chain of mental and physical consequences. But the good presented to the audience must be acceptable *to each person as specifically good for him;* it must not remain merely an abstract notion of good, or a good for anybody. It must have value enough to encourage a person to desire new habits and to reject the old ones that are incompatible with the purpose now to be obtained.

Sound Values Give More Permanent Results. Whatever is accepted as having worth-while value provides motivating force, but the intrinsically better and higher values will remain for a greater length of time as effective instigators of worthy resolutions.

Ideals, loyalties, and interests greatly influence the will. If they are chiefly products of the imagination or feeling, they cannot stand too much analysis. True, the preacher must use whatever legitimate means he can for persuasion, particularly those which are experienced in the concrete with emotional satisfaction, but he should remember that reason will sooner or later seek causes to justify a belief, even though it had no part in its creation. Sound values are found in reason and evidence having likewise emotional worth.

11. *Value in Motivating Phrases*

The repetition of slogans, sayings, or clever allusions, particularly during retreats or missions, awakens a kind of crusading spirit. The well-turned phrase often has real value in expressing some belief or viewpoint. Many of the pithy remarks of St. Albert the Great became household expressions in Germany. The three famous words, *liberty, equality,* and *fraternity,* heard during the French Revolution, although of little practical influence in creating liberty, equality, or fraternity among men, had power almost of life or death over them. Some religious dogmas, it also seems after analysis, have had only slight influence on the practical affairs of the world. Yet they are defended or condemned with vigor. If tersely cogent remarks about them are placed in a sermon, they do more than decorate it, for they actually have influence on belief, if not always on conduct. The clergyman, true to his vocation, however, will struggle with the problem of giving to these religious slogans and sayings a moral value by persuading men to accept them for practical application.

A Slogan Often an Affirmation.   The slogan may affirm views already held by the audience. A repetition of some idea, usually in an emotional setting, starts, as if by contagion, an emotional response in an audience. This group action strengthens the opinions of the weak, pulls from the fence the hesitating members, and gives the believers a new justification for their position. Robespierre, for example, with his ill-fitting glasses, painfully reading his speeches, would have failed as an orator had not his slogans, generalities, and masterful pretensions expressed well the emotional views of others. The preacher, knowing the truth behind the expression he employs, need have no fear of deceiving people by effective phrases. Phrases to him are but means to a worthy end — the salvation of souls.

Summary Phrases Must Be Meaningful. The preacher who has reflected on some arresting phrase may consider it very homogenous and illuminating; whereas his listeners, who really wish to understand the dogma, may find it confusing and inconsistent. Some slogans demand explanation in order to have greater value in motivation. Division will be found to be the most powerful rhetorical tool in aiding the understanding of the compact and compressed generalization. The preacher then can give a few ideas at a time, and give them force by association. The understanding of the part will soon give understanding to the succinct idea represented by the pithy slogan.

12. *A Shared Experience Necessary in Motivation*[8]

If the preacher chooses wisely among motives that affect men and impresses his arguments deeply on his listeners, he must feel their force himself. No listener can be aroused by religious truths while the preacher himself views them calmly, intellectually, smugly, or indifferently. A very bad mistake in any speaking, and a fatal one in sacred oratory, is to allow hearers to feel that their interests are not those of the preacher. He must partake of their perils, their fears, their hopes; when he speaks to sinners, they must not be astonished at finding him among them. He must be the first to be affected and concerned with the truth which he speaks. He knows his own feelings which have been impressed upon himself by reflection and meditation; these are the feelings which he must incite in others.

If the pulpit orator wishes to inspire his listeners with the desire for heaven, he traces for himself, after being enlightened by contemplation and faith, the most alluring picture he can paint of that state of eternal happiness. Then he conducts his hearers to the heaven that has been prepared for them, fixing their

---

[8] Sections 12, 13, and 15 are based upon material taken from Bellefroid's *Manuel D'Éloquence Sacrée*, pp. 264–268.

vision on the rewards, and awakening their emotions as they feel themselves transported to the celestial paradise for the possession of an immortal crown.

If he wishes to excite in the souls of his hearers the fear of hell or the hatred of sin, he represents to himself his being plunged into the fire and darkness of the lower regions. He tries to feel even the terrors of the consuming flames. He then tries to visualize what Christ suffered in His Passion of crushing sorrows. He will not have much trouble later in making his hearers feel the force of the eternal flames or the points of the nails which pierced the Saviour or the cruel anguish which crushed His Heart.

13. *Realistic Description Favors Motivation*

Assuming the speaker wishes to tell his hearers how to help the poor, he commences by instructing them in the obligations which are imposed upon them; he proves this point. He then speaks to their feelings and incites in them an emotion of compassion. He describes realistically the unhappiness all about him, showing everyone the evils and the sufferings brought about by need. He places them in a position where they can follow the happenings to be described. He may begin with general impressions and proceed to details, or he may start with detail and end with a general view. He need not lay bare his plan of description, but he must have a consistent viewpoint in it.

Although the audience may modify the images presented by the speaker, it is moved more by their quality than by their quantity. It is the personal view of the speaker that gives vitality to the picture and stimulates action. To further the purpose of motivation, the preacher can, after description, recall that it is Christ Himself who is suffering in the person of the poor. It is He who implores those who loved Him to give alms for the love of Him, and who finally assures man that he who gives to the poor in His Name is giving to Christ Himself.

When the speaker uses his imagination in speaking of mysteries, and when, for example, in order to inspire a fear of hell, or the desire of heaven, he undertakes to describe the other life by striking pictures, he cannot say just what he pleases in his descriptions. What he says must be certain, or at least probable. He should, naturally, base his description on divine revelation, avoiding all the arbitrary details that are found only in the imagination of some orator. Even in citing the texts of the Bible which are concerned, for example, with the celestial Jerusalem, the preacher must be careful to present as metaphorical that which is only metaphorical in order not to impart false ideas. As to hell, what the Saviour said of it is terrible enough to inspire fear, so that the speaker need not add his own description.

14. *Motivation in Relation to Audience Reactions*

The speaker is not the only source of stimulation to an audience. It is subject to many kinds of outside influences, such as those relating to personal comforts and discomforts, distractions, and contrary impulses. The preacher is more fortunate than most speakers in that many conditions help to sustain attention; yet he should be aware of these circumstances so that he may gain their help for emotional stimulation and may remove the handicaps that lack of attention would have upon his efforts.

Attention an Active Process. A preacher cannot drive thoughts disturbing the listener beyond the threshold of his mind. There they remain battling incessantly to re-enter the sphere of attention and to win the right to the spotlight as well as to dominate the mental and affective processes. Yet the preacher can always strive to make his presence and appeal more effective than the contrary stimulation.

The audience that is held in a state of expectancy will give better attention than the one that has settled down comfortably in the pews "just listening." Suspense is as vital to preaching as to the drama. Yet a preacher does not need sensational or eccentric behavior to gain attention. Well-organized material, correct application of audience psychology, good vocal energy to keep the listeners awake, and a wide variety of vocal and bodily expression are in themselves effective attention-producing factors.

Stimulating the Group Mind. The preacher is not dealing with individual minds when he is preaching but with a group composed of persons who have something in common. The individual is generally submerged in the group; as part of the group he is more submissive and credulous and responds more easily to emotional appeal than as an isolated individual. Routine activities such as singing, standing, or sitting make him more group conscious. The factor of interstimulation strengthens the group spirit. A person finds it hard to stand out against the crowd. He is inclined when in a group to run with the pack and to use less than usual judgment and reason.

The preacher who can make his audience give its approval to his thinking is, for the time being at least, the mouthpiece of the group. His expression of sentiments held in common tends to make a crowd homogeneous. When his remarks gain approval the audience is figuratively nodding its head and uttering, "That is what I always believed." The approval is a form of self-satisfaction. The audience, however, is not very often consciously pledging its allegiance to the speaker; generally it is living under the illusion that the speaker is a loyal follower of its views, and, therefore, he must be noble and learned, because he bespeaks what it would like to say.

Advantages Peculiar to the Preacher. The sacred orator has an advantage over most speakers in that he can crystallize group action by his mere presence in the pulpit. Most people tend to be docile in the presence of someone who represents financial strength, social prestige, or political power. They likewise feel, rather than know, the conveniences of being followers of one who represents a large following. The presence of the preacher renders an audience suggestible because he does represent a following, and moreover he has his power from a spiritual source.

Besides, the preacher is in a sacred place. The very liturgy and ceremonies of the Church render the listeners more suggestible by making the preacher a center of attraction. When the factors of suggestibility are already high, words which have stimulation value then come into use. These verbal representations are bound to produce effects because as words of God they are respected, inspire attention, arouse emotion, and direct thinking.

The preacher has two other important advantages always with

him in the pulpit; namely, the respect and understanding of his audience and the appropriate time for persuasion.

Since the beginning of its existence the Church has promoted an appreciation in the faithful of the true nature of the preacher's work. It has made it clear to the preacher, likewise, that it would be fatal to his success to remain aloof from people and their problems. Yet the preacher cannot live as two men — the holy man of the altar, and the worldly man of the mart. The Church solves the dualism by considering the preacher as essentially a pastor — interested in souls. Because of this interest, he feels his responsibility to be aware of the relation of worldly problems to religious obligations.

The preacher, in order to maintain the respect of an audience having mixed interests, cannot afford to become the mouthpiece for any exclusive set of persons, but he often can present views that in a parish establish equilibrium among groups or classes. Since his true work is the salvation of souls, he is not foreordained to preach in favor of some theological, philosophical, economic, or social theory. If the preacher becomes a political orator, his program will be judged for its political values, whereas if he preaches on religious subjects, few people will quarrel with his judgment.

Before the preacher even enters the pulpit, there exists a definite inclination on the part of the audience to accept his message. In other words, there are precurrent responses already in operation awaiting the preacher's presence to bring them to a head. A preacher should not throw away this advantage, but through additional suggestion build upon this foundation a stronger mental and emotional stimulation.

The second advantage to a preacher in arousing the attention and interest of the audience is the time factor. A religious ceremony intensifies intellectual attitudes and emotional awakenings. It prepares the mind and the heart. While a devotion is in operation it is the proper time to produce pious reflections and good resolutions. Religious rites which precede preaching prepare an audience for it, and those that follow it sustain its worth.

15. *Figures of Speech Which Help Incite Feeling*

Nothing is more natural in speaking than to use emotional forms of expression to give force, vivacity, and grace to a discourse. Among the figures are some that are especially impressive in inciting the affective states.

Exclamation, a sudden expression of some attitude, has worth in arousing feeling. *Apostrophe,* or an address to animate or inanimate beings, often stirs enthusiasm. *Personification,* a figure of thought, furnishes the preacher with many excellent means of animation.

Perhaps nothing is more eloquent, if not overused, than a sequence of *questions*. A preacher may use interrogation to pursue a hearer or an adversary and force him to submit to his argument. It is used very much to soften a rebuke which would offend if it were directly and formally given. "By this figure," said Maury, "the orator demonstrates and attacks, accuses and replies, doubts and affirms, disturbs and instructs." In brief a speaker uses questions sometimes in order to gain attention for a conclusion, a reason, a decision.

Giving the appearance of *doubt* in order to indicate reserve or to modify a reproach forms sometimes a fine emotional amplification which increases very much the value of a thought. "Whence shall I begin," exclaimed St. Ambrose speaking to a virgin who had fallen into wrongdoing. "What shall I say first, what last? The good that you have lost the memory of? Or the evil which you have discovered as lamentable?"

The preacher may hold the audience under *suspense* so that he may bring out something extraordinary, or keep it in a state of expectation before he advances a lofty idea or conclusion. He may appear reticent when he interrupts a train of thought as if searching for the right term, or for some expression, or when he hesitates to announce what he must leave to be understood.

Repetition, this figure of words is effective when it begins or ends many phrases or members of a phrase by the same word, or when it stresses one or the other thing, or when it repeats the phrase many times in the same terms. Here are some examples:

"You *live* and you *live,* not to give up but to confirm your bold-ness," said Cicero in his *First Catilinian Oration.* "How will you convert yourself," exclaimed the famous French preacher, Père La Rue, "when all your troubles will gather about you at your death? When every part of your body will be saying to you in the dissolution of their energies: *think of us?* When your servants demand their salaries they will say to you: *think of us?* When your business affairs will say to you in their confusion: *think of us?* When your family is desolate and your children scattered, they will say to you: *think of us?*" Bourdaloue remarks, "Your passions control you and often it seems to you that you will no longer master your ambition and your desires, *remember* and *think* that it is ambition and cupidity of man which ought to die. You will deliberate on an important matter and you will know what you need: you will *remember* and you will *think* what resolutions are fitting for a man who must die. . . . "

With repetition is associated *synonyms,* an assembly of many words with practically the same signification. They are used to strengthen an idea. Among other common figures of words that incite feeling are *metonymy* which replaces a name for one thing by that of another, *synecdoche* which expresses the more for the less or the less for the more, and *apposition* which makes use of a noun, adjective, or pronoun to strengthen some notion of its reference.

Exposition, an assembly of like thoughts for the sense although different in form has value as emphasis. This figure is employed to amplify the discourse with that fullness that characterizes eloquence, but should not be used if it does not improve mean-ing or bring out its many significations. *Gradation,* a figure of thought, also presents a sequence of ideas, images, or feelings which augments or diminishes the thought.

Deprecation (to avert by prayer) very frequently is substituted for reasoning in animated prayers. Many speeches have no other conclusion than a deprecation addressed to God, to our Saviour, to the Blessed Virgin, or to the saints whom the speaker is praising. Sometimes the hearers themselves are its subject matter. It can be vitally persuasive if it is well thought out and used with art. A similar figure often used is *optation* by which a speaker forms a petition that seeks to turn away unhappiness from himself or to gain happiness for himself or for others in whom he has an interest.

Imprecation, a solemn malediction against a person, place, or thing must be used with supreme caution in the Christian pulpit.

Inversion, a very useful figure of construction or grammar, is used to create a change in the order of words or a change in order of phrases.

CHAPTER VII

STYLE IN SACRED DISCOURSE

1. *Faulty Notions of Style*

"Preachers do some wonderful things unknown to the physical world," said Abelly. "Some possess the secret of having form exist without matter, while others have matter without form." Some preachers, in other words, find interest in style alone, whereas others think only of content. Either fault is to be feared.

A seminarian is inclined to follow the thinking of one or the other of two schools of training for creative speaking or writing. One group tells him, "When you have something to say, you will say it." The emphasis here is upon material and attitudes toward content and audience. The other group declares, "A student must acquire good taste in order to know and gain good style." Just as half truths appear as complete truths to the ignorant, so will obstacles to good style seem like virtues to be admired and gained by the one who holds speaking to be simply a response to a situation. To evaluate these opposing views the seminarian or the young preacher should know the qualities of style, the kind to avoid and the kind to acquire.

Without style certain attributes of a speech are of little value. Weak things said in good style may produce some results. On the contrary, excellent things, presented in an obscure style, with poor diction or bad grammar, will commonly be without effect. The dignity of the pulpit demands correct and effective speech. Nothing detracts more from a sermon than corrupt diction; nothing has more charm than truth expressed clearly, correctly, and harmoniously. It is no idle phrase to say that form embellishes and heightens subject matter. If, then, truth is dear to the preacher, he will secure for himself adequate means of expressing it. He can be assured that the test of preaching must be sought in the pews, and the pews sense good style in preaching.

2. *Qualities of Style*

The general qualities of style are sincerity, nobility, correctness, clarity, good placement, harmony, conciseness, preciseness, and variety. These general qualities should be present in every type of sacred utterance.

Sincerity. Of all the qualities of style, the one most essential to sacred eloquence is sincerity. Pulpit oratory must be free of all affectation and pretense. Of preachers who seek empty and sterile reputations for speaking pleasingly and beautifully without interest in the salvation of their auditors, and who thus profane the word of God and the Christian pulpit, St. Alphonsus Liguori[1] remarks, "They are enemies of Jesus Christ. The devil," he adds, "cannot stop the preaching of the Gospel, but he knows how to impede its success by helping these self-interested preachers."

Nobility. This quality of style is in opposition to triviality and vulgarity. It is not, however, antagonistic to simplicity; in fact, in using words in the right sense and synonyms accurately and effectively, a noble style is an aid to simplicity of utterance.

Correctness. A wrong word, a barbarism, an inappropriate term, an incorrect form will sometimes create more objections than a false thought or a defective argument. The use of idiomatic English, of language that conforms to the rules of syntax, and of constructions that belong to the language is necessary for a careful style.

Clarity. The preacher has a rigorous duty to impart instruction to his listeners. But he cannot give them truth or fulfill his mission well if he does not present matter clearly, correctly, and in a way that puts it within the comprehension of his audience. Rarely is the attention of the listener so entirely centered on any speech that he cannot get away from it for moments. Indeed, effort is required to follow and understand oral discourse.

The preacher cannot be too clear; consequently he must avoid obscure expression, bad constructions, too lengthy sentences, circumlocutions, metaphors and figures of speech above the intelligence of his listeners, pompous or pedantic words, phrases

---

[1] Quoted in Bellefroid's *Manuel D'Éloquence Sacrée*, p. 298.

too little employed or too newly coined; in brief, everything that may contribute to make his speech obscure.

"Propriety of thought and propriety of diction," said Macaulay, "are commonly found together. Obscurity and affectation are the two greatest faults of style. Obscurity of expression generally springs from a confusion of ideas; and the same wish to dazzle at any cost which produces affectation in the manner of a writer, is likely to produce sophistry in his reasoning" (*Machiavelli*).

Good Placement. Coherence is a quality that makes a speech flow, unifies it, and makes it easy to follow. This quality helps the mind to remember premises and to anticipate conclusions. Since a discourse becomes a sequence of impressions for the listeners, all connections among parts of the speech must be truly sensed, otherwise a break in continuity may result. The preacher must use effective transitions from one development to another development, or one point to another point. In general, he will distinguish the proofs, the developments, the members, the parts, so that the listeners can understand, without losing the dominant ideas, that he is entering into a new order of thought suitable to give more light or interest to the subject. These transitions may be divided into the perfect and the imperfect; the perfect when they contain a thought which is equal to that which has preceded it and to that which follows it; imperfect when they do not have close relation to either one or the other. If these transitions are skillfully used, varied, but related to the subject, they, in a natural way, help to maintain interest in the subject.

These transitions however do not give to style the kind of connection which is one of its principal qualities. Linking only unites the principal ideas of the speech. A connection is also necessary between the thoughts themselves and the phrases which serve to express them. To gain this result, the preacher must not only comprehend his subject as a whole but all his thoughts with their mutual dependence, their interrelation and connections. He must give particular attention to the sense of prepositions and conjunctions in order to regulate their usage. They aid style in making it clear and coherent.

Harmony. "I do not know whether they have ears, or what

these men are like," remarked Cicero of those who are not sensible of harmony. This quality of style contributes to persuasion by making the reception of a sermon more pleasing to the listeners as well as by giving emphasis to the thought and weight of the speech. Harmony results from the choice of words, a good arrangement of terms, proportion, and periodic construction. When found in sentences it builds up interest and maintains it to the end of the assembled thought. To get harmony, the preacher avoids harsh and disagreeable sounds, for the fault opposing harmony is discord. Mechanical harmony is brought about by the right choice of sounds. An agreeable effect comes not only from the arrangement of words but from rhythm and musical cadence resulting from the relation of stressed and unstressed words. An imitative harmony springs from copying the sounds found in nature. The preacher, however, must be moderate in using the factors which contribute to harmony, particularly periodic construction, for improperly applied, or overused, they may weaken the thought instead of strengthening it.

Conciseness. A concise style uses only as many words as are necessary to express the thought beautifully, simply, and precisely. Newman, referring to the writer who adapts himself to his subject matter, has said, "If he is brief, it is because few words suffice; when he is lavish of them, still each word has its mark, and aids, not embarrasses, the vigorous march of his elocution." Prolixity is the fault opposing conciseness, but the precise use of many words is not a fault if circumstances require a full explanation and treatment of a subject.

Preciseness. This quality is closely related to that of conciseness. Each idea should be represented by a proper term, and each thought should be briefly as well as rightly expressed; consequently, impropriety and redundancy are the faults opposed to precise expression.

Variety. "All discourses," said Fénelon, "ought to have their inequalities." Style must be adapted to circumstances, lofty or simple according to the thoughts which it is intended to express. The intensified and elevated expression of weak thoughts results in the most ridiculous of all faults — bombast. A careful criticism of the style of a speech before it is presented will disclose sentences which may be made concise, while others may need more comprehensive treatment in order to be clear. A moral, for example, may be reduced to a sentence, or a striking slogan. In another case, it must be treated in detail. Certain passages should be simple, even apparently careless and informal; others should be ornate, even elegant. A strong movement may be succeeded by a calm one; description may follow simple reasoning. The preacher will vary the parts of speech as well as the figures of thought, words, and construction. He will give variety, likewise, to transitions.

Style should always be checked for the repetition of words, pet expressions, and favorite constructions. Unvarying uniformity of style, and constant emphasis of terms bring only weariness and satiety. Still, a varied style must preserve a similarity of character as evidence that the speech has come from the same source and is not a mere borrowing of fragmentary bits or forms from many authors, held together by the thread of the narrative.

3. *Principal Kinds of Style*

Style is often divided into (*a*) simple; (*b*) moderate; (*c*) sublime.

The Simple Style. This is the style of good conversation, of writing as one speaks, assuming of course that one speaks correctly. It is adapted to the more informal types of preaching and to an ordinary, familiar kind of content. Opposed to the qualities of simplicity and unstudied graciousness are cheapness and vulgarity. A natural style is akin to a simple style in that it favors plain construction and homely words, and is opposed to high-flown expression.

Father Gisbert (author, *Éloquence chrétienne*) warns, nevertheless, against the sterility that may be brought about by a lack of instruction, carelessness, or fear of work; this is at times mistaken for simplicity. "Do not fall," he said, "into that popular error which makes a preacher imagine that preaching as the Apostles did is to think grossly, to express himself rustically, to speak without method, without purpose, without figures of

speech, without ornament, often without reason, and against good
sense." The preaching of the Apostles was indeed in general
very simple, but the results of their sermons appear to be
miraculous. Now, however, the ordinary means of persuasion
are sufficient for grace, and it would be sheerest presumption to
expect God to back up our preaching with the miracles granted
to the Apostles, and in order that the salvation of men might be
achieved. To do this would be to put His seal on laziness and
overconfidence.[2]

The average preacher need not be afraid of being too majestic
if he uses bolder conceptions and warmer and fuller developments
than he usually does. In fact, magnificence and simplicity are by
no means mutually exclusive. Barrenness must be avoided no less
than mere expansiveness, for both defeat the purposes of unity and
strength so vital to sacred discourse.

The Moderate Style.   Some kinds of sacred discourse, particularly for special occasions and special types of audiences, require
the qualities of the moderate style. These are elegance and
delicacy, and perhaps even finesse, a quality by which one
expresses less than he thinks in such a way that the listeners give
more meaning to his words than they actually denote or connote.

In seeking a moderate style, the preacher must not neglect
such rhetorical means as will sustain attention and give pleasure.
He does not banish, for instance, ornaments from the pulpit, but
he does avoid profuseness and particularly bad choice of figures.
Holy Scripture itself is filled with ornaments in the form of
figures of speech. Both Testaments contain fine examples of
persuasive means that any preacher may employ if he wishes to
succeed in reaching his listeners.

The Sublime Style.   The groundwork of any sermon must be
the familiar, the concrete, the specific, the simple, and the agreeable. For a superstructure, if it is to be sublime, must have a sturdy
base for its support. But in building this sublime edifice, the
preacher might well remember the advice of the older rhetoricians
who felt that the best style was one that had no appearance of

---

[2] St. Augustine, *de Grat. Christ.*, cap. 26; *de Doct. Christ.*, lib. 2, cap. 7; Epis. 55,
ad Januar., alias 119, cap. 21, n. 37.

being a literary production or, as a modern writer states it, "just off the production line."

Just as sacred eloquence has no value for its own sake but as a useful art, so the sublime style to have value must be useful. Yet the best style is transparent. Through it one sees the objects, so to speak, but forgets the glass. The sublime style is not secured objectively by simply striving for excellence. It comes from the man, the occasion, and the subject matter. It has the qualities of richness, force, even vehemence, and magnificence, reflections of sublime attitudes, noble thoughts, and strong emotions.

Richness comes from an abundance of ideas, striking comparisons, and colorful description. *Force* relates to the energy of the thought and feeling. *Vehemence* is an extreme of forceful utterance. *Magnificence* is a richness of manner raised to its heights. The peroration of the funeral oration on Condé by Bossuet has this quality.

According to Longinus, the sublime style has the quality of raising a soul to the heights, filling it with joy, and giving it a kind of noble pride, as if the soul had created what it alone experienced. This style can be suitably used only on special occasions, with proper subject matter, and before an intelligent and feeling audience. Sacred discourse will not be degraded if it is adapted to the occasion and the audience, and if the salvation of the audience is the chief concern of the preacher. The care with which a preacher prepares for those special occasions when a more formal sermon will incite motives for living a good life is evidence of his respect for the Divine Word and for what he believes is his duty toward his listeners.

4. *Figures Suitable for the Ornamentation of Style*

Some figures of speech contribute in a special way to the embellishment of style. Figures, however, should not be used merely for adornment; their function is to present thoughts more clearly, more vividly, and more beautifully. Rhetoricians commonly refer to three kinds of figures: figures of words, figures of thought, and figures of construction.

Figures of Words. Among the figures of words that have a place in sacred discourse, there is nothing more gracious or more forceful than a *metaphor*. This figure uses an idea that is familiar to the listener in order to explain another idea. The *allegory,* a figure of words which is only a developed metaphor, is extremely useful in making more agreeable an instruction which might offend. It is called an *apologue* when it teaches a moral lesson. The *parables* are qualified apologues. Our Lord Himself made frequent use of these figures.

Figures of Thought. Among these figures is *description* which presents an object under living colors and animated pictures. Anyone who lacks the power of vivid description will never be an orator, for it is especially by this art that the speaker arouses feeling. Description explains a fact in a lively and striking way, relates an event, creates a picture of manners and customs, paints a scene, and may leave in the mind a very strong impression of some emotion — fright, terror, admiration, or the like. By it a preacher may trace an ideal portrait without designating any person in particular — a flatterer, slanderer, vain man, vicious man, a virtuous man; or he may be more specific. By the use of *parallelism,* also a figure of thought, a preacher may compare and summarize in some manner two portraits. This ornament of discourse is pleasing if well used.

Antithesis gives much more emphasis to the thought and feeling; it consists in the relation or opposition of two ideas which have reciprocal worth. Contrast, on which this figure is founded, is one of the principal sources of beauty in style as in nature. A distinction must be made, however, between *simple contrast,* which opposes two objects, and *antithesis*, which relates opposing objects in a striking and formal manner. This latter, if overused, makes a style border on affectation. It must be used only when the opposition is real and not merely founded on words divorced from their sense. Antithesis may be secured by so arranging the words of a phrase that a noun responds to another noun, a verb to another verb, and the like, as in the following sentence: "A man, great in adversity by his courage, in prosperity by his modesty, in difficulties by his prudence, in perils by his valor, in religion by his piety."

Similitudes are figures of thought that serve not only to embellish style but also to instruct and to persuade. They are very useful in dealing praise or blame, in making ideas better known, and in securing more exact ideas.

Other figures of thoughts are *allusion* which consists in saying one thing in order to arouse thoughts of another thing; and *paraphrase* which uses a set of words designating an object or a person that a speaker does not wish to name.

Hyperbole consists in exaggerating the expression of an idea in order to emphasize its importance on the mind. This figure is generally out of place in sacred oratory, and fear of its use may bring some preacher to avoid strong expression. Yet an audience is no more willing to listen to a preacher who is unsure of his doctrine or his facts and who is constantly qualifying his views than to one who indulges in exaggeration and reckless assertion.

There is a kind of positiveness that leads some preachers into a hyperbole without their appearing bombastic. Hearers realize that they are conceiving an object vividly. Of hyperbole, Genung says, "Its exaggeration does not mislead it (reader's apprehension); it simply allows for the shrinkage" (*Working Principles of Rhetoric,* p. 99).

Figures of Construction. These figures consist in changing words within a phrase, omitting or adding them, primarily for rhetorical effects, although such practice does not, strictly speaking, conform to the rules either of logic or grammar. One common figure is that of *inversion* which changes the natural order of words; another is *ellipsis* which suppresses words in order to gain more rapid and forceful expression. The latter figure, common to oratory, must be used with caution, especially in reasoning where it might render the sense equivocal or ambiguous.

5. *Means of Improving Style*

It is possible to develop judgment to the point where it can discern the beauty or fault of a discourse. It can be trained to appraise emotional values, determine the worth of form, and know the diverse influences which affected the orator. It is good practice for students of the art of preaching to analyze sermons in which the rules of sacred oratory have found characteristic expression. They will be stimulated to greater efforts by great minds who have composed great sermons. They can feed their own minds with inspiring thoughts and observe the effects of successful motivation. They will find that models can awaken an appreciation of effective style.

Models.[3] Great orations should be read with pleasure before they are studied in detail for their application of rhetorical rules. Only after they are appreciated, should they be analyzed. From this study the student should learn (a) better invention, that is, proof he proposes to use, the intrinsic and extrinsic topics of worth to him, the values of the customs and niceties of sacred oratory, and the order and kind of emotions that should be aroused in persuasion; (b) better disposition of the content of his speech, that is to say, more appreciation of the proper distribution of parts — introduction, proposition, division, narration, discussion, refutation, and conclusion; (c) better understanding of the styles proper to various discourses — simple, moderate, and sublime; and (d) the action of the discourse, that is the proper use of gestures and vocal expression.

The seminarian will do well to study the effective styles of great orators and preachers, not to imitate slavishly but to reproduce their general literary spirit and to understand their application of literary principles. He can absorb much that can be mixed with the original elements of his own style. He can best learn to write or speak by writing and speaking under the guidance of some authority — textbook, teacher, or friend.

Further aids to good style are the reading of good authors, the learning by heart of bits of excellent poetry and prose, and the translation of good literature. In studying any author, the student must find the ideas the author wishes to express, and then the means by which he actually has expressed them clearly, beautifully, and precisely. If the student does not understand any term, he should look for it in a dictionary. He should evaluate

---

[3] For study of Catholic orators consult *Speech Models*, Duffey and Croft (Milwaukee: Bruce, 1943).

the composition of sentences for their effectiveness, beauty, and other qualities of style. Finally, he should find the values in the paragraphs, the different sections of the work, and eventually he can synthesize his views by considering again the total ensemble. He thus starts with a view of the whole (synthesis), completes a study of details (analysis), and returns to general impressions and conclusions (synthesis).

Just as good models can help develop good style, so can bad examples vitiate a number of good precepts. Bad speaking, mannerisms, and the superficial merits of associates may be considered virtues and readily imitated. The standards of diction or of grammar may be lowered instead of being raised by imitation of others. Style is affected, at least indirectly, by what the student comes to like or dislike in what he reads, hears, feels.

In studying various orators the student will note the characteristic differences among styles used by various races and nationalities. In analyzing the models of sacred oratory, he will find, for example, that the French preachers generally excel in their conceptions and means of persuasion, and that the English and American preachers often value usefulness, even if obtained at the expense of beauty. He will observe that political oratory in England and America has influenced the style and content of sacred oratory. Unfortunately, some modern preachers in America have modeled their preaching after the manner of a deliberative orator. As a matter of fact, some preachers do not consider sacred oratory to be a different genre from the legal and deliberative forms.

6. *Sacred Eloquence Distinguished From the Forms of Discourse*

Classification of discourse into three major divisions, demonstrative, legal, and deliberative, is according to the matter of decision and a time factor. Aristotle held that the deliberative speaking dealt with a concerned hearer who must consider a future measure as expedient or inexpedient; that judicial speeches related to the concerned hearer who must judge an accusation regarding a past action; and that demonstrative speaking was occupied with a hearer who could decide on the excellence of the speaker's style or the content of his speech, but not on the proposition, since the hearer is not in a position to secure immediate action.

Sacred eloquence resembles judicial oratory in that it deals with a consideration of some offense (sin) committed in the past. A criminal (sinner), however, is in the pew. No one charges him specifically with a crime, but with the mention of a crime and its circumstances he condemns himself. God is his judge, his defending lawyer, and his prosecuting attorney. The preacher speaking in the name of God presents facts, stresses issues, and appeals to the sinner to mend his life or suffer future punishment. The sinner is like the juror who must settle an issue about crimes or injustices, but unlike him in that he is also the criminal being judged for his sins.

The resemblance of sacred eloquence to deliberative oratory lies in this that the preacher lays down some proposition dealing with the future, and the auditor must decide whether the proposed action meets a need, and is practical, just, and expedient. The preacher stresses likewise utility, benefits, fidelity to principles, and the like.

Finally, sacred eloquence is like demonstrative oratory, which has as its aim praise or blame, in fact some rhetoricians have placed it in this class. Some sermons and instructions do not call for a decision on the part of the auditor, but may, like poetry, lead to contemplation. Some discourses may establish standards of conduct, right norms for social work, the practice of virtues, the appraisal of accomplishments, and the avoidance of vice. Often in the instructional discourse, the exemplary sermon, based upon the example of saintly men and women, doctrinal and controversial sermons, or in speeches for special occasions related to feast days, funerals, and solemn functions there is no proposition presented that calls for overt action on the part of the listeners, no bill is presented for a *yes* or *no* vote; yet the audience is stimulated to think and feel by the matter presented in the speech.

Sacred eloquence, then, has some characteristics belonging to the other forms, but is itself a distinct type principally because of its nature, its matter, and its form. The seminarian, nevertheless, can gain a better appreciation of preaching if he studies the style of all these types of oratory, understands their specific differences and particularly the distinguishing qualities of sacred discourse. He must keep in mind the proprieties of the pulpit, and the differences between secular and sacred oratory.

7. *Overemphasis on Ecclesiastical Style*

Although pulpit oratory has distinct characteristics of form, its style should be studied only after the general characteristics of all style are well known. Its form cannot be made so inclusive that ecclesiastical mannerisms are to be considered its chief virtues. A great preacher and teacher, Phillips Brooks, has said, "I do not think there is any such thing as a sermon-style proper." What he is really objecting to is the use of a kind of ecclesiastical dialect or jargon and a uniform type of composition. Dean Swift has condemned certain preachers in England for their clerical jargon and love of obscure words secured from Holy Scripture. In fact, some clergymen hold that no word is obsolescent if it is found in the Bible.

A clergyman is exposed to the contagion of pedantic terms, for the most part theological and philosophical, from the talk of his fellow clergymen and from the specific, but profuse terminology of textbooks on religious subjects. He is likely, too, to gather many sentimental terms, truly a pulpit dialect — "May we say," "Grant us," "In view of the last end," "My flock," "Our beloved congregation," "The brethren," "Brothers and sisters in the Lord," "Good people," "Our order holds," and many like expressions. Finally, he may employ what seems to him more gentle ways of expressing hard sayings and the "sins committed in Sodom," yet these gentle ways beget obscure expression which befuddle most parishioners.

Some preachers, sensing the dislike of the congregation for ecclesiastical dialect, go to the other extreme to seek an up-to-the-minute style; consequently, they unite with their own pet expressions the slang of the streets, the technical phrases of the stock market, or the popular sayings of the comics until their diction resembles that of a sophisticate — or a sophomore. The aim of the preacher is, of course, to follow the advice of Walter Bagehot who felt "the knack in style is to write (or to speak) like a human being," but the preacher must sense that the audience expects the cultivated human being, who thinks well, who warms words in his heart, and who speaks in conformity with the recognized norm of correct usage. After all, a good style comes from the right application of principles, not a different set of principles from those used to create a bad style.

Style in preaching tends either to realism or to romanticism. The first develops vividness and is factual. It can be artistic if it is a product of sane imagination and intellectual honesty. The second strives to reveal the inner life of the spirit, but its forms, under the influence of the imagination, may become nebulous and actuality may be overidealized. Style in sacred discourse, on one hand, tends to become very personal, and on the other hand, highly standardized in type expression. Either extreme is bad.

As a matter of summary, it can be concluded that the means of improving style are (*a*) use of sound principles in composition; (*b*) appreciation and right application of the specific quality of style belonging to sacred oratory; (*c*) study of good models in deliberative, judicial, and demonstrative oratory; and (*d*) avoidance of a narrow ecclesiastical style with its pulpit jargon and a monotonous formulation of subject matter.

PART III

KINDS OF PULPIT ADDRESS

Sacred discourse assumes several forms according to the matter which it treats, and the circumstances under which the orator uses it. Accordingly the different types of sacred discourse have their particular style and their particular plan. Each of them, while conforming in general to the rules which have been discussed, have, however, certain specific characteristics to be subjected to particular rules. In order to discover more facts about the different types and indicate the province of each, they will be discussed under two heads: (a) the less formal types of sacred discourse; and (b) the more formal kinds.

CHAPTER VIII

The Less Formal Types of Sacred Oratory[1]

1. *Catechism*

The term *catechism* comes from the Greek word meaning "by sound." Present usage relates it to a series of questions and answers. While it is not, strictly speaking, a part of pulpit oratory, it does belong to evangelistic preaching of which it is of the first order, and it is one of the principal duties of the preacher.

The Excellence and the Difficulties of the Catechism. Following the natural order, the Church looks upon fathers and mothers as the first instruments of teaching children. To the parents first, and then to other persons worthy of their confidence, she assigns the function of teaching the catechism. This instruction is of such importance in its results that no type of preaching can be compared with it. In fact, a good elementary instruction is the foundation for the whole edifice of religious knowledge. If this first groundwork is lacking, everything built on it in the following years will generally need much patching. But in this elementary instruction, it is not only the mind but the heart that is formed to love religion, to respect her ministers, and to observe her teachings. Religious notions, inculcated early in life, may later seem to have entirely disappeared, but often will be awakened suddenly to procure for some soul who has strayed from virtue a return to grace.

In proportion to the great benefits of catechetical instruction are its difficulties; this kind of teaching and preaching offers little attraction and requires much patience, tact, care, and perseverance. Yet a great number of holy persons testify to the

---

[1] This chapter is an abridgment from the author's translation of Bellefroid's *Manuel D'Éloquence Sacrée,* Livre second, Chapitres 1–3.

high value which they attach to this holy ministry, by performing it themselves. St. Francis de Sales, for example, very often discharged the functions of a catechist in his cathedral. Many famous preachers and members of the hierarchy have considered catechetical instruction their prime concern. Our divine Saviour Himself considers the blessings of instruction given to children as being bestowed on Himself: "Amen, I say to you: whatever you do to one of my least brethren you do to me" (Matt. 25:40).

General Means of Success. In teaching the catechism the great art is to make children love and esteem it. If they come to it with dislike, they finish by hating all religious teaching, perhaps for the rest of their lives. Hence the first concern of the teacher is his own attitude toward teaching. If children see that he is filled with ardor, they will understand the importance of learning and will also be drawn to enjoy the process.

The teacher must explain everything briefly and simply, slowly, and with good articulation. The order in which he places the material will contribute very much not only to the interest and clarity of teaching but also to the duration of the impressions.

Songs influence children in keeping them attentive; they enjoy singing, and while doing so are being instructed by the subject matter. St. Francis Xavier would sing the Lord's Prayer to them, and missionaries today find this method of singing of great help in instruction.

In following a sequence within a lesson, dogma is generally presented first, then the moral consequences. In both dogma and morals, the teacher should aim to stimulate the child's curiosity and to arouse his attention. A child cannot fix his attention on the same subject for more than four or five minutes; consequently, the teacher should vary the subject matter continually and mix in with it historical examples, parables, and comparisons which appeal to the young. A child likes distinctions and rewards. They encourage him to retain the responses which have value to him and attract him to the catechism.

The Lesson. The ideas of the catechism must be associated with the well-determined formulas which, if well known, will remain deeply engraved on the memory. As formulas are the same and never varied, it is necessary to question often and at length concerning them. But the lesson will become very wearisome unless the catechist makes this exercise of questioning interesting by the animated way in which he asks the questions, by his attention to each pupil, encouraging some who are afraid of answering or who hesitate, and by proposing challenges to the more aggressive. The teacher must have much recourse to memory, the most developed faculty in a child, but he must see that the child gets the meaning of what he recognizes so that he is sufficiently instructed in his religion. The teacher must take necessary time to explain formulas that have been studied, especially as a child is never anxious to attempt by himself to understand matter which has already been very difficult for him to confide to his memory.

Explain the Formulas.   The way to explain or develop a lesson, according to St. Augustine, is to make it "brief, clear, and true." The minds of children are vessels with very small openings, where ideas can enter, so to speak, drop by drop. Attention may be maintained if explanations are brief and to the point. Often a lengthy explication comes from faulty preparation. A catechist cannot plan and prepare a lesson too well if he intends to develop interest and attention in the important truths of the catechism.

The child will grasp the content if the teacher presents clear ideas by means of clear expressions. He must avoid too figurative meanings and technical terminology. He will have to study the characteristics of childhood in order to know the ideas of that age, to discover how ideas are presented to the child, to find out what sense he gives to words. A child, for example, will require some time to understand some words like *virgin, attention, distraction,* and a thousand like words. Although the child must be required to learn the formulas verbatim, a teacher can explain terms by common homely expressions without descending to vulgarisms.

Illustrate the Content.   A child needs illustration and also proofs. The teacher in drawing these proofs, generally from reason, should choose simple, striking ones. He borrows his examples from the objects the child sees every day. Illustrations may be presented under the veil of true history or stories. Everyone loves stories, and it seems a well-marked plan of Providence that most dogmas of our holy religion have in one or another way been related to some narrative.

Nothing is more useful in the instruction of children, and for that matter of adults, than a clear-cut, entertaining narration. Bossuet placed at the head of each lesson of his catechism a brief narration which served as introduction and explanation. Thus we read at the head of his first lesson: "Teachers will represent Jesus Christ at twelve years of age, listening to the Doctors, and asking them questions." In the third lesson before treating of the mystery of the Holy Trinity, he writes, "The teacher will relate the story of the baptism of Jesus Christ where the three Divine Persons appeared." Every teacher would be able in this way to treat the entire catechism and sacred history, especially the history of our Saviour, if he would take some interesting situation or some fact for a starting point.

Methods.   A teacher may present his matter by two methods. The first is the method of connected discourse; the second, and more suitable, is the method of questioning on all the subject matter. The first method cannot be used to prepare the children for First Communion as it would not be possible to fix their attention on the formulas. The second method causes the child to know the truths that the teacher has in mind. But questions must be asked with discernment. Suppose the teacher wishes to help the child understand the question "What is God?" "God is the Creator of heaven and earth, and of all things." A teacher can form this question: "Who makes our houses?" The child answers this question. The questioner continues: "Have you ever seen houses built by themselves? The mountains, the rivers, the stars, do they make themselves?"

Questions.   Questions should be precise, clear, and short. Children cannot hold many ideas at once. The language of the questions too should be simple, laconic, and meaningful. Idle questions, too subtle or imprudent questions, questions capable of arousing doubts on faith, dangerous curiosity, or bad thoughts must be avoided. The questions proposed ought to be such as the children can answer; a good answer encourages them to try another question. If they cannot solve a difficulty, the teacher must lead them by a series of questions to the answer which he wishes them to give.

In this religious instruction, as in all other instructions, the only possible method is to go from the known to the unknown, from the easy to the difficult. Sometimes, indeed, in order to awaken attention or curiosity, the instructor proposes a question which he knows the children cannot answer; but in general, all his questions must be within the comprehension of the group. If facts or stories are related in sequence and without interruption, in order that a very important circumstance or an essential point be better understood, the questions asked should be those that follow naturally from the thread of the story. Practical questions will dispose or develop in young hearts the seeds of piety, virtue, and truth, and at the same time communicate to minds the light of a faith.

2. *Homily*

The word *homily* is from the Greek signifying conversation or familiar discourse (*sermo*). This name was attached in the first centuries of Christianity to speeches given in religious assemblies in order to show, says Fleury, "that it was not a harangue, or a formal speech like those of the secular orators; but a conversation such as that of a teacher with his disciples, or a father with his children." Photius distinguishes a homily from a sermon in that the first is familiarly made by the pastors who would question people, or were questioned as in a conference, while sermons took on some of the manner of the ancient orators.

We may judge by what remains of the homilies of the ancient Fathers that their method of instructing the people consisted in the explanation of the Holy Scripture through which these venerable pastors gave advice and instruction. On Sundays and the feasts of martyrs, all the people assembled in the mother church where a priest or a deacon would read a passage from the holy books. Following the reading, the bishop explained what had been read, developing, paraphrasing, and interposing some moral reflections, stopping on each verse according to its importance. In the following meeting he took up an explanation of the part of the passage where he had left off.

These holy Fathers, endowed with fine talent, explained Holy Writ, which was all their theology, with great skill. They knew Scripture thoroughly, for they had studied it for many long years, and they used it continuously to nourish their souls. Their instructions were lively, sound, impressive, interesting, and eloquent. Sometimes they gave the form of a true discourse to their homilies. To this class belong those of St. Gregory Nazianzus and those of St. John Chrysostom addressed to the people of Antioch.[2]

Since the time of the Fathers, the homily, with some modifications, has continued in use in the Church. Today, the homily is "a simple, pious explanation of the Gospel or the Epistle of the day in which one follows the order of facts, and the truths which it contains, drawing from the principal texts an instruction suitable to edify the listeners." The purpose of the homily is not, then, as in the formal discourse that of inculcating some great truth by means of all the aids of the oratorical art. Its purpose is rather to edify and to nourish piety by means of the values of the sacred text itself.

In the real homily, the preacher begins by reading clearly and in a lively way a complete Gospel or Epistle selection, or such parts of it as he proposes to explain. He then proceeds with whatever preliminary explanations he considers necessary or useful in the circumstances of time, place, and people. He explains the motives which direct the Church to choose that particular sacred text for the occasion, and gives the needed background in

---

[2] Against the generally established custom, Chrysostom was only a simple priest when he had charge of speaking the holy Word. Almost all of what we have of the homilies of the Greek and Latin Fathers, we owe to some bishops. But one makes in the fourth century a glorious exception for the Greeks in favor of St. John Chrysostom, as in the fifth century for the Latins in favor of St. Augustine (354–430). Each had charge of preaching before being elevated to the episcopate because of his superior talents and his rare doctrine. Some rhetoricians term many of Chrysostom's homilies as mixed homilies: (a) story of parable with its principal application; (b) some analogous application of the same principle. Cf. Potter, *Pastor and People,* pp. 141–149.

the usages of the ancient law, as well as the customs of the Jewish people. He presents, in a word, all the historic or other details which shed light on the meaning of the passage or prepare the people for the instruction. He recalls pertinent facts from the text preceding the Gospel selection, for example, in a homily on the Gospel for the feast of the Blessed Sacrament: "For my flesh is food indeed" (John 6:56), under what circumstances and on what occasion the Saviour pronounced these words.

The preacher then proceeds, verse by verse, following the Gospel step by step, the book in hand. He explains first the literal sense; bringing out its meaning, and this with a certain warmth in order to maintain attention. If the sense of the text offers particular difficulties, he makes it clear by relating it to other texts of Holy Scripture, making use of the authority of the Fathers, the natural interpreters of Holy Scripture.

Grammatical analysis and philological discussion have no place in the homily. If the preacher meets some beautiful mystical or spiritual meaning that may well be applied, he should employ it to edify the listeners. He must be careful to inject such moral reflections or ascetic and dogmatic observations as naturally present themselves. But his choice must be good and his application appropriate to nourish piety among the faithful. He may descend into detail, but in style and content he must never forget the dignity of the pulpit. He finishes the homily by an emotional exhortation in order to drive home the truths, and to secure a salutary and strong impression on hearts.

Advantages of the Homily.   This type of instruction is apt for the inculcation of piety, borrowing its strength from the sequence and connection of the facts as well as from the words of the Gospel. In truth, it is the most pure word of God; the human reason plays the least part in the talk, and only comes in explaining the divine words. It can be used with the largest number of people because it is easy to find a moral application for the different classes of listeners. It can deal with matters which the speaker does not wish to touch upon directly or which would be out of place in another type of speech. Finally, distractions on the part of the listeners interfere less with the profit of preaching than if they happened in a more closely knit speech with sustained reasoning.

Disadvantages. In a homily the preacher covers many, or at least several, truths which the Gospel selection offers; consequently he cannot go very deeply into any particular point. Hence, the homily is not the discourse to be used when the preacher wishes to excoriate vice, or to make a strong impression upon people, inasmuch as amplification and other oratorical devices have no place in it. Nor is it generally suitable to audiences composed of informed or pious people, such as those in religious communities or in seminaries. The preacher must be able to gain and hold interest and attention, because in treating of several truths, the homily has no unity but that of the Gospel itself or that which comes from the linking of texts. The listener, not always seeing where he is going, may retain little because the development is not unified and is not concerned with a single point. The speaker can, indeed, avoid these inconveniences by placing particular truths under the development of a single principal idea,[3] thus achieving the rigorous unity of a true discourse. But in doing so he loses the principal advantages of the homily which have been previously enumerated.

Division of a Homily. In order to treat particular points, the preacher may divide the homily into many parts. The introduction will consist either of some commonplaces which he will relate naturally to his purpose, or matter which he must treat first, or perhaps some observations concerning the occasion. He may also say something about the divine Author of the Gospels or about the person concerned in his text. The introduction will be useful in that it will remove one of the great obstacles to the fruits of preaching — lack of faith or of respect for the holy Word. The body of the discourse will be the explanation of the

---

[3] Coppens lists the following selections from the Bible which are suited to the development of one chief idea: John 6:26–71; Matt. 6:19–34; 25:31–46; 1 Cor. 15; as well as certain narrations, parables, and all Christ's miracles. See also the homilies of Massillon, particularly, *On the Raising of Lazarus*. One will also notice that some single parables and some accounts of Holy Scripture are adapted to this kind of homily. Among these actions and parables, we cite in particular those of the prodigal son, the bad rich man, the faithless steward, the foolish virgin, the pharisee and the publican, and the conversion of Magdalen.

text, which should be held to three or four, or at most five, points. With few main headings, the preacher should be able to give more time to proof and to persuasion.

To compose good homilies, the preacher must have studied the four Gospels and must know how to use a concordance intelligently. Study of the Old Testament will furnish figures of speech, and a deep understanding of the Epistles will shed fuller light on dogma and morals. Excellent material can be found in the ascetical authors who have provided meditations on the Gospels. Many of the connected homilies of the Fathers are available in English translation. Fénelon, *Dialogues on Eloquence*, and St. Francis de Sales, *On Preaching*, may well be read for their ideas regarding the homily.

3. *Familiar Instruction*

This is the type of discourse usually given to the faithful on Sundays. It is divided into two parts: in the first, the preacher presents the order of feasts or fast days of the week, and like information. In the second, he instructs the people in their religion and duties. This type of discourse differs from the homily, which it has now frequently displaced, in that it develops only texts out of the Epistle and Gospel selection of the day. It has in common with the homily only the occasion where it is spoken, the simple style, and the general subject. Although it differs from the formal sermon in its greater simplicity, it still holds to some oratorical form. It ought also to be brief, and should by its nature contain nothing which would make Mass attendance distasteful to the faithful.

Although the ordinary subject of the Sunday instruction is a truth drawn from the Gospel or Epistle of the day, the preacher may, if the needs of the audience require it, choose his subject elsewhere. Although the unity of his plan, or even the isolated instruction may suffer, the familiar instruction does not require rigorous unity, and a pastor is always the judge of circumstances which require him to speak as a father to his own children.

The instruction should above all be simple and paternal without affectation. In style it should be as natural and animated as possible — the style of polite familiar conversation. If the preacher is filled with the zeal of the Apostles, he will not have to labor to adapt what he says to the intelligence of his listeners; he will know them and their needs. He can always be interesting and sound in explaining truth, making it loved, anticipating and solving difficulties, showing its practice, and applying its general principles to the circumstances of time, persons, and conditions. He can be simple without descending to the low or the trivial. All this does not mean that the preacher need not study to make the familiar instruction pleasing. Indeed, unless adequate preparation is brought to it, this form of discourse can fail more dismally than any other. Prayer and meditation are not the least part of the preparation which the preacher must undergo if he wishes to maintain good morals in his parish and work effectively for the salvation of souls.

4. *Conference*

This form of dialogue is one of the best methods of instruction. The philosophers, even the Saviour Himself, used it on occasion. Photius claims it to be the primitive type of the homily used by the ancient religious for mutual edification and instruction.

The great usefulness of the conference comes from its attractiveness and its suitability to arouse the curiosity. The fact that the audience is represented by a questioner gives the form a living interest. Furthermore it can go into a number of details and a host of practical cases that are beyond the scope of an oration.

The conference contains three parts: introduction; the body of the conference; and the conclusion.

1. *Introduction.* If there is a sequence in the conferences, the speaker, having announced the text, recalls the subject treated in the preceding session. He then gives such exposition of the subject as he feels to be useful, important, and necessary. He may divide the subject for discussion into two or three propositions which he presents in the form of questions. Thus, the French preacher, Brydaine, proposes in a conference on general

confession three questions: Is it useful to everyone? Is it necessary to many? Is it impossible to some?

2. *The body of the conference.* This part consists of questions
and answers. The questions sufficiently developed and appropriate
to the subject are asked by an interlocutor. His great art is to
arouse lively curiosity in the audience by provoking interesting
and instructive answers. The question is lengthy enough to
permit the questioner to recall first a few words of the exposition of the subject, or better, the previous replies; then he may
form the objections if there are any, or propose other questions
related to the principal question to be treated. The interlocutor
should explain the question in all its light so that the hearers can
understand it perfectly and recognize its importance.

If the purpose of the conference is to establish a dogmatic
truth, the interlocutor states the common objections according
to time or place. He should, however, take care not to go beyond
the limits agreed upon by the preacher. He should not present
specious objections which, since they have not been anticipated
by the preacher will elicit either weak or obscure responses. On
the other hand, the interlocutor should not make his questions
too easy, as the hearers will become suspicious that he intends to
leave the victory to the preacher.

If the conference deals with a moral problem, the interlocutor
must know the minds of the hearers so that he will understand
the reasons ordinarily advanced in excuse of their derelictions,
and will appreciate what are the usual occasions of sin for them.
The questions must be so worded that in them each person sees
his own thoughts and objections; thus he takes a more lively
interest in the replies which are provoked. Questions that might
lead to buffoonery and puerility are to be carefully avoided;
Christian instruction must always be serious.

The responses of the preacher should be clear, sound, and
authoritative. Before answering he should repeat the core of the
question so that the audience will have one more opportunity
to see it clearly. Then he answers as briefly as possible, giving
proof from Holy Scripture, the Fathers, and reason, along with

comparisons and examples. He need not hesitate to use feeling and persuasion where they are called for. His preparation must be thorough, for any hint of hesitation or embarrassment will lessen his authority. Although in style he speaks simply, he must never descend to the low or trivial.

3. *Conclusion.* In this portion of the discourse, the preacher indicates the results which should be gained from the conference. He must summarize the answers and indicate the profit to be drawn from each of the points, or insist on one principal result. He will do well to recall the obligations of the hearers and invite them to examine their obligations so that they may reform their behavior and make resolutions to do well in the future.

The Conference in Form of a Discourse. This is a familiar talk on a Christian truth or a religious duty, in which the preacher has little interest in the strict rules of other types of oratory. He discusses his subject, appeals to the good sense of his audience, and searches out for it the clear explanation of certain truths and certain duties. He reasons with his listeners and engages in a true familiar talk. He proposes strong objections against his case, responds to all of them, and solves all the proposed difficulties. Although this type of speech is hardly favorable to eloquence, it requires much art and method to be simple and very clear, yet to enter into so much detail of dogmas or duties.

In a retreat which a preacher may give to secular or religious communities, ordinarily a conference devoted to the particular duties of the different states of life is arranged for each day. The conference is preferred to the discourse since in it can be treated a number of practical things, some not ordinarily mentioned in the pulpit, concerning the duties and the functions of the holy ministry. Massillon affords admirable models of this kind of conference.

If a conference has for its object the defense of religion against heresy or impiety, or is an explanation of religious philosophy, or a sequence of instructions for the defense of Christianity, the preacher must consider religion in its fundamental principles; the proofs which establish them; the general reproaches which are made against them by enemies of religion; and under all these relationships he seeks to vindicate religion against the attacks of unbelief. He must understand how to argue in controversy so that he not only wins a debate of words, but conquers his adversaries in order to gain their souls for Christ.

Another type of conference may be found in the brief familiar talks and instructions given by St. Alphonsus Liguori. They partake of the nature both of the conference and an informal discussion. They have been explained by the saint in his work, *Practical Introduction on the Exercises of the Missions.*

5. *Announcements*

Announcements are neither sermons nor conferences properly speaking, but are simple counsels or notices that a pastor gives to his flock, a superior to his community, or a missionary to the people. Father Brydaine, the famous French missionary, calls announcements the soul of the mission inasmuch as they give value to sermons, awaken fervor, and inspire a taste for the exercises of the mission. In giving announcements, a speaker should neither declaim nor preach, but use a conversational tone, speaking easily and freely without study or constraint. When certain reflections or some short considerations are added to simple announcements, they must not appear to have been premeditated.

There are three kinds of announcements: (1) the ordinary simple and precise notices which explain the order and the time of the exercises; (2) the extraordinary notices, with well-planned phrases, that have for their subject some striking work or some important exercise, should be well motivated, expressed with eloquence, and given with effective vocal and bodily action; and (3) the special kind of notice that deals with the abuses to be reformed, reproaches to be made, and the practices to be indicated.

Announcements are addressed to the mind, and they must be written to emphasize the facts which must not be forgotten under any circumstances. They differ from exhortations which are addressed to the heart, and have for their purpose impressing the listeners with feelings and suitable dispositions, perhaps to approach the sacrament or celebrate a feast, or to fulfill one of the other duties which religion and piety impose upon them. Ordinarily, these latter are linked to the announcements and like them should be brief. Sometimes announcements and the exhortations produce more results than great speeches, but it takes tact, experience, and art to say little and say it well. As a final caution, the preacher should be reminded that he should avoid placing an announcement at the end of a sermon. It not only detracts from the effects of the sermon but loses its own force as an announcement of value.

CHAPTER IX

THE FORMAL TYPES OF SACRED ORATORY

1. *The Controversial Speech*[1]

Is there a place for controversy in the pulpit? St. Francis de Sales (1566–1622) questioned the expediency of undertaking strict controversies with the adversaries of religion, of attacking error or unbelief directly, or of treating matters of contention and indulging in disputes in the Christian pulpit.

Exposition Is Sufficient. Pope Pius X in a letter[2] to the late James Cardinal Gibbons directs that the doctrines of the Faith are to be taught to non-Catholics, as well as to Catholics, under the direction of the bishops, and by men well trained in presenting dogmas to sectarians and unbelievers. The Pope adds that "it pleases us that they [preachers] show no bitterness in their preaching, and their only purpose is a true and complete exposition of Catholic doctrine; which method much more easily opens the door of the true Faith to non-Catholics. For great is the power of Truth, and nothing more is required to make men love it than to know it intimately."

The same Pope in 1908, in a conversation with an American priest of the Paulist congregation, remarked that the exposition of the Catholic doctrines aided by persuasion would give Catholics and non-Catholics alike a real love of Catholic beliefs, but that rancorous contentions were of no avail, and he continued, *"Non possumus aedificare ecclesiam super ruinas caritatis."*

---

[1] Material for this chapter has been obtained as follows: Section 1, principally from St. Francis de Sales's *Preaching* and Maury's *Essay on Pulpit Eloquence*. Sections 2–4 are based on the author's translation of Bellefroid's *Manuel D'Éloquence Sacrée*, pp. 352–360.

[2] Letter to Cardinal Gibbons, September 5, 1908. *First American Catholic Missionary Congress*, J. S. Hyland and Co., Chicago, Ill.

Denunciation has too often left only smoldering ashes on the ruins of charity.[3]

The perfervid denunciation of any belief, so commonly found as a part of political oratory, does not belong to sacred eloquence. Many non-Catholics, for example, have certain erroneous but honestly-come-by ideas about the Church; ideas that the Catholic understands are without any foundation in fact. If these non-Catholics knew the real teaching of the Church, they would love its dogmas. They need to be told that what they think are the dogmas of the Catholic Church would be hated by most Catholics. The Church does not teach what many non-Catholics say it does, but only what Christ has directed it to teach, and if they study the dogmas they will find, with the light of faith, the truths of Christ.

Opposing Views Must Be Accurately Stated. Non-Catholics have the right to have their own views correctly explained. Many non-Catholics would, in fact, denounce the very views they are supposedly holding. Men are keen to notice any wrong statement regarding their beliefs, and can catch, as a rule, exaggerations as to the benefits of the new belief being presented to them. Once they feel, rather than know, the errors of exaggeration, they usually question what has been stated to be facts, or what has been enunciated as sound doctrine. The preacher is on safe ground when he presents the beliefs of dissenters accurately and objectively, and explains his own belief in specific exact phrases with enthusiasm and warmth.

Frontal Attack of Little Value. A sermon in which a preacher makes a frontal attack on the doctrines of other creeds antagonizes their members instead of subduing them. They defy those speeches in which a Catholic preacher presents a weak case for their religious views, and then proceeds to answer this case to his own satisfaction. Neither his analysis of the objections to the Catholic Faith nor his answers to the objections would generally be satisfactory to an actual opponent.

Disputes with adversaries of all religion are likewise of little benefit. Usually when the preacher challenges, they respond,

---

[3] *Ibid.*, p. 215.

gathering argument to oppose reason with reason, or authority by authority. Frequently, too, they are flattered by the importance the speaker has given to their difficulties and unbelief.

Spirit of Conflict Arouses Hate. "Religious disputes," St. Francis de Sales remarks, "do not work conversions." The Bishop of Geneva then goes on to say that when a preacher begins a dispute there are two viewpoints, but soon there generally enters a third element fostered by the preacher's desire to maintain his reputation. He hopes to gain some advantage in sustaining his opinion, and he values his superiority over his adversaries. He no longer looks to God for his success, but to himself. Then moderation in a dispute cannot be hoped for. The spirit of the storm in a contest cannot lead anyone to the port of truth. God, who lives in peace, wishes His creatures to deal with one another in the spirit of peace and tranquillity. Whatever is in the preacher's heart will find its way to his lips. If God is in his heart, he cannot have hatred on his lips. "Out of the abundance of the heart, the mouth speaketh."

The great St. Francis who was threatened with death by his enemies for holding to his Catholic beliefs later converted some 72,000 Calvinists by his gentle manner. When accused by some Catholics of being too gentle with those who differed from him in belief, the saint remarked, "I would rather account to God for too great gentleness than for too great severity. Is not God all love? God the Father is the Father of Mercy; God the Son is a Lamb. God the Holy Ghost is a Dove — that is gentleness itself. Are you wiser than God?" To St. Francis, persuasion came from a philosophy of peace that he had gained from humility, charity, and tolerance.

Religious Controversy Is Often Fatal to Catholics. Catholics who hear disputes are often scandalized when truths which they have always believed in and to which they have given their unquestioned assent are placed in doubt. Many people who never imagined that there could be any uncertainty in regard to certain truths now are unable to explain why they were brought into dispute, or why it was necessary to sustain them by reason.

The Illusion of Error. Controversy may weaken faith more than strengthen it. Sometimes, by an unhappy inclination of human nature toward evil, people are prone to be more impressed with objections than with the solid answers to them. There is some mystic illusion about an error; it lives by the very unreality which surrounds it. Most of the objections against the Catholic Faith have some element of fact and reasoning about them, but the erroneous portions have during the centuries gained an emotional appeal. Illusion keeps the error inextricably interwoven with the truth.

What is the remedy? — Must, then, the defense of religion be abandoned? Shall unbelievers and the impious attack with impunity any or all dogmas? Must these men be left to their evil ways, and may no preacher work for their conversion? The mission of the preacher is to save souls from eternal loss. Although direct controversy, which involves so many inconveniences, should be avoided, the preacher can follow by preference a plan that apostolic men have traced for him.

Method of St. Francis de Sales. Since some people aim to conceal the Catholic belief from others and make it odious by a thousand calumnies, St. Francis felt that when truth can be presented to men, scales will fall from their eyes; then they will carry in their hearts the desire to be thoroughly instructed.

In his sermons on controversial matters, he explained the doctrines of the Church, clearly and simply, considering objections against them as a part of his discussion, and not in a separate refutation, and in anticipating objections he weakened their force without seemingly meeting them head on. He sought, in the main, to establish the very truths from the texts of Holy Scripture to which heretics object. He gave forceful and clear exposition of the true sense of these texts as if he did not have anyone raising an objection against them.

His main purpose was to present to Protestants the true meaning of the very words of Scripture which they had made a chief weapon against the Church. He often used the first part of his sermons to treat the Catholic truths; then he gave over the second part of his talk to morality and piety. Protestants could not understand how he was able to prove the Catholic doctrine by the same passages from Scripture which their ministers had used to formulate the principal objections against Catholic belief.

In his public addresses, St. Francis sought patiently to persuade heretics to the Catholic belief without causing them either shame or confusion. He did not announce himself as a warrior seeking victory at any price, but as a good father who, truly touched by the troubles of his children, thought only to help them to truth, virtue, and happiness. He felt that moral sermons, accompanied and animated by devotional exercises were more suitable to convert, not only sinners in general, but even those outside the Church, than all the argument found in controversy.

Supporting Views. A great number of sound authorities support the principles and the methods of St. Francis de Sales. St. Vincent de Paul directed his missionaries to make good provision in dispute for humility, gentleness, and patience. He commanded his followers to give heretics evidence of much respect and affection, which, according to this man of God, were the means of opening the door to their hearts, and of carrying conviction to their minds. When controversial matter might appear in a speech, his preachers were advised to use Christian moderation and gentleness, and to detach themselves from everything that might appear to be invective, irony, or scorn. One will never persuade anyone he humiliates or estranges according to this saint.

St. Francis Borgia remarked that there are dangers in setting forth the objections of heretics in order to refute them, because the malice and the astuteness of the devil surpasses the most vigilant and prudent of men. He continues: "It will be ecclesiastically prudent to present with emphasis the proofs which establish the Catholic faith, and refute the errors which are opposed to it without having the appearance of responding to objections."

Father Eudes, a successful missionary among Protestants, was especially interested in establishing the fact that obedience to the Church as required by faith is just and reasonable. He found that, once this point was established, all other objections could be met by referring to the authority of the Church. This mis-

sionary cautioned preachers to speak of errors in such a way
that one who knew them would understand when the preacher
had refuted them, while one who had no idea of the objections
preserved his simplicity.

The student will find it of interest to compare St. Francis
de Sales's method in controversy with that of Cardinal Wiseman
in his *Lectures on the Doctrine of the Church*, of Lacordaire in
his sermons, of Cardinal Gibbons in *Faith of Our Fathers*, of
Cardinal Manning in *Reply to Gladstone*, of Lambert in *Reply
to Ingersoll*, and of Newman in his *Controversial Lectures*.

Persuasion in Controversial Discourse. Although an excellent
analysis of a truth may convince men of a new truth, additional
motivation is often required for persuading them to accept it.

Persuasion is aided when a reward is offered for a change of
belief. People are not inclined to abandon any belief until they
are sure that the new presents more security, more hope, or more
benefit than the old. Sometimes, of course, a person may be
disgusted with an old belief; when the preacher happens to
present a strong case against it at the right time, he tips the
scales in favor of the new life. Sometimes a sinner gives up sin
just as a man might give up smoking simply because he is
ready to give it up. Yet generally speaking the right incentive
must be presented at the right time before one belief gives
way to another. A reward, for example, may swing the decision
in favor of the change.

A person must be warned that a change of belief generally
upsets some habitual actions. A man is inclined to do what he
has been doing, and believe what he has been believing. He
persists generally in a habit since its operation becomes more
obscure to him and frees him from the necessity of constant
attention to the initiation and maintenance of a behavior. As
attention diminishes, actions become more machinelike, more
easily repeated, and more rapidly performed. In a word, the
behavior is more easily accepted. Aristotle has called habit
"a second nature." It is truly an acquired inclination which results
in pleasure or sadness according to the satisfaction gained from
it. The circumstance under which a habit is strengthened, as

well as attitudes of mind that intensify the habit, enter into any consideration of a change or a reform in a person's behavior. The preacher's real enemy in getting a person to relinquish a belief or to change a way of life is a habit of doing or of believing something.

Opposition to a new belief is often a matter of defending manners and customs. The causes of some beliefs may be found within the framework of manners and customs. Temperament, heritage, race, and place influence belief. Even social philosophy has colored a people's notion of God. For example, the Germans and the English express some of their own social views when they think of God as the Almighty. A racial characteristic is observed in the idea of the French that God is the *Bon Dieu*. The Spanish notion of God as *Señor* is distinctly Spanish. A better idea of beliefs would be obtained if they were considered in the light of traditional manners and customs.

Often, in arguing with himself against a new belief, a man is desperately fighting to defend positions taken in his past life. Sometimes it means that certain actions, satisfactory to him within the boundaries of the old practices, now must be avoided and indeed must be considered morally wrong. The defense of the past action or the justification of the traditional manner or custom sometimes outweighs the arguments presented for the proposed belief. Obviously men require sound proof and skillful motivation before they give up old beliefs embedded in customs and manners.

A new belief may upset a moral code. If the code of honesty of some men were questioned, it would be defended even though based upon some merely subjective criterion. For this reason a new belief should be judged in the light of the personal ethical system or the group-made moral practices of certain classes of people. It is important to compare the moral effects of the new belief with those allowed under the old belief. Usually people find reasons for their moral views and unless the preacher knows these reasons, he will have difficulty in finding common grounds for a discussion of religious principles or in using the proper motive to incite belief.

The average man realizing that moral order is necessary for the daily functions of business, of family life, and even of recreation is willing to accept religious restraints as part of law and order. He accepts what most creeds agree upon as necessary principles of social conduct, and he seldom opposes the more general moral principles of the Catholic Faith, for example the notion that sin is futile in bringing happiness to men. Yet conservative as he may be when engulfed in passion, he may fear retribution and seek to escape punishment. When someone attempts to force a change in his conduct, or show him the errors in his moral code, he builds a strong defense against the intruder. He realizes that the acceptance of a religious principle would upset his moral behavior or perhaps his notions of the moral code.

Often the preacher's problem in a controversial discourse is to determine what moral practice is being influenced by the new belief. A man may agree with the Catholic doctrine related to stealing, but be greatly opposed to certain teachings on falsehood. The preacher must know, too, whether the new belief is disturbing a moral theory or an actual practice. In a controversial sermon therefore the preacher must word his proposition carefully so that it covers the specific needs of his audience.

Success of a new belief may create fanatics for the old. Some men will hold out for an old belief on the basis of feeling. They may enjoy persecution or being crusaders. Having once accepted a religious belief, they feel confident that they are doing God a favor when they annihilate people who have a different religious creed. They may even destroy the symbols of an opposing belief. Their intense belief, irrational as it may be, grows more intense as another belief gains more and more adherents. Before a preacher can succeed in converting fanatics he must seek primarily to discover the advantages that are accruing to them when they seek persecution or when they become unreasonable zealots.

A new belief often begins with a doubt. A provisory doubt as to a belief or a mode of conduct is not always the enemy of the preacher. Any man may set up an inquiring state of mind in order to check the validity of some proposition or verify the foundation of some belief. This is not the doubt of the skeptic, but of the scholar who wishes to study both sides of a proposition. In fact, one can say with Bossuet that "He who judges as certain those things which are certain, and doubts those things which are doubtful is a good judge" (*De la connaissance;* Ch. i., Sec. 16).

Yet a negative doubt by which the mind refuses to judge between two opposite assertions, because it feels that there is no reason to affirm or deny them; and the positive doubt, by which the mind goes over and over the opposing propositions without affirming or denying either one, but accepting both as equally possible, are two states of mind that interfere with the preacher's purpose. Either condition must be removed before he can have success in establishing a new belief.

2. *The Sermon*

In a broad sense, this classification applies to every kind of connected and formal speech dealing with a religious truth or a Christian duty. The observations that have been made on sacred discourse in general may be fully applied either to the dogmatic or to the moral sermon. In this section, only certain considerations will be presented concerning two particular kinds of sermons — those on mysteries, and those for the investiture of the habit among priests or the veil among nuns and the professions of the religious.

A. Sermons on the Mysteries. Mysteries are (*a*) the essential truths and the incomprehensible elements of religion; for example, the Blessed Trinity, the Incarnation, or the Real Presence; (*b*) certain facts which, in a special way, enter into the business of our salvation; the Birth, Circumcision, Transfiguration, Passion, Death, Resurrection, and Ascension of our Saviour (the name "mysteries" is not given to those actions of the Man-God which have no immediate relation to our salvation; for example, miracles, although they are above nature); (*c*) the wondrous privileges accorded to the Queen of Angels and the principal events of her holy life accomplished in the interest of our salvation: the Immaculate Conception, the Nativity, the Annunciation, the Assumption, the Presentation, the Visitation, the Purification, and the like.

The Church has instituted feasts for the purpose of honoring the mysteries of faith and recalling them to the minds of the faithful. But the end which she proposes will not be attained unless the preacher has carefully instructed the faithful regarding these mysteries necessary to salvation. Souls are lost not only because of theft and murder but for unbelief as well. The mysteries are the principal subjects of faith, and even if the faith of the hearers needs no strengthening, a good address on the mysteries will be productive of much grace. Further, in order that the teaching of morals may rest on a sound basis, instruction in dogmatic truths is required. This is one of the principal concerns of the ministry of the divine word.

A preacher in treating a mystery can do three things: (1) prove it; (2) explain it; and (3) draw from it some moral consequences. Thus, in a discourse on the Blessed Trinity he can (a) set forth the proofs which establish the truth of one God in three Persons; (b) explain the belief of the Church concerning this mystery; and (c) consider this mystery from the moral viewpoint showing what we owe to the Blessed Trinity.

1. *To prove or establish a mystery*. A preacher must use strong proof if he wishes to avoid the risk of scandalizing the weak, or at least of diminishing a listener's respect for a mystery when in trying to prove it he creates doubt as to its certainty or strengthens objections against it.

2. *To explain a mystery*. A speaker must explain clearly, interestingly, with a kind of religious awe this matter that is often abstract, and consequently difficult to conceive. He would do well to recall here what has been said on the article dealing with instruction.

The preacher himself must be the first to have veneration for the mystery, to esteem its grandeur, and to appreciate the objections against it. He must realize the influence of men like Strauss, Renan, and others, who start with the premise that there are no foundations for miracles, prophecies, or mysteries in the Scriptures, or of Harnack who held that the disciples exaggerated natural events. Today rationalists often insinuatingly attack faith by questioning the mysteries,[4] and sometimes influence well-meaning Catholics into accepting plausible objections. The preacher, therefore, will find it necessary to be specific in the choice of terms and to avoid carefully low comparisons and trivial expressions. As the matter may tend to be dry, the preacher must try to treat it with warmth, expanding it with some ornaments, heightening it, and animating it. When necessary, he must introduce skillfully some proofs in support of his points, yet he should avoid formal argument. He can give truths plausibility without giving the appearance of wanting to prove them.

3. *Moral consequences.* The explanation of a mystery will be incomplete if the preacher does not indicate some of the moral consequences which flow naturally from the mystery he has discussed. As a matter of fact, he will grasp the occasion to present moral truths when they can be treated conjointly with the mysteries which serve them as a foundation.

A speaker can adopt one of the two methods of division:

a) For his first point, he may explain the mystery; for his second point, indicate the benefits which will flow from the doctrine. Or else, he may, in the first part of his address, speak of God finding in these mysteries His glory and, in the second part, relate how man finds in them his benefits; or again, he may take as the first point what God has given us in this mystery and, in the second part, show what we owe to Him.

b) The second method establishes a division in which each point unites doctrine and morals. Some sermons like those on the Passion present a particular difficulty, that of combining the historical order with oratorical unity. The historical order generally is more trustworthy and besides is suitable for moving, edifying, and instructing. The speaker then should use it at least for some points, and, at the same time, try to tie up the whole under a single viewpoint; otherwise, he will have a history and not a speech.

Here is a further example of divisions for a sermon: (1) the

---

[4] Cf. the *Syllabus of Errors,* July 3, 1907, regarding the errors, dealing with the interpretation of Sacred Scripture and the principal mysteries of the faith.

sacrifice of salvation, a point developed after the manner of the Epistle of St. Paul to the Hebrews; (2) the choice, preparation, and immolation of the Victim. This plan takes listeners from the origin of the world where the Lamb was prepared for immolation, down to the last breath which the Saviour gave forth on the cross.

The seminarian might find it to his advantage to read Bourdaloue, *Resurrection of Our Lord,* or he may use the following division from Bourdaloue to develop a fifteen-minute sermon. Text: Mark 16:6. Introduction: contrast Christ's tomb with other tombs. The glory of Christ's sepulcher. *Division:* (*a*) the principal proof of Christ's divinity and the foundation of our faith is the Resurrection; (*b*) the Resurrection is the pledge of our resurrection. *Application:* (*a*) to unbelievers; (*b*) to sinners; (*c*) to spiritual-minded Christians. Outlines might also be made of other sermons, for example, that of Wiseman on *Our Lord and the Blessed Virgin.*

   B. Sermons for Investitures and Professions. A formal sermon has come to be part of the ceremony of religious investiture or profession. There are certain points of interest to the preacher on these occasions which are favorable to eloquence:

   1. He may content himself with explaining the ceremonies and the prayers which the Church uses for the investiture or profession.

   He may indicate what the religious is interiorly renouncing and with what he is clothing himself. He recalls that the Church names the vestments of religion, the livery of humility, the ornament of chastity, the attire of the wise virgins, and the token of the vestments of glory.

   2. He may show the excellence of vows, as well as the obligations which they impose.

   3. He may demonstrate the advantages of the religious life in general, or specifically those peculiar to the religious order involved. He may proceed from the first consideration to the second, or vice versa.

   4. He may stress the spirit with which one should enter into the religious life, the duties attendant upon such choice, the obstacles and the difficulties which one will meet in entering such a state.

All the preceding reflections will be beneficial to the audience, particularly if the preacher should point out the vanities of the world and its dangers. The example of a person who has observed his baptismal vows and is now adding to them religious vows should show any worldly man that he at least should observe faithfully his own baptismal vows. The preacher should address some words to parents. He might stress the fact that they also have made a sacrifice, that there will be happiness and advantages for their child, and that benefits will accrue to them because the merits of the sacrifice will draw down heavenly blessings upon them.

3. Eulogy of a Saint

This solemn homage which the Church, through the mouth of her minister, pays to one of her saintly children is not only designed to honor him but to establish him as a model for the imitation of others. The eulogy treats not of some isolated traits, but of the entire rule of life, the assemblage of virtues, the complete and perfect model. This type of speaking is singularly useful in that it presents a moral that is intimately associated with its proof.

Introduction. The preacher may depict first the general traits that characterized the saint in order to incite attention, to make intelligible the plan of discourse, and to justify the references to the saint and to certain moral applications made in the body of the speech.

Proposition. The sacred orator must remember the end that God intends in creating saints and in manifesting by wondrous deeds the sanctity of His servants — that is to say he must offer us a living picture of the precepts of the Saviour and show us in some immediate way the Gospel in action. The speaker, then, will adopt as his end: (*a*) to honor, exalt, and glorify these friends of God and intercessors for man with God; and (*b*) to bring to his listeners the notion to honor and imitate them.

To gain oratorical unity as well as historical unity, the speaker must maintain a single viewpoint. A eulogy is more than a recitation of reflections. To obtain unity the preacher must discover some practical point which may not be applied indifferently to all saints, but some particular, peculiar, and eminent merit. This outstanding virtue, proper to the saint, will be the fundamental idea of the speech and will be its point of unity. The division will only present this idea under different viewpoints.

Division. Some orators make the body of the discourse an historical development with the moral being attached only as an accessory. Others take the moral element as the body of the speech with the life of the saint used principally to justify and apply the moral. This second method is good when the life furnishes few facts. Some speakers present a minimum of details in the life emphasizing rather the fact or the virtue which constitutes the saint's particular glory. The Church herself in her office is sometimes content to praise her heroes without going into the detail of their lives or their triumph.

A speaker should not confuse the principal epochs of a saint's life. It is extremely disagreeable to the hearers to be switched from a point dealing with the end of the saint's life to the beginning of it, or to hear something spoken of in the latter half of his life when his death has already been related. A still worse fault is to reserve all the moral observations to the second half of the speech. Moral teaching should be so distributed that the facts are always set in relief.

Bourdaloue divided his panegyric on St. Francis de Sales in this way: (a) by the strength of his gentleness he triumphed over heresy; (b) by the unction of his gentleness he re-established piety in the Church. This same orator, however, did not present one idea, but two in his panegyric on St. Peter: (a) faith of St. Peter; (b) love of St. Peter. His division in his discourse on St. Francis is preferable, since it has the two main heads leading back to a single principal idea of the speech.

Discussion. The speaker will choose the facts and examples most suitable to make the saint known, esteemed, and loved, and most adequate for moral instruction, the exaltation of virtue and the inspiration of his audience to greater spiritual efforts. Unless the preacher chooses to expose himself to the criticism of believing anything and acting without discernment, he must carefully avoid untrue or doubtful stories about the saint; yet he can hardly disregard miraculous works[5] entirely since they belong to the lofty conception of the saint, giving emphasis and luster to his virtue, and opening hearts to devotion and confidence.

But a preacher should limit himself to material suitable for instruction. He cannot propose for the admiration of his audience great natural talents, or the advantages of fortune, dignities, and riches, for from them he can draw no conclusions for instruction or imitation of the saint according to the listeners' state in life. Sometimes some hidden actions, a simple word, or a maxim are better means of making the character and virtues understandable than extraordinary facts and brilliant deeds. The facts of interest to the preacher are those which the listeners can imitate; consequently, he is deeply concerned with what kind of people will compose his audience and with the practical conclusions he will present to it.

The preacher must be allowed some leeway in describing the qualities of his hero. Poets have often created characters greatly superior to most superior men. These characters of fiction have often stimulated men to imitate their conduct. In depicting a saint, the preacher is not painting even an average type, but a model of some indispensable qualities. He can, it is true, go too far in exalting a saint or unwisely making comparisons among saints. On the other hand, he can make a saint too commonplace.

The preacher need not fear to mention, according to circumstances, the faults and weaknesses of the saint whom he is eulogizing. These things are: (1) for the glory of the saint himself who has atoned so generously and has risen to sanctity despite his digressions and imperfections; (2) for the glory of God who has shown by His generous gifts of grace His power and mercy; and (3) for the encouragement of misguided souls who may believe it to be impossible to return to God, and also for the consolation of converted sinners who understand that perfection is still possible to them.

The preacher ought to make good use of amplification, especially to the topics of circumstances that are designed to establish the facts and heighten the merits of persons or things. Contrasts,

---

[5] Cf. Second Council of Baltimore, Observation on Miracles, 139.

parallelisms, and relationships may well be pointed out. Rapid and striking substantial summaries will help to present facts. Among the factors needed to bring out detail is description, which has a definite place in eulogy in order that the hero and other persons in his life may be known. Bossuet, for example, in the funeral oration for the queen of England traces one of the most perfect portraits of the usurper Cromwell. The book of Ecclesiasticus can furnish the sacred orator with an idea of the eulogy and can give a number of texts suitable for explanation in the accommodated sense. St. Cyprian, St. Basil, St. Gregory Nazianzus, St. John Chrysostom, Bossuet, Bourdaloue, all have excelled in the panegyric.

4. *Funeral Oration*

Formerly this form of discourse was of great importance in sacred oratory, but today it is much restricted in use by the provisions of canon law and diocesan regulations.[6] Occasion may arise, however, when a funeral discourse may be permitted, consequently, a few basic principles may be presented for the guidance of the preacher.

Whatever is said in the funeral oration must not only be in accord with the dignity of the Christian pulpit, but also be suitable for religious instruction. On the solemn occasion of a funeral, the preacher finds his hearers prepared for persuasion, and in the presence of death their hearts are open without much labor to moral principles.

Inasmuch as a funeral oration is not simply a eulogy, the preacher must devote some of his time to instruction, yet if he only instructs, he is unfaithful to his subject. On the other hand, if too much of his speech is given over to eulogy, the souls of his hearers will not be nourished. There must be a nice balance between the eulogy and the instruction.

Proposition. The preacher should choose a proposition that depicts the merits of the deceased and will allow, in its development, fresh viewpoints rather than repetition of items about

---

[6] For attitude of bishops toward funeral orations, see *The Second Council of Baltimore*, 143; also *The Ceremoniale Episcoporum; S. Cong. of Consistory, Norms for Sacred Preaching*, AAS IX, p. 328.

the departed found in newspapers or magazines. If the preacher can find in the complete picture of the departed a single moral, he can use this to give unity to his discourse.

Introduction.   Deploring the death of the person has a natural place in the introduction. The scriptural text should be wisely chosen. The moral idea which dominates the entire speech ought to be awakened early and excite attention, but elements of the eulogy should be presented with it.

Body.   The preacher should present striking examples of his subject's life in relation to the moral idea he is developing informally. He should neither belittle nor flatter his subject. Weaknesses should be placed in opposition to virtues. The preacher need not excuse faults if he insists on the fact that the penitent sinner brings glory to heaven.

The speaker must pay scrupulous attention to the order in which he presents his facts. It is a fault to proceed indiscriminately from one epoch of a life to another. Unity can be established only by a correct assemblage of the facts. To develop facts and examples interestingly and persuasively, the preacher should use figures of speech, analogies, parallelisms, and striking pictures. Generally he will hide the formality of reasoning under a good amplification.

Conclusion.   The speaker should save some of the edifying circumstances of the death of the person for the conclusion of the discourse. Having secured interest in his subject, he strengthens it by stimulating, concrete language that is friendly and modest. Placing an appeal in the conclusion for the living of a good life can be effective. Recapitulation and reiteration of facts need not be made formal. A scriptural quotation usually makes a striking ending to a funeral discourse.

PART IV

DELIVERY

If visual and audible symbols are to have any value, they must hold some significance for each person using them. They are the external signs of so much conceptual material. But accompanying these linguistic elements of vocal and bodily expression are the various nuances of the voice and the different movements of the body. These are not representations of specific ideas, but rather, expressions of attitudes and emotional states. Lord Kames has well remarked that

The natural signs of emotions, voluntary and involuntary, being nearly the same in all men, form a universal language. This is a wise appointment of Providence, for if these signs were like words, arbitrary and variable, the thoughts and volitions of strangers would be entirely hid from us; which would prove a great, or rather invincible, obstruction to the formation of societies; but as matters are ordered, the external appearances of joy, grief, anger, fear, shame, and other passions forming a universal language, open a direct avenue to the heart (Elements of Criticism, p. 208).

A preacher deceives himself if he assumes that verbal expression is his only concern. His aim is to work on the heart as well as the mind of the listener, and therefore all the instrumentalities of expression and language are needed to make a sacred discourse effective. Chapters X–XIV will discuss the means that bring about sense stimulation in an audience for the purpose of stirring hearts, of gaining responses of the affective states, and of arousing moods and attitudes of the mind.

CHAPTER X

ACTION IN SACRED ORATORY

Action is another name for the art of expression, or the manner of suitably reproducing exteriorly everything which passes within the soul in such a way that all impressions which it has received itself are communicated to listeners.

1. *Nature of Action*

Delivery, formerly termed elocution, must now, as in the past, conform to the customs of the times. Modern listeners expect a more subdued manner of speaking than did those of a past day, yet action, as a response to situation, directly mirrors mental and emotional life as it is affected by environmental circumstances.

Voice is the principal and the most perfect interpreter of our thoughts; but it is not the only interpreter. The positions of the body, facial expressions, mannerisms, and appearances sometimes reproduce the ideas and the emotions even more strongly than the voice.

Action is natural to man. In a simple conversation he can hardly manifest vividly what is passing within him without enlivening his voice, and without his whole being entering into an expression of his thinking.

2. *Necessity of Action*

The necessity of action in sacred oratory can be well and succinctly explained by quoting a question posed by Bellefroid. "What," he asks, "ought the faithful to think when they hear a preacher deliver in a cold, languid, indifferent manner the most sublime, and sometimes the most terrible, truths, touching upon the most important interests of every human person — those facts relating to God, religion, souls, and eternity? Does he not believe these truths which he utters, or are they not important enough to him to attempt to convince his listeners of them?"

3. *Interpretation Is Placed Upon Action*

Some preachers are not aware of their own bad speech habits. Father Rapin, a distinguished professor of rhetoric, has remarked that some preachers study "theology, the Fathers, rhetoric, and everything which can contribute to their skill. They study everything but themselves and their bad pronunciation and their mannerisms; their actions and gestures scarcely conform to good breeding; their behavior is shocking. . . . But how can they neglect themselves so much without giving the impression to the audience that they neglect their listeners still more? What respect can they have for those to whom they speak if they do not have respect for their own behavior . . . ?"[1]

A seminarian may study not only his own action but also that of other speakers to observe the different forms that action may take according to the qualities of mind and body. Although outward manner may sometimes belie the quality within, it is, after all, the form which impresses people until the man himself is better known. Austerity may be the cold manner of warm kindness, or modesty may manifest itself in stiff, irritable stateliness; cleverness by pertness or bitterness; and pride by wise little nods and soothing mysterious tones.

Some of these expressions are more or less natural to particular ages or professions, and may be taken for what they are worth without much resentment on the part of the audience. What does antagonize listeners are mannerisms, generally acquired over the years, which are accepted as manifesting faults of character. The reserved manner of some preachers seems to indicate that they are aloof from the problems of the people. They may, in all truth, realize with Lincoln that the humblest audience warrants the deepest respect, but their external manner creates the wrong impression.

A young curate cannot afford to assume a patronizing or

---

[1] Rapin, *Reflections on Pulpit Eloquence*, Paris.

wheedling manner in his effort to suggest a fatherly interest in a congregation. He may be considered as a prime example of ill-informed conceit. Again, urbanity and charm of manner in a preacher, particularly if accompanied by a penchant for successful phrasemaking and stock outlooks on life, may be accepted as simply the technique of a professional pleader. The audience will become more interested in studying his graces and adroitness than his message.

The behavior of some preachers, perhaps arising from the notion of their detachment from the world, may be looked upon as an expression of impeccable respectability. Even reserved sincerity may seem cold and repellent to an audience and particularly to an audience of young people. Again the preacher, in his fear of the audience, may take on the external marks of rough superiority which will be easily misinterpreted. The seminarian should analyze his own habitual response-expressions, as he feels others may value them. Also, in studying the action of other men, he can better classify his own conduct, and, in particular, he can discover characteristic expression of attitudes and feelings that are helping or hindering his success.

Since the preacher opposes the strongest affections of man, he must call to his aid oratorical action. As long as religion makes any appeal to the senses of man for his own benefit, the sacred orator can enter into the spirit of this religion by making bodily expression an aid in elevating oratory into its rightful place of magnificence and ceremony.

4. *General Qualities of Action*[2]

The principal qualities which ought to characterize oratorical action are:

a) **Nobility and Polish.** With suavity and a certain seriousness (Quintilian). The definition excludes rustic, disordered, rough expression — everything that is too violent.

b) **Strength and Expression.** These factors exclude weak, languid, timid, fearful, soft, and effeminate action. May exclude, as well, all affected gentleness. Nothing is so persuasive and

---

[2] Translated directly from Bellefroid's *Manuel D'Éloquence Sacrée*, p. 388.

convincing as strong, ardent action used in the proper and necessary circumstances.

c) **Naturalness and Ease.**   These qualities exclude a dry, stilted manner, constrained and unnatural movements, affectation, and bombast. The means of acquiring naturalness in expression is the study of nature itself. She expresses herself without artificiality and without any effort to create an impression of vivid and profound feeling. The seminarian, if he has an opportunity, should study the masterpieces of sculpture and painting; better yet, he should, if possible, practice frequently under the direction of a man of taste who can give him sensible and worth-while criticism. However, he should avoid the teacher who will impose upon him all of his own mannerisms, vocal tones, and gestures.

d) **Unity and Propriety.**   The action will have unity if all factors of expression concur to express the same thought and the same feeling. The action of the voice, the gesture, the bodily manner, and facial expression must create perfect harmony. Unity cannot exist when the voice expresses one thing and the gesture another, or when the tone is animated and the eye is lifeless.

5. *The Proprieties*

These, according to Bellefroid, are either (*a*) common and ordinary, or (*b*) particular and relative:

a) **The Common Proprieties** belong to all orators, to all occasions, and to all speeches. Expressions of feeling, voice, gesture, look, even attitude — all should seem to say continually to the faithful, "Our mouth is open to you, O ye Corinthians; our heart is enlarged to you" (2 Cor. 6:11). The best attitude for any speaker, particularly a preacher, is this: "I have a remedy for you which will aid and comfort you." If his exterior manner is guided by restraint and wise reserve, and if the expression of his zeal is tempered, the preacher will gain the esteem and confidence of his audience. Modesty, the ordinary companion of true talent, can permeate the most vehement address; it produces respect for the word of God and for the preacher. *"Nihil ad conciliandum gratius"* (Quintilian).

b) **Relative Proprieties** are the concern of:

The orator himself — Age: action should be characterized in young men by modesty which, however, must not suggest indifference to the needs of the audience. In virile manhood action ought to be marked by strength and zeal. In older men it will be characterized by a paternal manner and an authoritative style. Other proprieties relate to *rank, dignity,* the *reputation* of the preacher and his *personal qualities.* They relate also to the greater or lesser *skill* which he has for a certain kind of action.

The audience — When the preacher has a *small audience of select people,* his action ought to be very polite and reserved; with an *ordinary audience of city people,* the action should be guided by the degree of authority the preacher must assert; before an *ordinary audience of distinctly rural people,* the preacher ought to use an action more strongly animated, full of firmness and assurance, but without any marks of pride or arrogance. In the *missions,* the preacher must have recourse to all legitimate means that will produce strong impressions.

The kinds of discourse — The *great moral truths* need expression of much force and energy; the *mysteries,* more grandeur and loftiness; the *panegyric* and the *funeral orations,* more enthusiasm; the *Sunday sermon,* the *conferences,* and the *general instructional talks,* more simplicity.

The parts of the discourse — The preacher should give the *text* very simply and not declaim it. He should deliver it with enough voice, however, that he may be well heard. The oral style of the *introduction* ought to be modest, reserved, and generally without much movement or gesticulation. Some salutation often helps the preacher to get into his stride easily and quickly, and saves him from toying with papers or creating useless delays while he overcomes his initial nervousness. In the *announcement of the proposition,* and in the *explanation of the division,* the preacher should refrain from gesticulation which might distract attention from his subject matter.

In the *narration,* action will be simple, passionate, or flowery according to the matter. In the *summary of the conclusion,* the voice ought to be firm and reassuring, with modulations more suitable to conviction than to emotion. In the *emotional parts of the peroration* itself, the action of the orator ought to be lively, and often very intense. In general, the preacher will apply to delivery this principle of Quintilian relative to discourse itself: "Let it always increase and grow."

The different types of composition — To animate a speech too much or too little is bad, but to do it at the wrong time, constantly, at every turn, is worse. Some ideas a speaker can convey better by little action. He instructs; he tells stories; he uses suggestion; his action cannot be too simple. He establishes principles; firmness and earnestness should be the principal characteristics of his oral style. Argumentation requires still more intensity and more energy. Everything passionate in feeling should be expressed either gently or ardently according to the feeling — tender or vehement. The preacher should regulate action so that he may work up to a more rapid rate or a more intense vocal force in particular passages.

Niceties. Besides the qualities which an audience expects to find in a preacher, there are certain niceties that indicate the preacher's inherent consideration for his audience. It is well for the seminarian to be observant of pulpit manner. He may have noticed at one time or another the finest pulpit talent going to waste because the preacher was saying something in a way which an audience would not accept. In every preparation for the pulpit, the audience must be kept in mind, and the seminarian can learn while in training to value circumstances which enhance the word, and avoid others that make talent and virtue sterile. According to Bellefroid, the niceties of preaching relate to (*a*) things, (*b*) persons, and (*c*) circumstances.

a) Niceties relating to things. Every time a preacher acquaints his hearers with an evil he must speak with caution lest his words be a stumbling block for some soul. In treating faults against justice or in reviewing procedures invented by man in order to enrich himself at the expense of others, the preacher must not by his treatment awaken cupidity in some while enlightening others against its effect or, in preaching on the sixth commandment, he must speak of it with certain precautions. A person who has not acquired a certain maturity and profoundness should not treat sex as if he were an authority on all phases of its activity. He first must awaken in his hearers a feeling of horror toward sex sins, and in his very manner of speaking the preacher will indicate to his hearers the obligation he has in speaking and how the very nature of the discourse should inspire the gravest of thoughts.

Any treatment of any serious moral problem like those related to sex should be associated with the motives of reward and punishment. Phrases relating to death, hell, and eternity must be intermingled with examples and illustrations. In treating any detail, the preacher may not alarm modest persons, offend delicate minds, or paint the vice in a way that those who have the good fortune not to know it, now have an interest in knowing more of evil procedures and techniques.

The skillful preacher can make a sinner realize the loathsomeness of his condition and seek enlightenment and satisfaction in the confessional. But this purpose can be defeated if the preacher yields to the temptation to paint vice in warm attractive colors, or to describe in detail worldly pleasures and entertainment. For a man supposedly dead to the world, it is a grave disparity to appear to know the intimate details of the ways and circumstances in which vice is made alluring.

A preacher can avoid the pitfalls of either rigorism or laxity if he embellishes virtue with all its charms, and shows its practice to be naturally good, at the same time not deceiving his audience as to the natural difficulties in practicing virtue. Man needs courage to face life's problems and a firm will to conquer his fondest inclinations. In dealing with explanation of duties, virtues, and vices, two general views can be held in mind: "How narrow is the gate, and straight is the way that leadeth to life: and few there are that find it!" (Matt. 7:14.) "For my yoke is sweet, and my burden light" (Matt. 11:30).

A final word in this section might be given to the proprieties of audience conduct: To let an audience get control of a speaking situation is dangerous for any speaker; but to allow a congregation to forget the sanctity of the Church is unworthy of a preacher. To bring sustained laughter by design into a sacred discourse is scarcely suitable because of the dignity of the pulpit, but it is likewise dangerous because the hearers tend to remain distracted throughout the sermon. Some innocent pleasantry which flows naturally from the subject matter may actually stimulate attention and interest, but any expression of uncontrolled behavior — noise, talking, moving about, and the like — is dangerous to the success of any sermon.

b) *Niceties relating to persons.* With individual exceptions, any person in any audience is more sensitive than the individual outside the group situation; yet a person listening to a deliberative, legal, or demonstrative speaker is far less sensitive, or "touchy," than when he is listening to an indiscreet preacher. One imprudent word may destroy the effect of the finest sermon.

No preacher can forcibly persuade the will of a listener. It submits of itself. The moment it is hurt or wounded it becomes childishly indignant and stubborn and refuses to give itself to the preacher. The "peeved" person forgets that the preacher is an instrument of God; forgets that he himself must accept truth. Generally when a man is admonished, he accepts the warning not always because of itself, but more for its relationship to the person giving it and the manner in which it was given. If he is displeased by something about the person of the admonitor, or by the terms used, his ears may remain open but his heart is shut. The preacher must try above all not to wound the delicacy or the susceptibility of his hearers, for if their hearts are closed, no good can come from his words and gestures.

No preacher should ever permit himself to humiliate his listeners. To expose a person, a group, or a locality to public scorn from the height of the pulpit is harmful to religion. A preacher who seeks to irritate, cures little. He loses his authority, and is generally put down as impudent or as an emotional upstart.

When presenting principles and making applications, a preacher should not enter into such detail that a local circumstance may be recognized or any particular person easily named or known. In small communities especially, precaution must be taken to avoid possible inferences as to personal behavior of parishioners.

On the other hand, a preacher is obligated not to speak in such vague generalities that vice or virtue cannot be appreciated. Listeners must know what a preacher means. To single out an individual for criticism is one thing; to hit straight at vice that is affecting the salvation of parishioners is another matter entirely.

A preacher must give the impression that he believes his hearers better than they really are. If he must deal with some major disorder, he infers that it is rare, or that those who are guilty of it are few. He often implies that no grave disorder is present among his listeners, but he must warn people of evil; consequently he signals out this or that disorder to show its terrible consequences. He inspires horror of vice, and in isolating the guilty, frightens them into believing that they stand almost alone.

In dealing with sinners the good preacher avoids invective and reproach. For them he has only compassion, as Christ had, who fastened Himself to sinners with indissoluble bonds. The preacher, while distinguishing sin from sinners, can flay vice and still find excuses for the slaves of sin without making their lives appealing to others. He has pity for sinners, and interpreting their conduct as favorably as possible, he imputes their waywardness to weakness of character, temperament, education, bad example, environment. He unveils the heaviness of their fetters and the violence of habits which tyrannize them. As the preacher becomes more indulgent, the sinner condemns himself more strongly and judges himself more severely. No sinner wishes to feel that a preacher despises him; he wants him only to have an ardent desire to help him return to the ways of God, which ways he knows will bring relief to his tortured soul.

Sometimes a preacher can mollify a stern direction by placing himself among the sinners he is addressing. At another time he may find a quotation from the Fathers or Holy Scripture which contains an instruction or a direction he could hardly give in his own words. Many of the best preachers used examples and allegories to present advantageously a particular, but necessary, criticism.

Perhaps at no time does the preacher need more precaution and diplomacy than when he must allude to faults found among fellow religious. To speak reproachfully, however, to a congregation of the laity regarding some ecclesiastic is never necessary. An allusion to a problem related to a clergyman may be necessary, but severe judgment is seldom justified. The preacher, likewise, should have and show great respect for civil as well as religious authority. People will become rebellious against authority if an interpreter of the law is constantly finding fault with, and criticizing, civil and religious authorities. Neither should one allow anything to escape from his lips that puts dogma in an unfavorable light or, for that matter, any teacher or writer on religious subjects. Among men equally clothed with a legitimate mission, some divergent opinion may and perhaps should exist, but the preacher should be on his guard against belittling either the works or the man because of difference of opinion in matters where differences are proper.

If the preacher should spare a congregation from offensive terms and behavior, he likewise should avoid the tendency to flatter it. St. Francis de Sales recommended the abstaining from any compliments that arouse sinful pride. He suggested the use of friendly terms which indicate that the listeners are the brethren of the preacher. If it is necessary to blame an audience, it should be done in a way that will not later prevent favorable reception of a remark regarding some good the audience has performed.

When the good of religion demands that the preacher pay homage to the presence of some important person, ecclesiastical or lay, he ought to measure his words so that he wounds neither the truth nor the person nor the proprieties of the place. Insincere flattery is never necessary. Every person has done some good in life. Honest achievement is worthy of honest mention. Praise also has a place. In petitions, especially in an exhortation that the people should walk constantly in the pathway of good, praise is pre-eminently effective in referring to past achievements of a congregation or parish, especially in speaking of the perseverance of pioneers and forebears in maintaining religion.

If the orator could in the distribution of the speech matter and the disposition of his speech keep the audience in mind, his pathway to persuasion would be made easy. While the orator is occupied with the important work of composition, he must never for a moment lose sight of the following considerations: as an instrument of God, he cannot direct souls with "mincing and diluted speech," to use Emerson's phrase; he must speak with the voice of authority, with firmness yet without stubbornness, with prudence and wisdom, with frankness and confidence; while holding the deepest respect for the views of others, he need not compromise his opinions; he must keep the esteem of his congregation, neither offending people with boldness or crude imprecations nor failing to contribute to their welfare and happiness. He advances nothing without proof and is neither presumptuous nor pretentious. He must have a general and specific end in preaching, and be fully aware of circumstances under which he will speak.

c) *Niceties relating to circumstances.* In addition to the niceties of things and persons which must be held in mind while composing and delivering a sermon, there is a certain decorum concerned with the circumstance of preaching. For example: the time of preaching has much to do with the manner in which it is received by a congregation. Canon law allows under circumstances that the sermon be placed at the end of the Mass, but to isolate a sermon without any chant or preceding ceremony places upon the preacher the whole burden of arousing interest and gaining attention. The ceremonies which precede a sermon prepare the heart and mind for it; in a measure they open the door for the entrance of the Holy Ghost. The ceremonies which follow preserve, sustain, and enrich the impressions gained from it, and often suggest firm resolutions to the listeners.

Sermons on Sunday should not be allowed to become a mere part of monotonous routine. The Church arranges for a variety of subject matter, which, although conforming to approved usage and diocesan statutes, can with a little preparation gain more variety of appeal if the preacher approaches it with freshness of purpose. One of the principal means of giving parishioners more interest in religious devotions is to make preaching an important part of the solemnities of the ecclesiastical year. Besides the special graces which are attached to the celebration of

Church feasts, more profit from the word of God can be gained because of the circumstances surrounding the occasions. Moreover, good sermons will help the people to understand better the mysteries of their religion, celebrate them more suitably, and draw from them the fruits destined by Divine Bounty for days of grace.

Preaching should be short. That thought has been stressed by St. Francis de Sales, Louis de Grenade, Fénelon, Alphonsus, and other teachers and preachers. "Mediocre preachers are satisfactory when they speak a short time, and excellent ones are boresome when they speak too long," said St. Francis de Sales. The Council of Trent, after prescribing preaching to pastors adds: ". . . teaching to all what must be known for salvation, and announcing briefly and skillfully the vices which people should avoid, and the virtues which they should follow" (Sess. 5, Chap. 2). Even the sermons of Bossuet, Bourdaloue, Massillon, Newman, Manning, and Wiseman were seldom as long as the revised and published forms. On the title pages of a number of his sermons, Bossuet has noted, "Written after having been spoken."

The regular Sunday sermon can seldom go beyond fifteen minutes and remain interesting. The more formal sermon can be extended to thirty minutes. After that time, some hearers are too weary to follow the speaker. A sermon too long for the circumstance of time and place causes the auditors to retire discontented with the preacher, and often very critical of the subject matter of the sermon.

It is questionable procedure for a preacher to assume that he must explain the Epistle and the Gospel, make announcements; plead for support of card parties, dances, benefits; and then give a résumé of the Catholic news of the week with critical observations on politics and art, especially concerning problems which may effect the Church. Today, with the variety of pamphlets and magazines available to the faithful, the preacher can refer to authorities rather than attempt to discuss so many fields himself.

6. *Gaining Action*

Expression, it has been noted, is a means of bringing the richness of meaning and feeling to an audience. To express well, according to Dr. S. S. Curry, one must first gain rich impressions, then wisely use the technique of good interpretation. Although the seminarian may learn the science of action he still must gain skill from prolonged and careful training.

This training must be twofold: educating the mind, and developing suitable co-ordination involved in total expression. The objective of this training must be (*a*) pleasing, expressive voice; and (*b*) a responsive body.

There is little use to drill for good tone, effective gesture, and good posture, and even gain these mechanically, if the preacher will not change habits that contribute to the acquisition of bad tone, chaotic gesture, and slouchy posture. Unless training stimulates mental and emotional action, it will become a technique of polishing a composition for some occasion, an exhibition in skill, a classroom or pulpit product not considered of any advantage to everyday activity. Action lives with a person twenty-four hours a day. Although it is natural to man as an art of expression, it is subject to planning in order to get this or that effect. It can be made mechanical, or it can be a reflection of honest, sincere, genuine feeling and clear, accurate, specific impression.

CHAPTER XI

Visible Speech

1. *Nature*

The term, *visible speech*, is sufficiently comprehensive to cover *all* action of the body. It has the same denotation as pantomime (Gr. *panto, mimos*) meaning today, "significant gesture without speech." All bodily action, intentional or instinctive, can also be called *gesture* which may be defined as the expression of thought and feeling by any movement of the body. The term *gesture*, then, it should be noted is not restricted to motions of the hands and arms.

Gesture has an eloquence which is proper to itself. It is a powerful help to the voice in giving body to thought, in making it evident and sensible. Dr. S. S. Curry, in his lectures to Harvard divinity students, emphasized the fact that verbal expression was not adequate for all purposes of communication. Man requires many of the symbols of a bodily language as well as the instinctive signs of emotions and feelings to interpret oral utterances. Furthermore, certain individual gestures alone are not enough. For example, a total bodily action may be required to explain a movement of the arm; or verbal expression may be needed to clarify the meaning of some particular gesture. Just as in the voice, a number of natural modulations mark different feelings, so too for actions of the soul and, to a certain degree, for the conceptions of the intellect, there are corresponding actions of the body. Whence the gesture, far from being entirely an arbitrary thing, is founded on the intimate relation which exists between the sign and the idea and between feeling and its manifestation. From this, one concludes that it is in nature that a speaker should study gesture.

Nature is indeed a good counselor, but it is a better one if it is cultivated or regulated, as in men of taste and careful education. Let the seminarian study the gestures of preachers who appear to excel in bodily expression, and likewise observe the gestures of people who have their emotions aroused. He must not, however, lose sight of the fact that whereas some gestures are common and belong to all men, others are, so to speak, personal, depending upon the particular manner in which an orator sees, feels, or conceives an idea.

In order to appropriate for himself and to make natural the pleasing gestures which he sees others use the seminarian must understand their significance and their suitableness. He must appreciate the relation between the thought and the sign, the feeling and its manifestation and must realize that the gesture he admires has been well conceived, that the orator has habituated himself to it and by skill given it grace and utility. To the observation of nature and imitation, the seminarian should join the study of rules which he can apply in frequent exercise under the direction of a judicious and enlightened friend.

2. *Stages of Development*

Specifically then, there are six stages to be covered in training for bodily expression. These are (*a*) understanding and gaining of poise and posture; (*b*) ability to relax; (*c*) appreciation of the representative gestures; (*d*) knowledge of manifestative expression; (*e*) development of skill in gesture; and (*f*) specific application of bodily expression to the various speech arts.

a) Poise and Posture. In the pulpit a preacher should have dignity tempered by modesty and firmness. He must hold a middle ground between unnatural immobility and ridiculous agitation. His body can be held straight without being stiff. His poise can suggest dignity without any element of haughtiness. After all, poise in the pulpit means the same good bearing one admires at the club, on the street, or at home. It is the consequence of a habitual reaction to values, motives, and traits of character. It is often judged by the audience, however, in terms of clothes, physical appearance, and bodily action.

Mannerisms. Habitual response may lead to good or bad posture. Some preachers, generally nervous and tense, fidget about, particularly in the opening remarks of the sermon, and continue with much purposeless action. They become intent on mere movement and fall back upon their habitual gesticulation. Some are fascinated by the pulpit itself, pounding away at it in vehemence or caressing it with tenderness. Others rise on the toes; bend the knees, play with papers, handkerchief, a watch, or parts of the vestments; in short, they indulge in habits that detract from the sermon.

A preacher, especially, must give appropriate grace or strength to his physical action and eliminate from it all the disordered and disagreeable movements, the contortions, rude and brusque gestures, and ridiculous mannerisms or tics, such as wrinkling of face, shrugging the shoulders, sighing, blinking, and knitting the eyebrows. However, in striving to attain polish and perfection in bodily action, as in everything else, the preacher must avoid any semblance of affectation. Some mannerisms may be pardoned in the preacher when they come from a tendency to be zealous or to speak from the heart, but when they are adopted simply to give grace to physical action, they can become an affectation.

Total expression required. One particular inclination on the part of the inexperienced preacher — not a question of grace or roughness — is the attempt to make one or two attitudes or gestures acceptable to the audience on the assumption that a few gestures are all it can expect of a young preacher. This assumption results at times from opinions that persist in establishing themselves in seminaries. Yet, as Macaulay says, "Vice sanctioned by the general opinion is merely a vice." So too lack of beautiful or strong bodily expression, even if tolerated by an audience, is still a lack of beautiful or strong expression.

Gesture is for any preacher a natural, not to say innate, way of avoiding repression. Rigidity is a consequence of nervousness or of suppression of feeling. The preacher who uses only a few gestures of the arms often gives the strongest indication that he is not aware of the relation of poise to mental attitudes and affective states. Bodily position is only a part of total expression. The question is never, "Do I use two or three gestures?" It is, "What is the total expression of the body for each thought and feeling?"

Co-ordinations of bodily actions gained from good habitual actions. Poise is related to good breeding which can be exemplified in any action of life. Pulpit etiquette does not sanction bad manners, even if brought about by a nervous strain. Self-consciousness, tension, and awkwardness are not necessarily confined to a speaker's platform or pulpit appearances. They usually are seen in his everyday activity. The grace and pleasing appearance which he seeks to have in the pulpit cannot be gained by special practice for a special speech. He must overcome by consistent effort the faults he is acquiring from his daily behavior. He must destroy bad behavior patterns, wherever they appear, before he can gain good poise and posture for the speaking situation. The right co-ordination of muscles and nerves must be a product of habitual response, under the stimulation of thought, images, and feeling.

Physical aspect of posture. The term *posture* brings to mind the images of framework, a chest, spine, and connected parts. The adjustment of the entire structure can be thrown out when one part is out of co-ordination with another. Bad posture indicates muscular constrictions and waste of energy. Since good voice depends upon good posture, the preacher must gain it not mechanically by some manipulation but by corrective exercises.

Good posture requires good bodily health. There must be a normal condition of vitality before one can properly adjust the entire framework of the body. Stretching exercises and drills that help maintain a proper proportion between muscular stimulation and relaxation are important in securing and holding co-ordination. Such activities as plays and games that develop a sense of personal worth and well-being help the body to function normally. Leisure for meditation and for bodily relaxation is a remedy for the continual excitement of work and intensity of interests. Posture, primarily a condition of control, is a balance between muscles in action and those in a passive state; it is a product of well-being, purpose, and harmony of mental, emotional, and bodily activity.

b) Relaxation in Relation to Poise and Bodily Expression. A seminarian, to relax thoroughly, must visualize himself in relaxed positions. He may relax better when he thinks of lying out on a beach in warm weather or resting in bed comfortably reading. As he builds the relaxing situation more and more pleasing to himself, he finds the body more and more giving up its tensions.

If he practices in a room where he will be free from distraction and if he closes his eyes as an aid to better attention, he will gain his purpose more easily. In every exercise, he must give heed to set positions and expressions, particularly in the region of the face, the neck, and the shoulders. In fact any person might well make it a habit of relaxing any part of the body that is constricted when he becomes conscious of this condition. The habit of relaxing the entire body two or three times daily is a great asset to a preacher.

Tension preceding relaxation. Some other persons find that they can relax better if they tense the body first. They work on parts of a body at a time, alternately and deliberately tensing and relaxing the arm, for example. They might, for instance, relax one arm and tense the other, then reverse the circumstances. In neck exercises, while the jaw is relaxed, and the muscles of arm and shoulder are equally relaxed, the head is slowly rotated. The muscles of the face can be tensed, then relaxed until a person observes the feeling of each condition. The tongue, "the unruly member" of the vocal operation, can be tensed, then relaxed. After the feeling is well noted, the person can many times during the day check his tongue habits. He may find that he habitually places his tongue against the roof of his mouth, or has it tightly set. In like manner, he can observe other parts of his body as they tense or relax under the normal conditions of living. A study of set bodily positions and habitual tensions will do much to help the student prepare his body for better visible speech as well as put it in condition for vocal responses.

Persistent hypertension. If the seminarian has met most of his emotional situations with a high degree of muscular tense-ness, he probably will be tense in any circumstance of speaking. Through a process of adaptation, however, he may gain sufficient control of himself to *appear* calm. Yet the hypertension will be really present, as can be observed in some physical patterns of action or in vocal responses. Even if the tension may be avoided in some situations, it may appear in particular parts of the body — the throat, the thighs, etc. Each person must analyze himself for inhibitions and tensions that are crippling expression and preventing him from exercising his ability to "let go," a condition which is a consequent of poise and relaxation. Per-sistent hypertension should be checked by a physician.

Exercises needed. Most teachers of speech agree that the first step in training for gesture is learning how to relax. If the seminarian will use exercises that bring about relaxation, he will not need to fold his hands beneath the chasuble or clutch at the pulpit.[1] He can relax his arms and hands. There is an act of volition connected with relaxation. When a speaker pro-ceeds to put his hands behind his back, he can oppose this desire as soon as he is conscious of movement, and then he can let them hang freely at his side.

c) **Representative Gesture.** The third stage in training for bodily action requires an understanding of the types of expres-sion. Language is both natural and artificial, its signs being man made or based on natural signs. The sign has three factors: the outward element which signifies; the inward fact which is signi-fied, and the relationship between the inward and the outward. The mind of the speaker must perceive the relationship between that which signifies and that signified in order to establish cause and effect, means and end, purpose and analogy. The mind of the hearer must gain a like relationship; in other words, language requires signs that allow a shared meaning between speaker and hearer.

Distinguished from instinctive expression. Expression as a generic term can be analyzed under its four aspects: (*a*) voice

---

[1] Consult the Appendix for several exercises of help in gaining relaxation.

language — symbolic or linguistic form representing conceptual material, often influenced by emotion; (*b*) bodily language — symbolic or representative gesture, which employs the body deliberately as a means of communication; (*c*) vocal expression revealing degrees of resolution, thinking, and emotional reaction; and (*d*) manifestative gesture indicating reactions of personality, purpose, and degrees of excitement or control. These four factors, each distinct from the others, nevertheless act in harmony and each reveals or expresses something not manifested by the others. Language, whether of voice or body, perfects thought since it clarifies ideas and simplifies their relationship. Nonlinguistic expression is primarily a personal reaction to a situation.

Symbols must be meaningful. If the entire body talks a language, one must look for symbols which have become meaningful. A certain pattern of action, generally the counterpart of a phrase, is related to the extension and comprehension of some thought. The patterns may be of strict form, or less strictly delimited, and their outlines somewhat hazy, but if the symbols have meaning, they are the basis of a language. These symbols can be acquired by observation of human action, by the study of charts, pictures of models, and the fine arts, and, when necessary, by training in symbolic expression of a business or a profession.

Characteristics of good bodily language. Bodily language is governed by the rules of a vocal language. Bodily "words" can change their significance; some of the approved and meaningful gestures of yesterday are without meaning today; some of those suggested by Quintilian or Cicero may have little or no significance for an American audience. Even the manner of Brummell, with his green velvet, gave way to D'Orsay, with his white shirt front, and neither style would be acceptable to a Republican convention that praised Calvin Coolidge's taciturnity. "Old-time" elocutionary poses have today slight value as a means of communication and less value as expression. They are not in the common experience of the hearers.

Speakers develop a workable vocabulary of words that are correct and appropriate. They must use bodily symbols likewise according to the rules of exactness, clearness, vividness, suggestiveness, propriety, taste, beauty, spontaneity, variety, and emphasis. Gestures as a language of signs may be used in a faulty manner by needless repetition, by indefinite representations and lack of coherence and unity. They may be too few or too many, monotonously used, wrongly timed, badly placed, or improperly co-ordinated.

d) **Manifestative or instinctive expression.** Attempts have been made to find a set pattern of expression for each known emotion. Yet these endeavors have failed. No grimace or bodily pose or manufactured pattern of gesticulation can be an incarnated form or a bodily resonance of a particular emotion. Still some specific facial action seems to enter into the expression of each emotion, and some changes in the grouping of muscles involved in any emotion may be felt. This consciousness of the muscular action in an emotional expression may help the speaker acquire a pattern of gestures. Bodily changes, however, are not in themselves emotions. A speaker must have an insight in some situation, then emotion becomes a consequence of meaning and intellectual discernment. The patterns of the emotional display, felt or observed, are caused by emotions and not the stimulus to the senses.

Instinctive responses to emotions cannot be catalogued. Expressions of love, hate, and anger are not restricted to formulas, yet audiences do tend to accept a type expression of emotion as well as some general expression modified by personal elements. Type expression can be analyzed into its parts; for example, the external expression of fear is composed of certain movements of the eyes, the head, the torso, and the legs. But when all these movements are built up synthetically from the general symptoms of fear, there is a woeful lack of bodily resonance ordinarily found as an actual accompaniment of fear. Obviously, a symbolic expression is better for the purpose of communication, but instinctive or manifestative expression best presents attitudes and personal reactions.

Arbitrary bodily action and instinctive expression interwoven. In bodily action, forms that communicate well and others that express equally well are inextricably interwoven. But just as the will is not the intellect, or the intellect the will, yet both work in certain mental action, likewise, linguistic and non-linguistic expression have a unity of purpose and response to the person himself.

It is the person who creates the expression, who is heard or seen or felt. Hence, if he is placed in a situation that calls for an emotional response, he may incite the external pattern of the emotion, a pattern strong enough to be recognized by another, and vital enough to reflect the creator's inward feeling. An example that might well illustrate response to situation as seen in some physical action is that attributed to Eleanor Duse, famous actress, who, playing the role of a faithless wife, stood alone on stage after a quarrel with her husband. While awaiting her lover, she toyed with her wedding ring. The on-and-off business became a symbol of her thinking and feeling. There are many significant expressions of feeling, even ideas, which we would not consciously express.

Similarity to vocal modulations. Bodily action, particularly non-linguistic action, is very similar to vocal expression. Vocal pause has its counterpart in bodily pause, not in a hesitation but in a moment of sustained animation, while the person awaits a response of some definite patterns of visible action. Stress in the voice relates to emphatic action in the body. Change of pitch and inflection are similar to the spatial intervals which gesture can establish for increasing and decreasing differences as well as distance. The tone color of the voice has its resemblance in the texture changes of the body which are shown by tension and relaxation. Rate is a time element, and the time factor can likewise be noted in the movement of the body. Tempo and rhythm are important vocal factors and equally vital to bodily action.

e) Skill in Gesture. The fifth step in developing visual speech relates to the acquisition of skill. Certain exercises have been found helpful in preparing the body for the various movements which enter into bodily expression. A few important ones are given in the Appendix; yet at best, they can only suggest to the seminarian the advantages of this kind of practice for his own development.

Application of techniques. After practicing exercises, the seminarian is ready to express some idea or feeling. Let him take some dramatic selection for interpretation. He should raise arms to the front, and hold them there until some thought or feeling in the selection suggests a change of position. He should feel every arm movement in relation to a general bodily action. The student will find that he is making some movement as he improves his interpretation.

Emphatic gesture. The student will probably observe that some expression of the body, particularly of the head or hands, coincides with the phrase containing the emphatic word. These gestures, so-called emphatic ones common to everyday conversation, simply indicate varying degrees of accentuation. They are serviceable but must not be overused, for all emphasis means no emphasis. They are made in a straight line rather than in curves, but arm or head action alone is not sufficient for the emphatic gesture. The entire body must represent the thought or feeling.

Order of Gesture. The first response of the body to thought and emotion is a general pattern. The second seems to be more accentuation of the reflection of the emotion in the eye and face. The third relates to the arms and hands. The fourth is the communication in words. If this order is reversed, the gesture will be awkward.

Locative gesture. After the student has developed some skill in using emphatic action, he can employ locative gestures, or movements which present to the imagination the location of an object. These gestures are closely related to descriptive ones which represent objects in a true and picturesque manner. As auxiliaries to the spoken word by a direct appeal to the eye, they generally correspond to a total phrase rather than to a single word. The pattern is a blend of movements.

But any pattern must be wisely used by the preacher, especially servile and rigorous imitation, and, in particular he must avoid pointing at anything he does not want his audience to become interested in. Persons seeing movement allow their eyes to follow it. If he becomes literal in his gestures, he generally is not adding much to verbal expression. The gesture should stimulate the imagination, and thus make the idea clearer, the scene more vivid, or the situation incite more feeling.

Using descriptive gestures. The sacred orator will find that he is seldom employing movement to the front of him in descriptive action as he does in those locative and emphatic gestures which reveal ideas and emotions directly to the audience. He is describing and pointing out objects to his side. He seldom indicates action as occurring behind the audience. People desire to see action to the front of them. Gestures to the back of the speaker common to platform art and the stage, have little use in pulpit oratory unless reference is made to the altar itself which may be directly behind the pulpit.

The affective gesture. This action, called by some the "suggestive" gesture, is the most noble of all patterns of physical expression, and is to be preferred when a speaker can choose among them; it is intended to express the feelings of the soul. In order to appreciate this gesture, the preacher must, as we have said in speaking of the vocal quality, consult nature. Each passion has some gestures which are suitable to it, but if the expression is crudely imitative, or consists merely of perverted symbols or symptoms of emotions, it will be weak and ineffective. Fear and sadness are restrained, being without much vigor or energy; the gesture expressing them is generally weak and languid. In bursts of indignation, the gestures are impetuous, violent, and excessively vivid.

A type of gesture appropriate to gentle affections is chiefly related to the hand which is directed to the chest, then gently brought away in the direction of the audience. The speaker bends the elbows in the gesture. In a general pattern of affirmation, he extends the hand toward the audience, the palms being low; another time the hand is on the chest. This gesture has come into use in protestation which is only in itself a strong and solemn affirmation. In aversion, the speaker makes a movement of the hand toward the left, and turns the head in the opposite direction.

Certain suggestions can be offered regarding parts of the body as they enter into the general pattern indicative of specific mental and emotional attitudes, and dispositions.

The head. This part of the body is so important in gesticulation that its movements must not be uncontrolled or aimless. Head gestures are of all gestures the most necessary, the most eloquent, and the most expressive. The head generally should be held easily upright in a natural position. Each of its movements has its own signification, and must be used for a particular need. Held easily high, the action suggests dignity; hanging low it manifests weakness or shame. Held high, it shows intense emotions and lofty thought. Turning of the head suggests shifting of attention. The head advanced toward the audience may suggest earnestness. Withdrawn it reveals antagonism. For an appreciation of head movements, the student should study the paintings of Ruben and Raphael.

The face, habitually calm, grave, and serene, ought to reflect the sense of the discourse. Nothing is more ludicrous than a sermon delivered by a preacher whose lifeless and expressionless face seems to get more blank as the speaker uses stronger words and more precise assertions. The term "dead pan" rather accurately describes such a performance, and the expression ought to be reserved for a certain type of comedy. The countenance should expand in joy, hope, and desire, taking on an air of happiness and satisfaction. By its tenseness it can well mirror indignation and like emotions.

Cicero maintains that after the voice it is the countenance which expresses the best of our thoughts; and the eyes, above all, give the life and expression to the countenance. To avoid giving an audience constant attention is to deprive the speaker of a great means of persuasion. Even in gesture, the eye, only on occasion, is on it rather than directed to the listeners. The audience must continually read in the orator's eyes those expressions of feeling that are penetrating his soul. Moreover, with his eyes he can indicate objects or questions or disconcert and even menace. Sometimes, however, the eyes might follow a gesture when the speaker is painting a picture. The speaker, for the moment then, is an actor who speaks in character.

Some preachers tend to develop bad eye habits. They shift their look about the church, stare out of the window, study the ceiling, and look everywhere but at their audience. This glassy stare and unfocused eye indicate a lack of directness, perhaps a vagueness of thought and attitude. The preacher is talking to human beings, and he must look at human beings, and they are not sitting on the ceiling or huddled *en masse* in the third row of the balcony.

The arms and the hands. Of all gestures, those of the arms and hands are the most varied. They frequently blend and go from repose to action, or vice versa. The hands in repose are often as expressive as in vigorous action.

Gestures of the arms should be a subject of special study. They should be made especially free and easy — not stiff, crude, or forced or fidgety or uncertain. They are frequently used in an informal manner centering action in the elbow, wrist, and hand, but those colloquial gestures are out of place in vigorous expression. In general, they commence and end with a thought, and they should be used especially with the most important and salient thoughts.

As the eye movement so that of the hand sometimes precedes for an instant the emission of the voice. One gestures habitually to the right. In giving variety to movement, one may make use at times of both arms; this action is especially necessary for the expression of vivid feeling or for painting some noble or terrible objects. More height and width in the entire arm action reveal more excitement and agitation. Anger and love, however, restrict arm movement. They are sensed more by total bodily action. The two arms should be used in a concerted manner, and with a certain harmony unless it is necessary to express different things, then each hand is used independently of the other. One rarely uses the left arm alone, this gesture being restricted to aversion, weakness, and horror.

Arm gestures can be made above the shoulders, in line with the chest or below the waist. The more exalted the thought, the more the gesture extends above the shoulders. Gestures of the middle area are expression of ideas and feelings common to

everyday life, while gestures below the waist, unless used loca-
tively, indicate debasing thoughts and feelings. The hand should
be well opened, and the fingers should neither be too tight together nor too extended. All hand and arm action must have firmness, ease, suitability, and naturalness. The hands should follow
the arms in their action, and never appear to be detached from
them in a way of separate action. The speaker never should
raise his hands toward the face in such a way as to cover it
even partly.

In definition, a speaker usually uses the rim of his hand. To
point out something, he employs the rim of the hand with one
finger extended. To suggest the giving of an object or thought,
he turns the palms of the hands up and extends his arms. To
indicate taking something away, he places the palms of the
hand up and then draws back the arms in a curve toward the
chest. To reveal, he puts the palm of the hand out and then
turns the fingers in the direction of the floor.

As a rule when the speaker makes a gesture to the front and
away from him, he moves his head backward. There is consequently opposite actions of the head and the arms in most gestures.
When a specific gesture has been completed, the speaker may
begin another meaningful movement or let his arm hang relaxed at his side.

f) **Application of Bodily Expression to the Various Speech
Arts.** In preparing for the physical expression required in
preaching, the seminarian might choose selections that give a
variety of response. Selections from stories and novels that have
epic value create and suggest viewpoints as well as imagery.
These will call not only for a variety of vocal modulation but
also for physical expression that reflects vivid imagination and
dramatic insight into a life situation.

The student, too, will realize that, as a clergyman, he will
have many opportunities to use practically all forms of public
speaking; hence, he should practice selections in deliberative,
judicial, and demonstrative oratory. Debate, for example, not
only is helpful in improving the ability to analyze subject matter,
but it stimulates a crisp, direct kind of physical action valuable

for instruction and controversy. The various kinds of demonstrative oratory are of use in giving variety to a preacher's style. After-dinner speaking, for instance, has special advantages for the student in keeping his physical action direct and "human." The physical action that reflects the oratorical spirit makes ideas clearer, impresses aims, gains consent, actuates conviction, and even entertains.

A dramatic situation, or the drama itself, arouses the student's dramatic instinct, and by his taking on character he is sympathetically identifying himself with human nature in life situations. The physical action of a drama requires the entire gamut of expression. The seminarian, of course, is not practicing to be an actor. But in using recitations, poetry, dramatic reading, or scenes from a drama, he is employing a first-class medium for the development of physical expression. He will find the farce to be splendid means of making scenes, situations, and characters live principally by pantomimic action.

Finally, the lyric offers specific training to the student in the rhythm of action. It refines action, it unites vocal modulations to bodily movement. As each specific idea of the lyric must be accentuated, physical expression becomes more distinctive and more personal.

Suggested exercises.[2] A good exercise for learning gesture is to portray a definite character like a middle-aged banker and then apply in succession to it certain qualities, for example, austerity, bashfulness, generosity, despair, excitement, outspokenness, or curiosity. Let the student choose situations for this character, keeping in mind the emotions that he would have. Let him have in mind a definite time and place. Let him admire something, hate it, be surprised at it, worry about it, and the like. He should build his own situations and express his ideas for emotions; if possible he should see his characterizations in the mirror. His improvement will depend upon practice and interest.

Interpretation should be begun with the head held easily erect,

---

[2] In Chapter XVI under the discussion of interpretation, selections from the New and Old Testaments will be offered the student who seeks a means of developing his abilities to express himself by action.

with the weight of the body held easily distributed on both feet, with the base neither too wide not too narrow. When the weight is on both feet, the body is not in a strong action. A narrow base may be a sign of weakness; a wide base suggests everyday ease or, if unusually wide, arrogance. A very wide base, with weight evenly distributed, may indicate fear. Repose has a narrow base with weight on the back foot. Antagonism calls for a wide base. Generally, as the speaker works himself into action, his weight shifts to the forward foot. The speaker should be always prepared to make transitions with the feet, either to the left or the right, or to the front or the back. Let him show in his total physical responses the conception of the thought and the emotional reaction, but he should emphasize the specific expression — perhaps of the arms and hands. Let him remember that action precedes words.

The following types of exercises may suggest to the seminarian ways of practice for visible speech.

Stand easily erect, arms dangling loosely at the sides, eyes closed; as you inhale allow your arms to rise gently to chest level. Keep wrists and fingers relaxed. Then open your eyes, step forward, and energize your wrist and hand as you make an appropriate gesture to illustrate the sentence: *This man is here.* Repeat the same exercise, and at the proper time point the index finger as you say: *I am pointing at you.* Suggest then by gestures that you are reaching for an object; you are warding it off; you are revealing it to the listeners. Practice gesturing with a number of phrases locating or describing objects; first use one hand, and then the other. Write sentences that will contain emotional values that you may interpret.

Suggest the physical action of each person in a group who is seeing a girl about to leap into the street from the ledge of the eleventh story of a burning hotel. Express horror, anguish, attention, awe, etc. Individualize your images and ideas. If it is of help, write out a dialogue between two persons at the window of this burning building.

Establish a character, a place, a time, a situation. Let another character approach the scene and exclaim, "I am glad to see you." Write a number of sentences for the dialogue between these characters. Feel each character. Avoid giving only a few representative gestures. Reveal some of the qualities of the characters. Distinguish between a transient action and an action that comes from bearing, or the deeper conditions of the character, for example, seriousness, philosophical, neurotic, etc. Learn to appreciate that response to situation is the only way you can train yourself in manifestative gesture.

What would be the general standing or sitting posture of a person who was happy? Sad? Proud? Despairing? Defiant? Cringing? How would each character talk? Walk? Choose a situation. Give some person, with one of the above characteristics, words to speak and appropriate visible action.

After working on situations you have created for your characters, you might interpret selections from literature. There are many good texts for interpretation, as well as for platform art, that contain excellent material for physical expression. You also can collect your own matter, being guided in your choice of selections by the desire to get content with emotional appeal. You can then reflect in pantomime your interpretation of character, mood, situation, and place.

CHAPTER XII

Voice

1. *Purpose of Training*

Voice training is nothing more or less than a cultivation of functions, but if these are to be used correctly, the person himself must be trained. The larynx and the extrinsic muscles connected to it are the same in the cultured and the uncultured person. Yet, assuming the organs of voice are free from physical or pathological disturbances, the cultured person who has skill in using these mechanisms will get modulations from his voice that the unskilled and uncultured cannot. Even in drills one cannot work directly upon the voice. The person behind the mechanism must always be considered first. The stamp of his creating intelligence is upon the vocal product.

Some seminarians, perhaps realizing that training in voice has in certain instances led to artificial methods of speech, are prejudiced against any voice instruction, feeling that voice is a product of nature, not nurture; consequently, they accept the voice as it is. They may agree that certain qualities are pleasing in another's voice, or that a strong, well-modulated voice would be a benefit to preaching, but they will do nothing about studying voice production or even vocal expression. Yet in their own way some of them may try to change a tenor voice to a basso, or to get power by vocal constrictions, usually with sad results.

The seminarian who has wisely observed what training can do for a voice will improve his own organ. He must realize with the great orators and rhetoricians that simply knowing the facts about voice does not make it a better one. Yet knowledge should be the basis for the art of speaking. Observation, study, and practice — all are necessary operations for the seminarian who wishes to train his speaking voice.

A good voice, an expression of personality as well as a product of a bodily function, is one of the important assets of an orator. The time spent in practicing oral reading, singing, and declamation will be helpful in developing vocal responses. The study of music in particular will have a double benefit — training the ear for harmony; and giving skill in the right use of pitch.

The student has seven immediate interests in voice training: (1) He must realize the social aspect of vocal culture. (2) He must understand the physical basis of voice. (3) He must learn to co-ordinate activities involved in vocal effort. (4) He must evaluate his need for remedial work in vocal training. (5) He must develop breathing techniques in order to meet the needs of voice production. (6) He must initiate tone successfully. (7) He must learn to modulate his voice. This last requirement is of such importance that it will be treated in a separate chapter.

2. *Social Aspect of Voice*

The standard of good voice differs somewhat with places and peoples. A native singer or speaker of China would seek a tone color and pitch not always acceptable to Western ears. Some teachers of voice in Germany favor a strong pharyngeal coloring; some instructors in France make a good voice an "affair of the nose." Yet the student has a general notion of the type of voice that seems agreeable to persons of good taste and is adequate for his needs. He has some appreciation of the qualities of voice and speech necessary for successful communication and expression.

A guide to these qualities will always be the reaction of cultured people to the intensity, pitch, and resonances of any voice. People who have the faculty of appreciating the beautiful are in general agreement regarding certain vocal qualities which have been universally admired. They make the laws of beauty the basis of the norm of a pleasing voice. Climate, education, race, and the like, may bring about variations in the standard of a good voice, but people of culture can always distinguish the accidentals from the essentials since taste for the beautiful is something proper to man.

3. *The Physical Basis of Voice*

A student can help himself to a better understanding of his vocal problems if he has a better understanding of the anatomy of the oral and nasal passages, the larynx, and the musculature involved in breathing. Anatomical charts may be examined for the appearance of the various muscles at different stages of their functioning. Many texts on voice[1] go into this matter in detail, and also treat of the physics of sound in relation to voicemaking. With the aid of a hand mirror a student can also observe the position of soft palate and the tongue when he engages in a yawn.

The two vocal lips, composed of muscles covered by membrane, are attached to the cartilages composing the larynx. Since these lips or wedges can stretch lengthwise and laterally, have thickness and elasticity, they can assume positions when their edges come into sharp contact conducive to the creation of various fundamental pitches. In short, the structure of the larynx with its intrinsic muscles is suitable to function as a sound producing mechanism. It has the properties of a vibrating string — length, mass, and tension; it is subject also to the effects of subglottal pressure. The actual activity at the vocal fold is an involved complexity of balancing functions, the nature of which has not been definitely determined. When the edges of the vocal lips are retracted by the action of the muscles, the open space between the lips (glottis) allows the entrance or expulsion of breath. The larynx may be thought of as a valve, opening and shutting, and vibrating in relation to activity throughout the entire body, and in conjunction with the direct impulse created by the desire to speak. Strong emotional states create tension in the body, consequently, also in the intrinsic muscles of the larynx. Hence voice obviously is a product not of one valve, but of the entire body.

---

[1] The author's text, *Voice and Delivery* (St. Louis: Herder, 1941), has an extensive bibliography of texts on voice and diction as well as numerous drills for voice production and vocal expression.

The vocal lips set into vibration by the breath stream from the lungs create sound with its three properties of intensity, pitch, and quality. Any human sound (tone or glottal pitch) has its full complement of component parts, that is to say, overtones or resonances — all of which are either intensified or absorbed or modified in the connecting chambers of the throat, mouth, or nasal passages. Since these cavities can vary in size, shape, and texture, various resonances may result. For example, the many positions assumed by the tongue, lips, and soft palate create vowels and consonants, other names for frequencies or resonances; and accompanying these practically fixed resonances are those frequencies composing what has become to be known as tone color. Thus, we speak of a sharp *e* or a harsh *g* or a mellow *oo*.

Soft surface tend to dull or absorb the high frequencies belonging to the resonated laryngeal-created pitch. Hard surfaces intensify frequencies. Thus certain vocal placements are conducive to certain qualities of tone, some mellow and others bright. Tones are often named by their anatomical location such as a throaty tone, a nasal tone, a forward tone, a head tone, or a pinched pharyngeal tone. A better explanation perhaps relates qualities to the kind and relationship of overtones. A mellow tone, for example, has a strong fundamental and a few and comparatively weak overtones. A rich tone has a dominant fundamental and first five overtones.

Certain conditions are necessary for a well-made tone:

a) The proper opening of the throat is required so that the inhalation of air is unrestricted, and the preparation for voice is established, namely a relaxation of the parts involved in voice-making — the jaw, tongue, soft palate, throat, and vocal lips.

b) The filling of lower areas of the lungs with air; thereby the action supplies the raw material of voice under a pressure, yet does not interfere with the demands of the body for its constantly renewed supply of oxygen.

c) A constant pressure against the vocal lips creating thereby the laryngeal pitches which are in turn resonated in the oral and nasal cavities. These fixed resonances are termed vowels and voiced consonants with their accompanying qualities. Energy is required to produce sound. Change the energy, and a change occurs in sound. The breath stream may create, under the permeating influence of the desire to speak, either musical sound or noise. Vowels are basically musical elements; consonants are noise.

d) A releasing of the breath stream with varying degrees of pressure through the partially opened vocal lips is the basis of the sounds, either plosives or fricative in nature. Both kinds of noise are resonated in the oral chambers and generally intensified by the actions of the oral agents. The plosives are created by the breath stream being blocked until its pressure is built up, and then it is quickly released. Observe action of the soft palate and tongue in the explosive *k*, and the lip action in the explosive *b*; some speech sounds are caused by the breath stream being forced through narrow passages. Observe the tongue action in creating with the hard palate a tubelike channel for the fricative *s*.

e) The proper placement of the laryngeal-made sound in the oral and nasal channels in order that the consequent resonation be socially pleasing without impairing in any manner the fixed frequencies which are known to the human ears as vowels and consonants.

4. *Co-ordination in Vocal Effort*

Voice is directly related to thinking, feeling, and volition. Some seminarians may feel that any vocal modulation, inflection, for example, may be acquired simply by imitation. It is true that seeing another perform some action may stimulate a whole series of co-ordinated activity, but vocal modulations are by nature spontaneous and a response to inner life. When thinking, for example, is vague, some vocal modulation will express this vagueness; when some emotion is changing the tension of the intrinsic muscles of the larynx, or the texture of the pharynx, the fundamental pitch of the tone with its component overtones is being modified. For each time a student will use a modulation of the voice or body voluntarily and mechanically, he will employ twenty or thirty modulations which have resulted from stimuli being distributed to proper muscles in the right order and sequence.

Co-ordination means a *working together*. What is working together in a vocal effort? Nerves, muscles, organs in an animated body. Some actions are under the control of the will; others are involuntary. In fact, much of the mental and emotional activity in relation to speech has been turned over to physiological mechanisms, and is no longer a continual conscious process. Many actions become fixed in habits, and we are not conscious of them or only dimly observe their functionings.

Study of Physiology and Psychology Important in Voice Training. If some of the facts about these actions of the body are known to the seminarian — the workings of the central nervous system, the autonomic system, the endocrine system of glands, and the like, he will understand better the functioning of factors involved in voice and speechmaking. But thoughts and emotions are more than physical consequences. The study of physiology may give a good background of the working of the body, but the knowledge of rational psychology, which the seminarian has probably gained in his course of study, will help to explain the intricacies of the relation between the physical mechanisms and the spiritual mind. The principles concerned with the relation of sensation to thought, the kinds of imagination and their workings, the processes involved in reasoning, the nature of language, the influence of volition, these and other psychological facts are important to the proper understanding of the speech functions and the real vocal responses.

Skill Required. In addition to understanding the facts of the co-ordinations that exist in the body for the purpose of furthering the speech functioning, the seminarian must develop skill in using these processes. Some of these co-ordinations are highly diversified and complex, for example, the muscles around and in the larynx should be relaxing while the muscles concerned with inspiration are contracting. Some of these activities are now used skillfully; some need to be relearned, and some, no doubt, should be discarded. Perhaps even ideals, attitudes, and desires need a revaluation before proper co-ordinations can be established. In any case, drills for better functioning are necessary before much progress can be expected in better vocal efforts. They can, if properly devised and performed, establish desirable habits of action and can eliminate bad habits that are creating interference of effective responses. The student must have a clear understanding of each drill. He should practice most voice or speech drills as if he were in an audience situation. He should make voice training speech training, and speech training voice training.

5. *Remedial Work in Speech or Vocal Training*

It is well for the seminarian starting voice training to realize that he may at some time have difficulties of speech and voice belonging to four classes of defects or disorders: loss of voice, loss of speech, faults of speech, and faults of voice. Their causes may arise from structural defects, functional disorders, emotional upsets, or environmental circumstances. The physical apparatus may be faulty; the body may not be functioning properly; psychological causes may account for the lack of co-ordination; and certain environmental conditions may be creating physical or emotional upsets. Texts devoted to speech correction go into this matter of deficiencies in speech in detail. Here we can only suggest some procedures for overcoming difficulties that are upsetting co-ordination, either in speech or voice.

Check on Sensation. As senses play such an important part in speech or voice, they should be checked for proper functioning. The eyes, for example, may be used in such a way as to be the cause of bad reading, or if they are not accepting the proper visual stimuli, the speaker may not be reacting effectively to his environment. The ears may have suffered some disaster which prevent not only proper hearing of words, but right evaluation of pitch, intensity, and quality of sound. In cases where general hearing loss is suspected, or where difficulty arises in the determination of certain pitches, hearing should be checked by an audiometric test. Brain disorders generally affect speech or voice; in fact, any difficulties related to the central nervous system, the brain, and organs of sensation should be diagnosed by experts who can determine their causal relation, if any, to vocal deficiencies.

Structural Defects and Pathological Disorders. Since speech and voice require the use of certain cavities of the mouth, nose, and throat, any structural defects in these members may bring about bad vocal conditions. There are only certain limits to structural deviations within which organs or organic parts can operate successfully. Some compensatory measures may be used, it is true, but certain deviations in teeth, lips, jaw, palate, nose, mouth, and throat structure may prevent proper conditions. In any case, imperfections in the oral and nasal passage should be examined for possible causal relationship to speech defects. Not all vocal difficulties are due to structure, for some are by nature pathological having as their source some infections, growths, or disease in voice-producing mechanism or in the resonating cavities. Generally speaking, these troubles make themselves known, and their causal connection with vocal disorder can be determined.

Wrong Functioning. Many difficulties of speech and voice, in fact most of them, rise not from defective conditions, but from strain and tensions brought about by wrong functions. Bad vocal qualities, high weak pitches, weakness in vocal strength are usually indication of incorrect action. The student must realize when he feels strain in speaking that he has expended too much effort in some operation. Hoarseness, for instance, is generally caused by wrong action of the vocal machinery. It is difficult to overuse a normally functioning voice, but many people who have average quality in conversation develop hoarseness as soon as the machinery is called upon for some extra work. A husky tone comes usually from strains, and may be caused not only by persistent wrong use but by various infections. A physician generally should make a diagnosis where huskiness continues.

A breathy tone is a typical example of lack of co-ordination among the forces involved in phonation. The expiratory breath is out of control, and there is a consequent lack of proper phonation and resonance. If a person cannot use his voice well, whether his difficulties be pinched metallic tones due to hypertension, or weak tones caused by lack of vocal support and throat tension, he must learn the art of vocalization. The use of drills to establish proper function is the best procedure when disorders associated with phonation and resonation arise.

Psychic Disturbances. In addition to conditions arising from pathological disturbances, structural defects, and functional sources, co-ordinations are upset as well as created by psychic causes. The sanguine, the choleric, the melancholic, and the phlegmatic differ in their vocal expression as they do in other behavior characteristics. As Lewes declared in his lecture on style, "A picturesque talent will express itself in concrete images; a genial nature will smile in pleasant turns and innuendoes; a rapid, unhesitating, imperious mind will deliver its quick incisive phrases; a full deliberating mind will overflow in ample paragraphs laden with the weight of parenthesis and qualifying suggestions" (*The Principles of Beauty,* Chap. 5). The vocal manner will differ in persons just as verbal expression differs. The strong, rough voice of the ill-educated man must be deficient in those niceties of vocal modulation possible to the man of education who produces voice correctly.

There is a correlation between the incarnated forms and the mental and emotional forms nurtured by the person himself. No man who has the physical organ of voice properly responsive can disassociate the strength of his mind and heart from expression. Likewise, no man can escape giving some symptomatic expression to conditions associated with fears and self-consciousness. Sometimes these attitudes lead to establishment of the very noticeable symptoms of depression and anxiety. These reactions to the conflicts of life often bring about such vocal changes that the audible sign becomes significant in determining the progress of the disasters.

Behavior that arises from compensatory technics, negative attitudes, defense reactions, and sublimations should be observed for its relation to speech or voice upsets. For example, some students cover up their fears and feelings of inadequacy by overcompensating, thereby becoming bold and assertive. These qualities of behavior probably have upon voice a worse effect than shyness, an opposite condition of the exaggerated security attitude, but they generally arise from the same cause. Overcompensation over-stimulates the entire nervous system while it is under the strain of fear. Not only are the major muscles affected, but the intrinsic muscles of the larynx suffer. The main trouble, however, is the disaster it creates in vocal co-ordinations.

Psychic disturbances need not be of major importance to be a cause of improper voice production. Even the transitory emotional states one encounters in the everyday work have their reflection in voice and in speech. In brief, then, not only do the emotions influence vocal properties for pleasing results, but they can be a major cause for vocal disasters, principally because they work directly on the organs involved in voice production, and on the many co-ordinations necessary for breath control, phonation, and resonation.

The Environment. Environmental influences not only determine many of a person's beliefs and attitudes of mind but many of his patterns of behavior. The adult as well as the child imitates much of his own surroundings. Poor speech and poor vocal quality are freely imitated, and the student will generally speak the language with the tones used to convey this language which are consistently coming to his ear. Speech and vocal expression are reflections of experiences. Many factors in speech and in voice will, therefore, manifest repression, exhibitionism, and like reactions to the conflicts arising out of any environment. Not only are superficial mannerisms and idiosyncrasies reactions to the desire to meet or to fight an environment, but many of the deeper modes of conflicts arise from self-interest opposed to society interest. In the absence of pathological or functional disorders, many speech and vocal defects can be attributed to the state of discord among ideals and values in conflict with desires for the future or with past experiences. The erroneous bases of un-co-ordinated and abnormal vocal action often must be sought in a person's reaction to his environment.

Specialists Often Required for Diagnosis of Vocal Ills. Any disorder lasting for a period of time requires expert diagnosis. Although good training may prevent many vocal and speech disorders, certain circumstances may give rise to particular conditions. There are adequate facilities in this country for vocal diagnosis, and many serious consequences are often averted by advice regarding proper vocal methods. Even the most experienced speaker may develop mannerisms harmful to good vocal production. When conditions indicate some vocal deterioration, or when bad speech habits persist, like hesitation, lisping, or mumbling, a speaker should consult a specialist in voice rehabilitation.

6. *Breathing Techniques in Relation to Voice Production*

This process depends first upon preparation for breathing. In the pause, occasioned by a preparation for a new thought with or without much emotional accompaniment, occurs a physiological change in the throat, namely a relaxation of the back of the tongue, an expansion of the pharynx, and an opening of the vocal lips. After this preparation, breath, generally by the way of the mouth, rushes into the lungs through this expanded channel.[2] The diaphragm, a muscle and a partition between the chest and the abdominal cavity, descends, and the lower chest muscles and back muscles go into action to create an all-round fullness in the middle of the body. The raw material for voice is thus assured.

Vocal initiation of tone follows when the breath stream is immediately brought into contact with the vocal lips, yet the air may be wasted before or during phonation. If breath is lost before production, one of the serious faults of breath control, the speaker may not have sufficient breath to complete the representation of the thought he is about to undertake; if breath is wasted during the vocal production of the phrase, the vowels and voiced consonantal sounds become breathy and the breath consonants usually become exaggerated in their fricative elements. The *f, s,* and *sh* sounds require much breath, consequently need not be unduly emphasized. After a phrase the excess of breath should

---

[2] Mouth breathing is generally recommended for speech because it allows greater ease in relaxing the throat. Nasal breathing should be used under other conditions. Within a speech are many occasions when a speaker can return to nasal breathing. Sometimes much of the breath for speech has been taken through the nose during a pause, except for a little amount that finally came through the mouth. Yet it was this last operation which opened the entire throat passage.

not be held. If it is, the action prevents the proper reception of the new inhalation which prepares the oral channel by expansion, and by enlarging the lower chest, it creates a condition for vocal support. Breath control begins, therefore, with the process involving the proper preparation in the pharynx by inhalation, but, as a term of operation, it is more generally applied to the sustained exhalation governed by the conditions of phrasing.

The Act of Breathing Differs With People. Some persons breathe deeply and slowly; others take shallow breaths, but breathe more rapidly. Either extreme is bad for voice production. The normal rate of breathing, generally rhythmical, is approximately fifteen to eighteen times each minute, but in breathing for speech the rate depends mostly upon phrasing and is irregular. Most people have ample breath to support a tone from the tidal air which is the air flowing in and out in ordinary respiration, but they take breath in at the wrong time, perhaps as a result of emotional reactions, or they cannot use rightly what they have received. Nature sees to it that a person always has a big reserve of air on hand. Phonation is work, and as the mental and emotional activity consumes energy, nature must protect her air supply. But she does not give the skill to control its functioning for speech.

Delsarte, the great teacher of pantomime, has remarked, "The accentuation of the fundamentals brings power." Breathing for voice is not a new kind of breathing but an accentuation of a natural fundamental process. A moderately deep breath draws enough air into the lungs for normal speech operations. If too much air is taken, the speaker attempts to control it by tensing the laryngeal areas, and thereby interferes with good initiation of tone. If too little air is drawn in, the reserve of air is affected, but of more importance the type of breathing which gains little air tenses the chest muscles and upsets the co-ordination of opening the throat.

The Intake. Inhalation is both an active and a passive process. The open throat is mostly a result of the operation in which outside air rushes into a partial vacuum; it is also a consequence of a desire to speak or sing. The depression of the diaphragm and the raising of the lower ribs involve activity. The lungs are practically passive and merely responsive to the breathing operation itself.

Exhalation. This process is normally a relaxing one inasmuch as the muscles put to work in inhalation are returned to original position, or at least to a less expanded condition. In speech this operation must be controlled. The speaker must learn to direct the outgoing breath actively yet smoothly and evenly. The diaphragm must relax *gradually,* as must also the muscles that were involved in lifting the ribs and contracting the abdominal walls.

Excessive Tension Upsets Co-ordination. The student is warned not to force the muscles involved in breathing into excessive activity, for tension will spread to adjacent muscles. Let him constantly imagine that breathing is an effect. Once the breathing has been centered, let the muscles work practically automatically. Strain is a waste of energy when an action extends over and above the minimum requirements of getting work done. Tension is required only on parts working. Stress, strain, elasticity are in a relationship. When a stress is removed, the matter must spring back to its unstrained condition. Tension, therefore, has its balance in relaxation, and unnecessary tension prevents work from being done and destroys the elasticity of the matter upon which it is working.

Drills Are Important. Exercises may be taken that give the student an appreciation of the function of breathing and that develop skill in gaining the art of making and supporting tone. These exercises[3] should be welcomed by the student, but he should remember that exercises, as Dr. S. S. Curry has often declared in his lectures, "are for the practice room, and not for a display of technique before an audience." Good vocal conditions are needed by the speaker, but not to be demonstrated as ends in themselves. In observing the breathing of other persons, the student should not be deceived by accidental variations; the principal movements of correct breathing for speech are approximately the same in persons who breathe diaphragmatically.

---

[3] Exercises for breath control will be found in the Appendix, pp. 274–276.

7. Initiation of Tone

The raw material of voice, the breath stream, striking the vocal lips drawn close together produces vibration. The action is one of many acts in the total co-ordination of voice-making. The act of willing enters the process not so much in the determined execution of the action, as in the person's acceptance of it. On the other hand, these actions involved in phonation are not self-starters; the assent for speech generally calls into play all the necessary physiological processes which respond in a habitual manner. The unit control is in the person who desires, and directs the action. He has learned to perform, and the body has become responsive to him. Emotional reactions create tension in the vocal folds, influence respiration, change the oxygen content of the lungs, and effect the rhythm of breathing. Phonation, then, is not a mechanical closing of the vocal lips, but is truly a total bodily activity often incited from mental and emotional causes.

When the vocal lips are tensed and taut, they produce higher pitches; the lips when thicker and longer cause lower pitches. Each voice has a range of pitches. The number of pitches of a range differs with each person and likewise the median speaking key differs, but, roughly speaking, it is about halfway between the highest and lowest pitch of a range. Intervallic pitch goes higher or lower from this median position. The student must use different pitches when he practices drills for proper phonation.

When tone is being produced, the student must strive to become conscious of overtenseness in the neck muscles, or more specifically in the extrinsic muscles of the larynx, i.e., muscles with one attachment to the larynx and another to some neighboring part — chin, spine, sternum bone, etc. When tenseness persists, exercises for relaxation should be used. He will find that, as a rule, he must start relaxing the larger parts of the body — head, leg, arms, etc., before he can work directly upon the throat muscles. Some people, by proper methods of inhalation and through the power of the images can secure more direct control of the larynx and immediate musculature. Some teachers, however, would have students forget the larynx entirely and imagine the tone as coming from the center of breathing. It is true that too much attention on how the larynx is functioning may cause tensions there.

When vocal exercises have brought about a correct adjustment of the larynx by the conditions of posture, by proper inspiration, and by the control of breathing from the efforts of the strong muscles of the lower chest, abdomen and middle back, the student can focus his attention on the end result of voice and speech. He can determine correct vocal action by a freedom from tensions and strains, by the sensation of diaphragmatic control, by the aural sensation of a pleasing tone, and by the assurance that, barring disease and accident, good posture and constructive thinking, and healthy feeling will maintain the musculature involved in voice in a condition for functioning.

CHAPTER XIII

Vocal Modulations

1. *Nature of Vocal Modulations*

The voice is sound, and therefore composed, as all sound, of three properties — intensity, pitch, and quality. Since the energy at the vocal folds created by the breath stream takes the nature of a glottal pitch with all its potential overtones, any change that takes place above the vocal folds will create various modifications of the sound, and any change in the pressure of the breath stream will likewise be observed as a modulation. Yet no matter what pitch may be sung or spoken, the fixed resonances of vowels and consonants will not be materially affected by changes in the glottal pitch. One can sing or speak *me* on many pitches of the scale without materially changing the vowel or the consonant. Vocal modulation can, therefore, be studied under two aspects: (*a*) the properties of voice considered within the province of vocal expression; and (*b*) the properties of voice related to the formulations of audible symbols thought of as comprising the subject matter of diction (the content of the next chapter).

Vocal Modifications of Symbolic Expression. A speaker may communicate his thoughts, yet give little of his own reaction to them. He gives speech sounds that have become the symbols of oral communication, but he must have vocal expression in order to give his own personal reaction to the audience situation. He uses emotional signs that may or may not be accompanied by the audible symbols. Involuntary expressions are always coming and going throughout the body, and manifestation of volition and emotion are present in speech. They are nuances of tone, varying rates and habituated patterns of rhythm which express with great veracity the inner life of our animal as well as rational nature. They are rather obvious in conversation as natural responses, but in public speaking they may often be inconsistent with the speech situation.

The Vocabulary of Vocal Expression. Pause, stress, change of pitch, inflection, tone color, and rate make up a vocabulary of delivery valuable to the speaker. They become the mediums of interpretation and clothe words with various sound patterns that aid persuasion. Each modulation is a vocal implement charged with emotional energy which can be transmitted to a hearer. If the current of emotional flow is low, the hearer may get some meaning, but his feeling is at a low ebb; if high in power, the feeling in the hearer is high. Despite its importance, however, this agency of voice should not be made an end in itself; it is rather a means of interweaving expression with communication so that the ensemble expresses denotation and connotation.

Since these modulations are not, strictly speaking, a language and seldom need to be consciously made and only arise out of a response to a situation, they should not be acquired as a language, but from circumstances. The speaker practicing vocal modulation should put himself in a speaking situation that calls for changes of pitch, inflection, and the other modulations. If he cannot devise these situations for himself, he can find practically any life situation in good literature.

Consequences of Vocal Modulation. A twofold result comes from good vocal modulation, first, in relation to the speaker and, secondly, to the audience. In reference to the speaker: as vocal modulation is a natural response of the organism it aids better vocal production. A well-modulated voice lasts longer, preserves physical energy, preventing waste and serves to make a good impression for the speaker. In connection with the audience: good modulation is pleasing. It is an aid to making subject matter understood and is a material factor in securing attention and good will.

Certain factors of vocal expression now merit attention:

2. *Intensity*

The strength of the voice depends on the intensity of vibration in the larynx and its consequent resonation. Good attack, of course, is aided primarily by adequate breath and proper breath control. Vocal force is known under various terms — stress, accent, volume, emphasis, and the like.

Carrying Power.   A voice has carrying power under the following conditions: (*a*) as a response to the speaker's idea of the distance that the tone must carry; (*b*) a sufficient amount of energy at the vocal folds while the tone is being initiated; (*c*) ample resonance in the oral and nasal chambers, and (*d*) an adaptation to acoustic circumstances. Consequently, while practicing for stress and emphasis, a speaker should associate loudness of tone with proper use of pitch and quality. He should use his eye to recognize the distance his tone must carry, then the brain, receiving the message from the eye, will stimulate the muscles to whatever motor activity is involved in creating more intensity at the vocal folds.

Touch, a Result of a Mental Act.   Although physically a stress is an application of vocal force, psychologically it is a pulsation of the mind — a mental discrimination of centers of attention. The proper touch on the vowel indicates a volitional act of mental attention. The remedy for emotional drifting is a firm stress. Associated with correct pause, vocal stress gives rhythm. Let the student read the following passages of Holy Scripture: Matthew 5:1–10; Psalm 102; and John 14:1–22. He should indicate the centers of attention with a definite stroke of the voice, and have his inflection change with ideas; let stress indicate his vocal control.

Distinct and Correct Utterance Helps the Carrying Power of Voice.   The student must apply stress to words and consonants consistent with English usage and the requirements of interpretation. He should let the mind locate the centers of attention for emphasis, then stress syllables according to the laws of correct pronunciation. He must give the proper duration to a syllable, but not materially change it, because he gives it an accent. He must not deliberately change the quality of the vowel, because he stresses it. He should not exaggerate the tendency in speaking English to pronounce every unstressed vowel as a neutral one, for example, the *a* in sof*a*. He will be better understood if he speaks distinctly, for a loud voice even with emphasis may not be carrying meaning to the listeners.

Intensity Must Be Consistent With Interpretation. Volume relates to the characteristic loudness or softness of voice as applied to the interpretation of an oral composition. The student might read John 10:1–18 using volume consistent with the interpretation, yet remembering that enunciation, proper stress, and the predominant characteristics of loudness or softness cannot be divorced from good vocal quality.

Faults to Avoid. (*a*) Lack of support. Many speakers do not breathe often enough. Generally, however, the condition is a fault of breath control. Tone must be sustained. (*b*) Lack of resonance. Placement of tone is important. (*c*) Misconception as to the proper placement of emphasis. (*d*) Wrong pronunciation of words due to wrong accent. (*e*) Monotonous stressing of words preventing the natural rhythm of the English phrase. Each successive idea has not the same importance. The forward movement of the sentence must indicate appreciation of points of concentration, and places of subordination.

Emphasis is a tool of emotion as well as a sign of intellectual discernment. A preacher who stimulates the vocal mechanism in the same monotonous pattern has a wrong attitude toward life. He is uninterested in his surroundings and lacks convictions. A change of force in the voice is an early sign of interest in happenings. Most faults related to intensity are not directly associated with the problems of phonation. Many people who speak so softly as to be almost inaudible *wish* to speak softly. The attitude a person has toward a loud or soft voice has much to do with the voice he accepts for himself.

3. *Pitch*

There are two kinds of pitch, intervallic (steps) and inflectional (slides). Intervallic, or a change of pitch by steps, occurs anywhere within the sentence; it is caused by the prevailing mood, and by the mind discriminating one center of attention from the other. Change of pitch, then, should accurately manifest the distinction and often the sequence of ideas, particularly the subordination of ideas as well as the emotional content stimulated by various images. As was said in an earlier chapter, certain emotions have wider changes of pitch than others. Anger and nervous fear tend to a wide range, whereas love, hate, affection, dignified feelings tend to a narrow range, but not necessarily to a decrease in the number of pitches.

The Dominant Pitch. The pitch of a voice relates to fundamental pitch of a complex sound made in the larynx with the overtones resonated in the oral and nasal cavities. It may be high, low, or middle. Physically, it is determined by the frequency of vibrations. This frequency of vibration at the vocal folds is affected by their length, mass, and tension. The shorter the length and the greater the tensions, the higher the pitch. The deciding factors for the key, i.e., a predominant pitch level, should be the mental and emotional interpretation of the subject matter itself, the needs and comforts of the audience, and the vocal ease of the speaker.

Each speaker has his own best pitch level which he can determine by experiment. Too high or too low a pitch at the beginning of a speech is uncomfortable for the hearer and soon becomes uncomfortable for the speaker because he is soon at the limits of his own pitch range. This range is determined by the structure of the larnyx and its functioning, but a high-pitched or a low-pitched voice can be used in all of its range, and each pitch can be made resonant.

Wrong Use of Pitch. An audience can understand a change of pitch much better than a change in volume, but a speaker in using intervallic pitch should avoid its two faults: monopitch, and singsong. Monopitch reflects monotony of thinking. The speaker should not try to grasp such a broad and lengthy comprehension that he fails to realize the import of the context. Let him read the ninety-first psalm indicating where the pitch will change when his mind takes different views toward the successive ideas. He must not go high, then low, then middle just to make a change or to avoid singsong. When he puts his mind on making a vocal modulation, he cannot focus upon what he is saying. In conversation, pitch changes as well as key changes are a free natural response to reason and emotions. Vocal transitions should be greater when emotional and mental transitions are more intense.

How to Secure Good Pitch. A student should observe how people use pitch effectively, and how the faults of pitch detract from good speaking. Then he should learn to judge the use he makes of his own pitch, and lastly, he should practice the drills found in books on voice and diction. To determine his best general pitch, he can sing up and down the scale, keeping good quality on each pitch, and testing the quality of each pitch by increasing and decreasing its intensity. The placement on each pitch is frontal or forward, particularly in the lower pitches of the voice. He may prefer as some people do to use a hum in singing the scales. By stopping his ears with his fingers, he can determine the pitch level of the hum in relation to good quality and volume.

Imitating the voices of other people gives a person an idea of the range of his own voice, its pitches of quality, and its best pitch level. Somewhere, about the median between the highest and lowest note, will be found a pitch where speaking is easy, and from which point change of pitches can effectively be made. The student should avoid using high or low pitches that are without good quality. He should also observe that there is a direct relationship between intensity and pitch. If the pressure on the vocal folds is increased, the tendency is a rise in pitch. To maintain pitch at a desired level is an art. If he must speak loud, he must control the tendency to speak only on high pitches. Many preachers speaking in a loud high voice have chronic disorders of voice.

Inflectional Pitch. An inflection is a wave or bend of the voice during the emission of a sound. Direction of inflection indicates antithesis, sequence of ideas, questions and answers, contrasts of emotional and mental attitudes, and quotations. The inflection is straight to the degree it represents direct, serious manifestation of thought. The voice is inflected *lower* when it manifests a certain finality of thought or a positive, even commanding, attitude. Inflection tends to *rise* when it indicates a certain doubtful manifestation of the mind, unfinished thought, surprise, or a questioning or looking-forward attitude of the mind. Not every sentence with a question mark calls for a rising inflection. "What are you doing?" may call for a falling inflection, since there is a finality of thought. When using the falling inflection, the student should avoid losing the support of tone. The inflection bends downward, but the vocal support is not diminished, nor is the pitch necessarily lowered for the end of each thought; otherwise, the audience will not hear the last part of a sentence.

Kinds of Compound Inflections. There are two compound inflections. The rising-falling is often heard in sarcasm and insincerity. It is an inflection to be avoided in conversation, and formal speech, unless irony, sarcasm, or perhaps a subtle relation of ideas is deliberately intended. The falling-rising shows that the thought is being influenced with an emotional reaction of uncertainty.

Length of Inflection. How long should an inflection be held? The answer depends upon the emotional and intellectual content. Long, positive inflections indicate clearly vigorous thinking, and an appreciation of the importance of the concept. The abrupt inflection often indicates degrees of excitement, and often a colloquial spirit. The abrupt inflection is not something to be avoided. Conviction may be decisive. The meaningless short inflection is a sign that the thought has not been realized.

Faulty Use of Inflection. Some preachers have a bad habit of making every phrase complete in itself, when they should indicate the forward progression of thought by rising inflection. Others tend to close each sentence with a rising inflection — an affectation condemned by many of the early speech teachers, but a fault which still persists among preachers. Professor Winans of Cornell University related the cure of faulty inflections to proper phrasing, a very appropriate connection, since good phrasing distinguishes idea from idea, scene from scene, and mood from mood. If a student learned to phrase well, he would inflect his thought in relation to sense and feeling. In conversation, his inflections are probably normal, because he has an attitude toward what he is saying, but when the student memorizes a selection, he may not have very definite attitudes toward his ideas; so he pronounces words and gets viewpoints afterward.

Drill. Since inflections are closely related to the standards of language, it is well to use them in such a manner that the rhythm of the English sentence is not destroyed. For practice the student might accentuate every shade of meaning by proper inflections in the material of the following citations: 2 Corinthians 11:16–30; Mark 3:31–35; Isaias 5:7; Matthew 25:14–30; John 4:1–26; 10:1–21; 1 Corinthians 15:12–58; Psalms 21, 22, 80, 107.

4. *Quality*

Older textbooks attempted to teach a specific vocal and bodily pattern for each emotion. Psychologists now hold that each emotion, as we know it by name, is not so specially expressed; rather one group of emotions tends to create within the body repressive characteristics, and another group to create expansive characteristics, but within each group there is considerable overlapping of behavioristic expressions. Consequently, adoration and love will have basically the same pattern with some particular variations, principally caused by individual responses to situations.

A person may have a resonant voice of good quality, that is to say, a voice with a pleasing arrangement of overtones, but he may not in passing from one idea, or one situation to another, use good tone color as an indication of his intellectual insight of the subject matter or his response to his imagination. A speaker cannot play on one or two emotions. Every conception has its own connotation as well as its denotation. Every attitude has its reflection. Just as the ore in a rock has the telltale mark of a mine, so often the hard vocal quality is only a reflection of a cold, calculating mind. Feeling, then, to secure good vocal modulation, must be specific, and not a nebulous kind of physiological reaction divorced from a specific experience.

Expressions of Emotions. Bellefroid remarks that each one feels passion in some different way, and expresses it with individual differences. Sorrow places a weight on the heart and troubles it; the voice suggests this weight, becoming languid.

Although sorrow may burden the heart, an expression of sorrow should not suggest despair. All the great orators, as well as the great actors, have been able to suggest in their expression of sorrow a great reserve of control. Weeping suggests the loosening of control, while sorrow can reflect faith and courage. In the death struggle of Laocoön we see the man with the children being slowly crushed to death by the serpents. There is a majesty of power in the man's features. It it written in each furrow of his tortured face. The sorrow incited by the Saviour on His cross brought no despair to Mary, even though her heart was pierced. Expression of sorrow, then, and of deep grief, should have nothing about it that suggests weakness, such as emotional whining and a singsong drifting. If the preacher discriminates ideas and feelings, and if he avoids the sustaining of one emotional mood, there will be less drifting. Grief and sorrow should rather convey suffering tempered with strength, even a spiritual acceptance of anguish.

Bellefroid says, "Pleasure and joy dilate the heart, and are expressed by vivid and animated accent. Anger is fiery, hurling the soul into disorder, and is expressed by violent, strong impetuous tone," but hate is cold, calculating, and has level pitch, and even color. "In admiration, the tone will be uncertain, breathless, confused, because the soul has become expectant of what it wants, and of what it approves."

Tone Color. Color, good or bad, is always in the voice. In order to get proper quality, the student must realize that the character of the secondary vibrations determines tone color along with the degree of tension in the vocal mechanism. The texture of cavities has much to do with vocal quality. The very walls of the oral and nasal cavities are softened or roughened according to the emotion dominating the person. Not only is the texture of the cavities changed, but their size and shape are affected. Under the influence of some affective states, tension may become so great that vocal power is lost, or the quality of voice becomes husky or aspirate; in other words, conditions in the body induced by mental and emotional states prevent clear resonant tone.

"Can you give me a specific exercise for this or that improper vocal quality?" is a request heard in most speech clinics. The quality of a tone must always be determined in relation to pitch and intensity. The extremes of a person's range may not be as pleasing as more median pitches. When a speaker can produce some pitches with good qualities, then he can experiment with placement for other pitches and volume. If no structural abnormalities, no defective functioning of senses or pathological conditions are present, then inefficient phonation and poor resonation must be caused by a lack of skill in voice production, or are a consequence of a way of life, persisting emotional states and attitudes. Quality of sound is peculiar to the instrument itself; in voice, the person himself, a consequence of his skill and power.

The immediate solution to better vocal quality, assuming vocal conditions have been established, is learning the art of interpretation. The material for speech must be analyzed, and evaluated for its emotional content, then the student places himself into the situation which is arousing the emotion; his sense of imitation, or perhaps better, his own dramatic instinct, arouses responses. Let him interpret the following excerpts: Matthew 26:36–46; 2 Kings 18:1–33; Isaias 29; Psalm 54; John 21:15–23; Luke 10:1–16; 12:27–34; 15:11–32.

5. *Rhythm*

This element of expression may be considered in three ways: (*a*) mental rhythm, (*b*) emotional rhythm, and (*c*) expressive rhythm. The mind thinks rhythmically, a kind of pulsation or stress on one center of thought and a leap to a new center of attention. A center may be considered subordinate to another center, or co-ordinated to it. Thinking manifests itself in types of phrases, each phrase arranged in a form with varying degrees of emphasis and pause. Attention to the grammatical arrangement of words is helpful, but not sufficient; the mind must apprehend the importance of the thought. Each emotion and each conception has varied forms within the total pattern, and manifests itself in vocal expression and physical action.

The student should keep in mind in the excerpts for practice the natural rhythm of the English phrase, avoiding singsong, unnatural stresses, and word-by-word delivery. He should aim at conversational naturalness, think well, and think aloud through the medium of vocal expression: he should interpret the selection considering the thought the author wished to convey and the emotions arising out of scene, situation, characters, and mood. He should accentuate pause, and stress with definite pitch changes appropriate tone color and rate. He will find the following excerpts of interest: John 10:14–21; Luke 6:27–38; 13:22–30; 16:19–31; Matthew 23:14–39.

6. *Duration*

This factor is not a property of sound but rather a time factor. How long should vowels and consonants be held? How long should pauses be held? According to the nature of the English language, some vowels are long; others half long; and still others short. What the mind centers upon affects duration. The emphasized word gets more length of sound. Vowels and consonants, however, should be pronounced in accordance with English usage and the requirements of interpretation.

A sense of rhythm prevents the clipping of vowels or the slurring of sounds. In more formal speaking, vowels and consonants tend to be better sustained, while in conversation, more lightly held. When words are given their right quantity and accent, the rhythm of the word aids in establishing recognition for it. If the rhythm of a word is incorrect, a listener has difficulty in getting a shared meaning from it.

Time Factor Determined by Circumstances. Neither the rights of interpretation nor the rights of pronunciation are supreme in themselves. Each process must aid the other, and together serve to transfer content to the audience that must recognize a sound pattern and interpret it as a sign of thought and emotion. If the rate of speech, which depends upon the quantity and the duration of the individual sound as well as the pauses, is too fast or too slow, the audible symbol is changed beyond easy recognition. Improper rate is fatiguing to an audience. When the sound pattern becomes monotonous, it diverts attention from its thought content. The student must be trained to use a rate consistent with pronunciation, interpretation, and audience comprehension. He needs variety in rate since it is as necessary to good speech melody and rhythm as variety in pitch or in vocal force.

The rate used by the speaker should not interfere with the effectiveness of any vocal modulation. "To go slow," for example, does not mean every word should be given the same value. A slow rate means that the total number of words spoken in a given time is less than the number of words spoken when the rate is more rapid. The personal style of the speaker, tone production, pronunciation, enunciation, interpretation, audience reaction — all enter into the question of how fast or slow a rate must be.

To modulate a tone for effective duration, the student must sense that the sounds in many words can in themselves suggest images and incite emotions. If a word like *kick* or *halt* is prolonged, its sound effects are lost. If the vowels in the word *groan* are clipped, the emotional values of the word are weakened. Likewise, when the natural balance between vowels and consonants are upset, a listener has difficulty in recognizing the symbol, and the connotation of the word is frequently lost. Each syllable has a proper duration. If a consonant is unduly prolonged or separated, or if the vowel is drawled, the rhythm of the word is upset; for example, observe the fault of holding final consonants, bed*uh;* or prolonging initial sounds, *funny;* or making two successive and like consonants in English two separate prolonged sounds.

Drill. The following citations from the Bible refer to passages which are to be used for practice in pronunciation and rate: Luke 9:28–36; 11:1–5; John 20:24–29; Romans 13:1–7; 3 Kings 2:1–10; Psalm 6.

7. *Pause*

Dr. S. S. Curry has maintained that pause is the most neglected of vocal modulations, and the one most important to the speaker, as well as the actor. Many students beginning public speaking seem unable to pause before a phrase in order to give the mind time for the formulation of ideas. During a vocal pause the conception of thought, a spiritual process, is completed in the mind, and the bodily resonance of the thought is functioning. A thought must gain representation before it can accurately and effectively be given to an audience. Not only must the thought become significant to the speaker but its emotional accompaniment may often be required to incite him for the sake of audience reactions. Pauses are designed not only for the preacher but for the listener so that he may have time to comprehend a thought.

Pause, a Physiological Need. In addition to this relationship to thinking, pause has a physiological cause in that a speaker must take time to fill his lungs with air. A new breath, however, is taken more as a reaction to a thought and feeling than as a consequence of a need to support life. There are always certain pauses that are utilized to sustain life. Some of these pauses are used mainly for this purpose, but the speaker who has breath control will not let a physical action interfere with conception of his thought. He will gain ample breath for physiological needs when breathing for speech, without pausing deliberately for breath. The need of breath is determined by the phrase and by the requirement of voice production; the place of breathing is mostly established by the demands of interpretation.

Pause Not Hesitation. A pause may seem long to the beginner when it is actually of short duration. If it is an act of hesitation, it may be of seconds or minutes. Hesitation is generally an absence of action, or perhaps little action, mainly chaotic; it is a place where one trying to think is not succeeding very well. In a pause, real action is taking place — breathing, thinking, and feeling.

Influence of Language on Pause. Breath groups are greatly influenced by the nature of the language; for example, in some tongues, pauses occur at the weakest point of a phrase, while in others, they come where emphasis is the strongest. Pauses then should be related to phrase, clause, and sentence structure, and, as far as possible, pauses should be made the occasion for breathing that the following phrase may have its proper bodily support.

Faults. Bellefroid says, "Avoid two excesses: (1) tiring the attention of the listeners with a grouping of too many words without a pause, and clouding the meaning by grouping words that should be separated; and (2) chopping the speech, and breaking it up into any kind of phrasing, or multiplying the pauses."

Emphasis. Pause, like stress, may be used to indicate emphasis which directs the attention of the audience to the salient words of a phrase, and acts also as a kind of vocal punctuation, but, like punctuation marks, may be wrongly applied. A preacher who uses pause correctly is reflecting his understanding of the sense of the passage. Appreciation of pause is the first step in the cure of monotonous reading and speaking.

Drill. The following citations will direct the student to passages with various types of phrasing and emotional values, thereby giving him opportunity for proper appreciation of pause: John 10:1–18; 15:1–17; Romans 8:1–11; Luke 1:39–55; Matthew 8:23–27; 17:1–8.

8. *Phrasing*

The thought must be represented by vocal or bodily signs. Because a thought may differ in its connotation and its denotation, the phrase, as a group of words, will vary in its length and in its structure. Phrases consequently differ in form according to the different languages.

Proper phrasing indicates a person's control of a language. It is a consequence of centering the thought. This process is a mental act; phrasing is a matter of words, but words so arranged that they represent thinking in terms of so many units. The act of centering indicates a speaker has an understanding of the relative importance of ideas. Some he co-ordinates; some he subordinates. It also is a sign he values emphasis, not only emphasis by force, but emphasis by any of the vocal modulations — pause, inflection, change of pitch, rate, or particularly quality of voice. It is by these modulations he distinguishes thought from thought, image from image, and situation from situation.

Phrasing Aids Meaning. The ability to center the thought is an effective way to transfer thinking to another. With proper phrasing a listener gets the thought simultaneously with words; with bad phrasing the listener must wait until the phrase is completed. He probably is given too large a unit of thought to grasp. The chances are that the speaker is rattling off words, perhaps at a monotonous level without any discrimination of thoughts.

As a thought is but a part of a larger unit — reasoning, so is a phrase a part of the larger unit — a sentence or a paragraph. A speaker then makes a logical phrase a means toward an end. He values successive thought units. He separates a phrase from other phrases in order that the particular phrase may be understood. But he does not separate it to the extent that it appears to be disjoined from the next greater unit. Phrases, therefore, lead forward to the comprehension of the next phrase. Emphasizing everything and anything, hitting every *and*, *but*, or *so*, a kind of word by word speaking, is monotonous; in like manner, so is succession of disjointed phrases.

Relation to Rate.   Good phrasing can be secured without interference with a pleasing rate. Some speakers with rapid speech have good phrasing, while others have poor phrasing, but so do some of those who speak slowly. Both types should think more, feel more, and show consideration for their audience by using an appropriate rate consistent with the material, and its interpretation.

Faults of Phrasing.   Improper phrasing, particularly throwing together words at random, or repeating words until the breath is exhausted, may be due to wrong breathing, but more frequently the fault lies in wrong mental and emotional action. Pauses due to hesitation or faults of memory will not occur to a person who is skilled in phrasing. Breath control, proper thinking and emotional responses are the cure for wrong phrasing. The speaker must learn to establish a proper sequence of ideas, and then correctly interpret this sequence. Generally, articles are joined to nouns or adjectives, adjectives to nouns, pronouns to verbs or related clauses, verbs to subjects or predicates, adverbs to adverbs or verbs, prepositions to their subjects, and conjunctions to following words.

Phrasing and Coherence. Every paragraph can be written to conform to the rules of coherence, with a main thought well expressed and a series of sentences interlinked to give strength to the structure. One thought is expressed in one sentence; another sentence gives echo to this same idea, possibly another sentence amplifies it, illustrates it, or restates it. Proper phrasing will interpret these sentences for the listeners as well as relate the major ideas to those of lesser importance. But if the speaker fails to keep this connective relationship clear to the hearers, he destroys by his delivery what in composition he has made a virtue.

Drill. The following references are to passages especially chosen for their suitability for correct phrasing: Matthew 3:1–12; 7:24–27; 1 Corinthians 2:6–16; 14:1–5; 2 Corinthians 9:6–15; Ephesians 4:1–24; Hebrews 10:19–25; James 3:1–18.

Summary. We have seen in this section that each thought and feeling has its own proper intrinsic energy which finds expression in vocal modulations related to intensity, pitch, and quality of the voice. It is well, then, for the preacher to make vocal modulations work in his interest. He must learn, for instance, that in proving a point, particularly a proof from authority, a preacher speaks firmly and with a sense of affirmation. In argumentation, he develops warmth and earnestness. In persuasion, he gives his voice a natural tone penetrated with the feelings of his heart. His tone in the introduction is simple; in the proposition and in the division he speaks clearly, confidently, and more slowly; in ordinary narration, his utterance is simple and smooth, but has variety and emphasis to distinguish situations, circumstances, persons, and time; in the body of a discourse, he has force and a serious convincing tone, taking care in treating the main points to draw their conclusions with strong intense tones. In brief, he uses vocal modulations as effective instruments to give further values to the types of composition — narration, description, exposition, and argumentation.

CHAPTER XIV

Diction

Authorities on preaching declare that the study of diction should not be treated as a course separated from the subject matter of sacred oratory, but should be made part and parcel of it.

1. *Audience Reaction as a Test of Diction*

If a seminarian allows himself to use poor grammar, to repeat faulty diction and errors of articulation, he will continue to have faults that later in life will interfere with his ability to persuade others. Henry Ward Beecher, in a lecture on *Oratory*, defines it as "the art of influencing conduct," and he added this significant thought, that the influence was truth "sent home by all the resources of the living man." Argument and instruction are among the resources available to the preacher as ways to gain the purposes of preaching, but each of these requires (*a*) correct diction, a matter expected of preachers, and (*b*) effective diction, a matter of positive values to all speakers.

Words of value to oral discourse have such qualities as the familiar, concise, concrete, specific, and the like. As long as verbal expression requires these kinds of words to make effective the speaker's thought and feeling, they should be adapted to the type of composition — narration, description, argumentation, and exposition; to the intellectual level of the audience; to the spirit of the occasion; and especially, to the kind of speaking — sacred oratory, for instance.

The effectiveness of words can easily be checked by audience reaction. Words that make meaning clear, a scene vivid, or a mood valuable are creating conditions within the listeners which they manifest by interest and attention. Effective diction can be fairly accurately judged by these two qualities in an audience. If another quality be added; namely, responsiveness to the speaker's purpose — these three qualities give an ample test for an effective diction.

The Words Which a Preacher Uses Must Be Intelligible to His Audience. When the speaker realizes that the pattern of symbols he sees, remains practically the same from year to year, while the audible symbols he uses are only evanescent happenings and that the spoken word is gone with the death of its vibrations, he will seek words that do not need several evaluations before they are understood. The listener must be able to grasp thought at once and form a judgment from rapid impressions. The words of value to him are the ones which send messages over the same well-marked pathways of the brain, the deep-grooved channels, words that stimulate the same or similar cortical associations. If "the best brain work seems to be wholly independent of consciousness" (Galton), there is slight value in making a brain labor with new or complicated impressions derived from audible symbols, half-meaningful or over-saturated with meaning.

To make his diction effective a preacher must choose the exact word to convey his thought to the audience. And equally important he must seek the emphatic word. For *happy* he may find a circumstance to substitute *joyous* or *sunny*. Such a substitution may make a meaning more intense. By avoiding worn out expressions and general words, he can escape the criticism so often leveled at preachers that they deal too frequently in general terms. Words have picture values or feeling tones. The specific word incites the individualized image. There are many words, for example, that will give specific impressions for the general notion of *walking*.

2. *Faults of Diction Common to Preaching*

Of the many faults of diction usually listed in relation to speaking, there are some that seem to be peculiarly associated with preaching. For instance, triteness of expression has no virtue. Indeed it would pay a preacher well to keep a black list of trite expressions as well as a glossary of faulty terms. Then too there is jargon! Perhaps as Phillips Brooks remarks, some preachers "are deadened to their sacred work by their constant intercourse with sacred things"; consequently they are unaware of their dependence upon a kind of ecclesiastical diction. As a matter of emphasis, it can be said that this technical language, like all such language, should be used only in relation to special subject matter employed for listeners who can share its meaning.

Jargon employed to express theological or philosophical ideas is nothing but jargon, despite its high association. There is no special English for the pulpit, only good English, but nevertheless English suited to the nature of sacred oratory, just as it is adapted to the deliberative assembly.

Some preachers straining after fine writing and "literary" language fear the homely word and the connotations of certain common terms. Even if their terms do convey some meaning, they do not put listeners into a situation where the meaning can have value. The seminarian must start with the principle that feeling is not always quickly aroused, but develops with thinking. The right words start a feeling on its surge, other words intensify it, finally the homely familiar words that incite vivid imagery and emotional association set off the spark that gives feeling its climax.

There are preachers who, realizing that affected, overcareful speaking often suggests lack of sincerity on the part of the orator, seek to express their thoughts simply and graciously and to exclude any appearance of a labored and heavy style. Although they use the homely word under certain circumstances they fear the connotations of certain common terms. In view of their moral obligations, preachers should examine any word for what may be associated with it; but in striving to be gracious they will have to guard against being ridiculous. "Legs," for example, must be called neither "nether extremities" nor "the lower limbs." These expressions put one in mind of the rule quoted in Longfellow's *Kavanagh* which forbade the young ladies to "cross their benders." A delicate diction may be tender and dainty and refined, but it may become so fastidious as to become fragile and weak.[1]

---

[1] A. S. Hill, *Our English* (Harper and Brothers), gives further examples.

3. *What Is Good Diction?*

In addition to effective diction there is good or correct diction. Is good speech accepted speech? Any youngster can tell when someone's speech sounds "funny." But what sounds "funny" to one may be praised by another. The test of diction is not, "Is it accepted speech?" except with the qualification: "By whom is it accepted?" One uses good language as a social obligation. But there must be some norm established for it. The usage of the cultivated class is such a norm. This broad standard equally opposes vulgarity and pedantry. Conformity with this standard is encouraged by good speech habits and associations with cultured people.

If a preacher's ideals, breeding, and character are expressed by his choice of words and the correctness of his diction in the expression of his thought and feeling, then he has certain obligations to himself to avoid the use of words offensive to cultivated people. First of all, he must avoid provincialisms and unidiomatic expressions. The preacher is expected, by reason of his training and education, to be able to speak a language based at least on a national standard of correctness. He cannot as an educated man use such expressions as *had ought* for *should*, or *listen at* for *listen to*. He cannot say *to choose between right or wrong* for *to choose between right and wrong*. Provincialisms and unidiomatic speech as violations of correct English are not expected from the pulpit.

Then too there are vulgarisms often used by uneducated people that do not belong to sacred discourse. If such expressions as *between you and I* are constantly heard, the listeners will not classify the preacher as belonging to the educated class. He must check his discourse, and particularly his extempore speaking, for improprieties and the overuse of colloquialisms. Words that may be proper in easy intimate conversation are hardly appropriate in a sermon or a more formal type of instruction. No doubt people who expect power, charm, and vigor in the diction of a preacher will be disappointed when they hear him use slang. They will feel that he is either lazy in his thought or poor in his words when they observe that he habitually prefers the use of the vagabond, short-lived word to that of accepted English.

The Use of a Dictionary. To maintain a standard of good English, a dictionary is required, for, as a collection of words, it is the result of reporting the pronunciation of cultured people throughout the civilized world who speak English correctly. Variant pronunciations can be expected; for example, the *ah* sound is used by some cultured persons in those words which other equally cultured persons use the vowel sound in *pat*. If the seminarian will consult a dictionary, he will find variants reported for other vowel sounds. When they are in the speech of the cultivated class, they are socially accepted as correct, but all variants are not so received. The *au* sound heard in *past* is not correct, or is *esk* allowed as a variant of *ask*. Obviously, the importance of knowing how to use a dictionary should be impressed upon seminarians. Usually the introductory remarks of the large international dictionaries give the necessary information on how best to use the book. Texts on voice and diction go into this matter in detail.

4. *Articulation*

Breath is the raw material out of which voice is formed, and voice is the raw material out of which speech is formed. The fundamental tone is the result of phonation. The resonances of the oral and nasal cavities are the voice products for the making of the vowels and the consonants. Speech, a conventionalized sound pattern, depends upon articulation to fit together the isolated parts of its audible pattern. But not only can parts be wrongly fitted together as in mispronunciations, but they can be fitted so tightly that the ear can scarcely detect any variation in the audible pattern from the start to the finish of the sentence which represents the thought, or they can be fitted so loosely by the sluggish action of the machinery of articulation that speech becomes indistinct, and good vocal modulation is prevented.

The remedy for faulty articulation lies first in correcting the mental and emotional habits of the speaker; secondly, in discovering wrong action of the lips, the tongue, and the soft palate; and thirdly, in practicing the right action which will lead to acceptable speech. Drills for enunciation will be found in public speaking texts and in books devoted to voice and diction.

Good Diction Does Not Interfere With Communication. Diction considered in terms of words is a result. In terms of functioning, it is a skill in modulation or composition, a putting together of certain resonances — some more musical than others, some more noisy. Some students have come to believe that the "pronounce-every-syllable" style of speaking gives excellent communication. Nothing can be farther from the truth. Such a style centers attention upon a forward movement of words and not upon thought. It gives all syllables the same stress or duration, creating an overprecise enunciation inconsistent with the demands of pronunciation. For example, assimilation, or a process which allows a sound to be affected by the preceding or following sound is allowed in some words, although slovenly speakers use it wrongly.

Good Pronunciation Generally Gives Good Enunciation. Sounds correctly made tend to be clearly made. The first element in good enunciation is the right formation of vowels and consonants. The student must have clear images of the operations involved in securing the sounds of language. In speaking, there is no additional lip action or tongue action over and above the specific action used in making the vowel and the consonant. Mouthing of words, and an exaggerated use of the lips or facial muscles, actually interfere with diction. If the student secures good vocal quality, then pronounces words rightly, he will generally enunciate carefully and distinctly.

Articulation Need Not Interfere With Vocalization. Enunciation need not be acquired at the expense of good voice. A sound from the oral or nasal cavities may have a variety of tone color, yet still maintain its characteristic form which the ear classifies as a certain vowel or consonant. The organs of articulation and the organs of voice are not two separate machines, but many parts, nerves, and muscles are involved in both functions of voice production and speech proper; consequently, if articulation is performed in a tense, unnatural manner or in a slow unwieldy action, phonation will suffer as well as enunciation. In some cases, vocal disorders affect articulation; nasality, for instance, a condition that may be brought about by failure to raise the soft palate during the production of the vowel, or lack of nasal resonance created by a failure to lower the soft palate during the formation of the *n* and *ng* sounds, creates speech difficulties.

No Dualism Between Word and Sound. The nature of the vowel and consonant was discussed in the section devoted to voice. From the viewpoint of diction, there is no sharp dividing line between voice sounds and consonants in many of the resonances. A good division from the viewpoint of the speaker is to consider the vowel, when rightly "touched" in a syllable, as giving carrying power to the voice; and the consonant, when rightly fitted to its accompanying vowel, as creating distinctness and clearness in speech. Vowels, diphthongs, and consonants, it is true, are modifications of sound, the vowel being musical, and the consonant being noisy. But as the vowel and consonant unite in the audible symbol to make a pattern of sound, and as several patterns are again united to make the word or the phrase, obviously the niceties of enunciation must be combined with vocal modulations in order to assure the transfer of meaning.

Aims. The objectives to strive for in diction may now be enumerated: (*a*) real desire to improve articulation and to change habits of speech, if necessary; (*b*) true understanding of the norm of good diction, and a desire to conform to its requirements; (*c*) knowledge of the exact formation of each vowel and consonant; (*d*) easy, precise action of the machinery involved in articulation; (*e*) ear training in order to hear each sound used in speech, and to recognize the characteristics of its resonances, for example, the vowel in *me* if rightly made is crisp and brilliant; but if wrongly formed, it is metallic, possibly shrill, or flat and quacklike.

5. *The Vowel in English*

Since good pronunciation is an obligation to the sacred orator, it might be well to recall here its four major faults: (*a*) unnecessary addition (ath*a*lete); (*b*) unnecessary subtraction (p'haps); (*c*) wrong substitution (dooty); (*d*) misplaced accent (al'-lied for al-lied').

A word can be wrongly unstressed as well as wrongly stressed. The student should use duration and force, which are the elements of accent, to secure the rhythm belonging to English speech. Each language has its own natural rhythm, and faults of rhythm offend not only the laws of vocal expression, but of languages.

A speaker who realizes that his vowel sounds are influenced by a dialect or a foreign tongue should consult special teachers of speech. Two tendencies should be avoided by the speaker — the habit of clipping sounds and the habit of drawling them. Some vowels in English are not pure vowels and have on-glides or off-glides. Some vowels are practically pure vowels, and should not be lengthened in diphthongs.

Let us indicate here some examples of the more common faults of pronunciation. The short *i* as in the word *city* is sometimes heard as the *e* in *me*. At the end of a word it is sometimes heard as the first vowel in the word *day*. Both sounds are to be avoided. The first vowel sound in *day* should not be nasalized. The vowel in the word *pet* is in some words wrongly lengthened; it is a short sound. Many words having the sound of the *ah* in *father* are also heard as the *a* in *pat*. Where there are two approved pronunciations, the speaker has his choice. The short *o* sound is frequently mispronounced either being raised to a higher vowel as the *aw* in *awful* or lower to the *a* in *father*. Neither is the short *o* sound.

Confusion exists regarding the sound of the so-called "glide *r*." In the words *farther* and *father,* the first vowel sound is the same. Many cultured people, however, turn the tongue slightly toward the roof of the mouth while pronouncing the vowel *ah* followed by a glide *r*. This action produces an inversion of the vowel. The degree of this inversion varies with sections of the country. In fact excepting in stage diction, inversion of any vowel may be heard, but particularly for combinations of *ur, ir, or*.

A diphthong is a union of two sounds in a glide. It is made during the single emission of a sound. Neither element of the sound should be isolated from the other and stressed. *High*, for example, is wrongly made as *hahee*. Both elements of any diphthong should be given with its own proper sound. *County* is heard as *kyaoonty*, with the *a* heard as the vowel in *pat*. Triphthongs are a fusion of three sounds pronounced with a single vocal emission; *fire, pure, hour* are words containing triphthongs. A fault of diction occurs when words like those enumerated are pronounced in two syllables.

Many textbooks have lists of words commonly mispronounced. Make a habit of studying these texts, and also look up in a dictionary words that you hear pronounced differently from your own pronunciation.

6. *The Consonant in English*

Consonants create difficulty for some speakers. Like vowels, they are subjected to the same four faults. Sounds are unnecessarily added, for example, *t* in the word *often*. One consonant may be wrongly substituted for another. Thus *t* is heard for *d* and *p* for *b*. Final consonants are frequently wrongly subtracted from the sound, for example, *beat* for *beaten*, and some consonants are wrongly stressed.

P and *b* should be strongly made, or weak lip action will produce mumbling. *M, n*, and *ng* are nasal sounds. *T, d*, and *n* are made above the teeth on the gum ridge, and not on the teeth as is the common practice in European languages. *T* and *d* are often dropped in careless speech. *L, m*, and *n* are sometimes used correctly as a syllable, as in litt*l*e, chas*m*, and bitte*n*. *K* and *g* are explosive sounds, and should not be made fricative. The *th* sound is not a *t* sound. It is made between the teeth. *F* and *v* are labial dental sounds, not lip to lip continuants.

The English *r* is not trilled even in the interest of enunciation. In dialects, it is wrongly added to some vowels. It should not be confused with the sound produced as an inversion of the vowel *ah*. The consonant sound is made with a single flap of the tongue.

S is a single sound in English, and it should not be given as a *ts* sound. *Z* is often wrongly substituted for *s*; *abzurd*, for example. The *s* sound may be taken as an example of a consonant that often causes trouble. It is made by a narrow groove formed down the middle of the tongue with the dental ridge the upper side. Through this channel the breath stream is directed. If the stream is too wide, the friction may be lessened and the sound may seemingly slide out over either side of the tongue. The front of the tongue, generally the tip, must be well up to the palate to form *s* correctly. The sound must not be overstressed.

Further analysis of consonants may be secured from any good speech text.

PART V

PRESENTATION AND INTERPRETATION

If a speaker is going to use the symbols of speech effectively, he must employ the proper method of presentation, and perhaps of greater importance, he must give life to the symbols. He must vocally realize and physically manifest the potentialities of the material he has prepared for his hearers. In a word, he must interpret for others what he has set down as his experiences. The success with which he does his work will depend greatly upon his own understanding of these experiences, and the control he has over the agents of interpretation. Chapters XV–XVII cover the main notions concerned with the methods of presentation and the literary interpretation of content.

CHAPTER XV

Methods of Presentation

All Methods of Value, If Suitable to the Audience. A sane observation was made by Professor James A. Winans of Cornell University that a well-equipped speaker should be able to use any of the methods of presentation. The preacher, in particular, because of the nature of his work in and out of the pulpit, must be ready to adapt himself to every speaking situation.

1. *Reading*

Some nineteenth-century rhetoricians asserted that reading prevented a speaker from properly presenting his matter (Blair, *Lecture* 29). They felt no orator could read with the fire and animation necessary to hold the attention of an audience if his eyes were glued to a manuscript. Bellefroid speaks of the reading method, as generally used, as "a cold and insipid thing." Others refer to it as "a way to give a speaker a kind of foliage, but no fruit." Many observed that the preparation for this method took considerable time and required burdensome work. Even great orators cried out against the labor of writing sermons. "I am required," said Massillon, "every day to learn my lesson as a pupil." Another inconvenience attributed to the method was the inability of a preacher who was burdened with a manuscript to catch the enthusiasm of an audience, and, when he had it, to strike quickly to gain immediate consent to his proposition.

Skill in Reading Can Be Acquired. If all the difficulties against reading from manuscript were insurmountable, there could not be good radio speech today. Yet political speeches, as well as announcements, which are read from manuscript (script), are heard over the air. They have all the elements of persuasion working on the listening audience. The radio theater uses prepared scripts. The truth of the matter, then, is that rigid adherence to a manuscript need not prevent effective speaking. A good reader does not feel its presence is in any way interfering with his utterance. As a matter of fact, its use gives him a certain security, and an assurance that he will escape the tendency to digress and will stick to his purpose.

Oral Reading Is an Art. Reading is more than a method of communication; it must be also effective expression for an audience. Some preachers are aware of listeners, but have little interest in their reaction. To gain the attention of the listeners along with verbal expression, there must be visible speech and vocal modulations. Symbols are not rich in themselves. Their value rests in the results they have upon two parties, the listener and the speaker. In reading, for example, the visual symbols must first affect the reader before his audible symbols can influence the listener. The art in reading, then, is twofold — getting the thought and the emotion and transferring both to an audience.

A preacher must not only write his sermon, but read its content effectively; he must be two artists — the writer and the reader. He may do well with the reading of his own material, yet that is not enough, for he must learn to interpret another's thoughts, for instance, those found in books. He must not only communicate ideas, but for example in reading sermons or Holy Scripture, he should read so very well that he gives pleasure to listeners. A New England lady records her impression of an Anglican minister reading from Scripture, "I had heard the Bible read before, but not until I had heard it read well did I learn to love its language and the grandeur of its thoughts."

Good Reading Conveys Meaning and Feeling. Oral reading can give meaning to a selection which may escape the silent reader. As great an artist as Shakespeare could not write a complete drama. He put down on paper so many words, but left a portion of the work to the actor who, by pantomime and vocal action, could make a scene and characters live. Yet Shakespeare and the actor still do not supply all the meaning and the imagery to the play, for the listeners, out of their experiences, add color, light, and shade to scenes; some, in fact, may in their imagination change a location from Denmark to East St. Louis. There is a trinity behind every reading — the author, the reader, and the listener, and each must contribute his share before oral reading has value.

Good Reading Requires Practice. Good readers have worked to gain knowledge and skill in the art of reading. Some preachers are content to assume that the skill in reading learned in the early grades of school is sufficient to interpret orally any selection. Many of these men have spent years in getting religious subject matter ready for vocal or bodily expression. They know the meaning of what they read, but they lack the skill to communicate meaning to another or to express viewpoints. Often their attitude toward good reading has come from a false notion that expressive reading is artificial. The question can, then, be rightfully asked, "How much expression is required in reading?"

Good Reading Is Not Acting. A preacher must first of all realize that an oration or selection is not read with the same techniques of dramatic art as are employed on the stage. Impersonation is seldom required in oratory. The preacher, hence, needs to be only as expressive as is consistent with the demands of the literary type in which he has placed his subject matter, with the interests of the audience, and with the customs of the people. Some passages from the Bible, for instance, call for more physical expression than others, but when it is required it must be more than gestures restricted to arm action. Every line of the selection or of the sermon must be read with the entire body participating in its interpretation. In short, the preacher must learn the technique of platform art.

Preparation for Oral Reading. Whether the matter to be read is Holy Scripture, a sermon, an announcement, or some author's work, preparation must be made for delivery. The preacher will find his remote preparation in his own reading of the Gospels and Epistles. He must understand the meaning of each excerpt from a Gospel, the purpose of the Church in using the particular selection for a Sunday or feast day, and the aim of the author in telling such and such an event. He will also need proximate preparation each time a Gospel or an Epistle is to be read in public, not so much to get meaning as to give expression to this meaning, otherwise his vocal interpretation may defeat the purposes of his literary interpretation.

For this task of acquiring meaning and feeling, a few suggestions are now offered:

a) An interpreter should read through his selection — whether it is his own composition or that of someone else — for his own enjoyment.

b) He should know the purpose of the writer. Is it to interest? to convince? to persuade? When he finds the author's intention, he formulates it for his own understanding in a sentence. In addition to the chief purpose of a selection or speech secondary objectives may be noted; for example, the author may wish to arouse images, to create moods, or to express a philosophy of life. Where one author has a desire to be logical, another has an emotional bias. A speaker can read or interpret the content much better if he knows what was going on in the author's own mind.

The interpreter may gain an insight to an author's purpose from examination of the title page, the preface, and introductory matter. An author generally expresses his thought regarding the scope of the work, his viewpoints, his limitations, and bias. In trying to understand the author's view, the interpreter must be open-minded in getting it before he decides to interpret his thought. If the interpreter thinks while he reads, he can compare his present views with new ones proposed to him.

c) Once the purpose of the writer has been determined, the sequences of the parts of the matter should be observed. If visual marks will assist the eye to find main heads, or subheads for oral reading, the reader should use these devices. When reading aloud, one can easily get lost in detail. If topical sentences are underlined, better emphasis may be secured. Some readers find it helpful to mark certain pauses for the taking of breath, a procedure that would create bad vocal conditions for others.

In grasping the meaning of sentences, the reader can note the restatements, illustrations, and amplifications. The purpose of connectives, if understood, helps to make reading intelligent.

As a climax is a ladder which must have a lower rung as well as a top one, the reader will have to find this lower rung in order to build the climax successfully.

d) Reading will be more expressive if the reader understands each reference or allusion.

e) Emotional content may be found in the large or the small units of thought. It must be sought out and expressed with appropriate vocal modulations. Mood is found in all subject matter, and if it is known and felt, it incites a variety of vocal modifications.

f) Summarizing each paragraph into a sentence or briefly outlining the selection helps some readers gain an understanding of the material, and the procedure aids in preparing for more effective expression.

g) Paraphrasing a selection often gives a reader a better sense of the sequence of ideas.

h) The means an author has used to gain a rhetorical effect will also be found as an aid to interpretation. Some writers favor intrinsic topics; others prefer the topics from authority or those of circumstance.

i) In preparation for oral reading not only must the denotation of words be understood, but the effect of their connotation upon an audience must be appreciated. The order of words must be observed to prevent fumbling which occurs when the reader is unprepared for a peculiar arrangement of words or an unusual sound combination.

j) Oral reading is given for either the audience or the imagined listeners. To gain directness, the interpreter in practice should ask questions that a listener or interlocutor might ask, and answer him in the words of the subject matter. When a selection contains remarks of characters, the reader can question these characters, and then in the words that the author has given these characters, the reader can answer his own questions.

k) The pronunciation of words should be verified, particularly the names of people and places. As many words found in Sacred Scripture are not ordinarily heard in conversation, they may easily be mispronounced when they appear in the matter to be read. The preacher must also know whether some of these words have been Anglicized.

l) The grammatical arrangement of words might also be observed to gain further ease in articulation. Sometimes even a well-worded sentence is difficult to read.

Mistakes in grammar and in composition are not always caught until the content is read. The use of *this* in an indefinite reference, for example, might create confusion when orally read, or the *which* clause added to another *which* clause could bring about an obscurity in meaning. Common faults, then, of diction, grammar, and rhetoric may be caught in the content if the preacher will look it over carefully previous to the oral reading. He will often sense that the material does not "read right."

Oral Reading.   When the composition is made suitable for reading, the reader then must apply the skill proper to its oral interpretation. The vocal and literary technique will be discussed in Chapter XVI, but a few suggestions, particularly applicable to reading, will be given here.

Control of Situation.   A good reader feels what he is reading, but he does not let his feelings control him to the degree he cannot be master of his surroundings. The audience expects a reader to be spontaneous in his reading. It enjoys his expression as he discovers ideas, gets pleasure in imagery, and reacts to the behavior of the author's characters. Although the reader often does not talk directly to his own audience in platform art, as in public speaking, he is always aware of its presence. Yet to live his characters, the reader cannot hold his complete attention on the audience, the printed page, the typewritten manuscript, or the microphone; neither can he be so absorbed in interpretation that he is unaware of actual conditions in the church.

Empathic Responses.   If the interpreter knows the effect an author intended when he employed words in some special manner, he must try to secure this effect in his delivery. If an author's intention was to arouse an empathic reaction in the audience and to stimulate motor activity, the interpreter must use physical expression to gain this result. In brief, whatever results have been obtained in practicing for public performance should not be lost in the actual reading before the audience.

Faults of Oral Reading. The most common faults of reading have been discussed in connection with voice and vocal modulations. They can therefore be enumerated here without further explanation. Faults of pitch, for instance chanting and singsong, are common. The attempt to read as one would talk sometimes gives the appearance of an unsympathetic concern for the content; a reader can hardly be casual, for example, with the story of the Passion. The halting manner and rapid rate are both faults of oral reading. The desire to enunciate words precisely sometimes causes the preacher to lose the natural rhythm of the English language or prevents him from obtaining a forward movement to his reading. Then too there is wrong phrasing. When eye actions, mental reactions, and the motor activity of speech are unco-ordinated, reading must suffer. In brief, then, faults in oral reading can be summarized as those arising from improper silent reading, from wrong literary interpretation, and from misuse of vocal and bodily action. Finally, most of the faults observed in speaking caused by an inability to relate subject matter to an audience can likewise be attributed to oral reading.

Another group of faults arises from mechanical difficulties and from the improper handling, while reading, of a manuscript or book. In Chapter XVII, related to microphone technique, mention will be made of the effects of holding a book or other copy in certain positions. Also, a few points will be offered regarding the proper way to prepare a manuscript for easier oral utterance.

2. *Memoriter*

Teachers of sacred oratory who believe that all speeches should be written and well memorized start with the assumption that beginners in speech have certain difficulties to overcome, such as physical mannerisms or vocal peculiarities. They feel that skill in expression would be endangered if students begin too soon to improvise. These advocates of the memoriter method claim that a speaker must form a style and acquire by study a number of sound and varied discourses of interest to potential audiences. They, therefore, counsel a student to undertake in the beginning of his career the task of composing speeches and learning them by heart. They further feel that if he accustoms himself to writing nothing but what is sound and constructive, he is learning to make good plans, to establish good sequence of thought, and to devise proper developments for his discourses.

Certain Disadvantages of the Method Can Be Overcome. Certain advocates of the memoriter method claim that memory will become lazy and stubborn, if the preacher first gains skill in extempore speaking without thorough training in written discourse. Yet memorized speaking tends to exaggerate certain elements of delivery and weaken others — for example, the volume may be increased, or the change of pitch and tone color may become unnatural — although preliminary training should emphasize the fact that no element of conversation should be neglected in the enlargement of all factors of delivery.

Some students develop bad habits by giving a memorized speech before they have learned to form sentences easily and correctly in front of an audience. Having something to say is only part of the speech problem; to say that something correctly and effectively is also of importance, and according to some teachers the first factor to be stressed in training. If errors of diction, vocal production, or bodily action are corrected in the beginning, they will not be perpetuated by repetition. A student may write well and memorize well; he must also learn to speak well.

Some teachers who have had experience in teaching seminarians believe they should commence speech work by writing out simple instructions. The students may gain ideas by the proper use of the topics — intrinsic and extrinsic, after the manner explained in this textbook in connection with the invention of thought. They must learn to deliver these instructions memoriter with the directness of conversation. When they have some ease in talking to their classmates, who compose their usual audience, they can organize more elaborate compositions which are again delivered memoriter with attention given to vocal expression, bodily action, and audience psychology.

The advantage of the memoriter method seems to outweigh its disadvantages, for this means of presentation secures all the benefits of preparation, all the well-placed images, and the well-planned construction. It is especially valuable for the speaker who has gained ease before an audience, and who can think at the moment of delivery. It is likewise of worth to one who can avoid the disadvantages of the method such as placing attention on words and not on thoughts, or speaking without enthusiasm in a kind of half-direct manner with a quiet restraint which the speaker feels is a product of dignity, but which the audience accepts as a lack of interest or indifference.

Delivery Must Be Remembered When Writing a Discourse. The experienced preacher will not compose a sermon without anticipating the needs of the audience, even the inspiration required to arouse attention and feeling. Whatever is not in the speech when it is composed cannot be manufactured before the audience, since the speaker is chained to a fixed pattern of words. Communication of thought and feeling is not entirely a matter of delivery. If the stimulation for a varied pattern of vocal expression and gesture is not in the thoughts and feelings of the prepared material, the chances are expression will be inadequate, or inappropriate. If impelling motives are not worked into the woof and warp of the composition, persuasion can hardly be accomplished by the art of delivery.

If a preacher could, as it were, write his speech in one breath, the ensemble, sequence, unity, and vivacity of the sermon would gain much, but under the influence of composition an orator, working without interruption, may become fascinated by his thought and art, and compose without regard to the needs of the audience. Then, when his mind is tired by too long-sustained work, he finds he has lost a sense of values, and cannot return to a progression of ideas serviceable to listeners. There is a better chance of remembering the purpose of the speech if the orator holds to the middle ground, working without interruption, and avoiding anything that can stop the flow of the mind and cool the imagination, yet not obstinately sticking to composing when the mind tires.

Polishing and perfecting material and style are always necessary. Even with long habits in writing with fire, enthusiasm, and correctness, a speaker still needs to improve a sermon in order to make it harmonious, sustained, and sound, and in particular, to place thoughts and feelings more suitably for listeners.

Faulty Memory. Some speakers, although convinced of the advantages of the memoriter method, are subject to memory lapses which bring about hesitations. They may lose the thread of the ideas, and their intervals of silence cause nervousness and embarrassment in themselves and their hearers. Nothing makes an audience more anxious than a speaker who is always on the point of forgetting his speech. An audience, we have noted, expects a preacher to speak with inspiration. It is not prepared to admit that even a prepared sermon is created for any other group than itself. But the illusion of the preacher using a prepared sermon as though it were being inspired by an audience is not possible when he must stop to consult his memory, or when he talks as if he were reading words from a mental manuscript. For the memoriter method, then, the memory must be subjected to discipline and training.

Daily Drill Is Memory Training. Teachers of seminarians, following the lead of Quintilian (*Institutes,* 11:2) who knew the value of training the memory for oratory, advise those who are expecting to be preachers not to miss, during their philosophical and theological courses, learning some selection each day, even though it may be only of five or six lines. This procedure, remarks Abelly, "cultivates the memory and forms a style like that of the author whose diction and construction the student has confided to memory."

St. Bernard became so familiar with Holy Scripture that he was able at any instant to quote it in his writings. It may be true that memory training was overstressed in previous centuries. The mind must be formed as well as filled with facts; yet it must have something to work on, and memory training gives assurance that the ideas and images will be available for use. Memory depends upon observation of likeness and contrasts and a variety of distinctions. The ability to note these differences is good mental training.

Memory Can Be Trained. Although some teachers of speech maintain that a memorized discourse never can have the qualities of good speaking, the history of oratory demonstrates that many of the best speakers have used the memoriter method throughout their lives. They used it successfully because (*a*) they could memorize well, and (*b*) they could re-create their prepared thought and clothe their mummified symbols with emotional values. A well-memorized sermon can be good if delivered rightly. In the words of a great French orator, "The best of my sermons are the ones that I know the best."

If the seminarian can apply what has been presented in this text about vocal expression, he will be able to re-create his prepared speeches before an audience, and now to make it easier for him to memorize well, a few suggestions will be offered:[1]

a) The time and the place most suitable for learning by heart will vary with individuals. But a person will memorize with easy mind when he is calm and free from distractions. Experience will show him whether he can memorize best while walking or in the silence of his room.

b) As to the function of memory itself, the student understands that he recollects only his own states of consciousness in relation to what has incited sensation within him. In other words, he remembers his own reaction to persons and things. What has impressed him strongly and clearly is subject to easy recall. The emotional element, then, is at the base of a good memory, and the idea, which is clear to the mind and strong enough to fight against other ideas seeking to gain entrance into the center of consciousness, demands and receives attention.

When two ideas are brought into association, each idea will be better remembered. Order, therefore, is a great help to memory. If a composition is not well arranged, it is difficult to unite and to co-ordinate in the memory disjointed and discordant thoughts

---

[1] Many of the ideas for this section were taken from Bellefroid's *Manuel D'Éloquence Sacrée,* p. 381 f.

confusedly thrown together on paper. If a speaker is having trouble memorizing a speech, he should check it for its logical arrangement and structure, and for his own emotional reaction to the content. He must be sure of the ordering of the material of speech, of the progression and the linking of ideas. If, while speaking, he happens to miss the thread of thought, he will not lose himself entirely, for generally, one idea or two ideas will be held in mind, and soon, by association, the sequence will be remembered.

c) Frequent repetition of the same state of consciousness brings strength to the memory. On the other hand frequent repetition will induce in the speaker a coldness toward his matter. His work, nevertheless, is to memorize his material by repetition. And if the content, which first of all seemed to have filled him with ideas and to be capable of making a very strong impression upon him, now appears insignificant, he should not let his courage ebb at this situation. He should remember the truths which he intends to announce are those which the Son of God has apprehended in the bosom of His Father. This thought should encourage further efforts in memorizing material and in valuing it for oral utterance.

d) Memory acts somewhat differently in different persons. One has a stronger intellectual memory for ideas, another has a propensity for a sensible memory for images. Even within these forms of memory are other differences, such as memory for color or form or different types of ideas. Then, too, one may have a strong visual memory but be weak in recalling auditory images. Generally speaking, most preachers find it easy to memorize a speech after getting an idea of it in its entirety, then running over it a few times relating sentence to sentence, paragraph to paragraph, and subheads to main heads, taking advantage of their visual memory to relate meaning to certain marks or symbols. They use their visual memory to recall well-managed alignments, unequal margins, changes of type or writing, and even arbitrary signs which may serve as points of recall.

Some preachers, however, find that their auditory memory is stronger than their visual one; therefore, they repeat sections aloud, and relate ideas to various types of vocal modulations. Some other preachers have developed an artificial culture of memory. They relate ideas to places, to names, to noticeable objects in the church, to prominent parts of the edifice, or to some connecting link which appears to be strong enough to force the recall of what has been associated with it. Whatever the preacher has found to be of strong value in aiding the recall of his ideas and images should be used in memorizing his sermon or any other content.

e) When a student decides to use the memoriter method, he should learn every word of his discourse. He will by this practice habituate his memory to retain faithfully what he has confided to it. In the sequences, also, he must attach particular importance to details, to enumerations and amplifications, and to emotional passages, in a word, to everything which can be rightly interpreted to improve delivery.

From what has been said regarding the nature of memory, it is obvious that bodily action and vocal modifications should be associated with the verbal symbols while a person is memorizing a speech or a selection. The body tends to accept a pattern of action that has been repeatedly impressed on it, and the mind tends to recall the thoughts it has already thought. When physical action is related to mental action, both patterns tend to be recalled because the factor of association is strong. Nothing which has affected the soul or the body is lost to either the soul or the body, and what has strongly touched either is generally readily recalled.

Final Preparation for a Memorized Speech. In addition to the suggestions offered regarding ways of memorizing a speech, a few points might be presented concerning the final preparation for a memorized speech. When the preacher is practicing his speech before delivering it in public, he will visualize his audience as it will actually be. He must give this body of listeners a certain width, depth, and length. In this final oral practice, he should check his enunciation and pronunciation. He should think also of the etiquette of the pulpit. In fact, he should make a quiet survey of things with which he cannot be occupied when he is finally in the presence of his audience.

In the Pulpit. One of the well-known preachers of the Middle Ages advised young priests to clothe themselves in a holy fearlessness when they entered the pulpit. God's help is present to them. They have solicited it by fervent prayer; they have prepared themselves by laborsome work, undertaken in the sight of God. They need not fear the criticism of the listeners who ordinarily are the most indulgent censors and easily satisfied listeners.

In the pulpit, the preacher should not lose his eye control of his audience. If he evades the eyes of his listeners, he may find it difficult later to talk directly to them. He must look at the audience as though he were to hold a conversation with it. He thus can familiarize himself with the different objects which he finds in front of him, and evaluate particularly the different grouping of people. If a word escapes his memory, he must replace it with another instantly as this is no time to lose the thread of his discourse. If he is off the main line and cannot return to the right road, he should continue with his general purpose expressed in some general reflections. Generally, some thought, a transition, a word, or something will be found that will get him back on the track. Often coolness saves the speaker; an instant of reflection will be sufficient to regain his sequence of ideas.

A preacher, like all speakers, must avoid the causes of distractions. Too much curiosity or anxiety on the part of the speaker concerning the reaction of the audience may make him nervous or impatient, a condition which will be reflected in the audience by inattention, and distraction.

The practice of St. Francis Borgia which he recommended to his Jesuit brethren speaks for itself: "It is a very holy practice, which never fails of having fortunate results, to make for three days before the sermon some devotion to the three adorable Persons of the Holy Trinity, invoking the Father, praying to Him to fortify the memory of the preacher and that of his listeners, supplicating the Son to enlighten their understanding, and asking the Holy Ghost to inflame them and incite their wills."

3. *Extempore Speaking*[2]

Henry Ward Beecher in his *Yale Lectures on Preaching* remarks

[2] One of the best books on extempore speaking is that of Rev. M. Bautain, *Art of Extempore Speaking*. It is often paraphrased by modern authors. Another book of value is Dr. Richard Storrs's *Preaching Without Notes*.

that great preachers may have had certain natural abilities, but were, in the main, the products of training. All preparation for preaching is arduous, and the seminarian must have energy and persistence to get himself ready for its trials. If he wishes to be an all-round speaker, he will practice the extempore method of presentation, but he will find that no form of presentation requires more training than improvisation.

Advantages. Improvisation was practiced by the ancients and by the holy Fathers. It offers many advantages to a preacher because if he can use the extempore method, he can speak on most any occasion, and on almost any religious subject he has studied or read. The method is useful to one who must preach very often, saving his time and much labor. The extempore speaker speaks with much more completeness and naturalness, with conviction and persuasion, with less formality, but more inspiration. He is much better understood, although not so orderly or concise, perhaps, as when he has his pen in hand. In adapting himself to the understanding of his audience, he presents in a better manner what he has to say, and, as master of both the subject matter and the style, he can adapt his material to the different classes of persons which compose this audience.

This method has some advantages that the memoriter method does not have. For example, the extempore speaker can follow and observe for his own direction the more or less vivid impressions that the discourse is making on his listeners. If they remain indifferent, he delays on the development of a thought. If they are not being impressed, he notices this. Is the way open which conducts them to persuasion? He can see what is being understood, and what is not; he passes on from what is understood, but he delays on what is not. Do the listeners seem to be distracted and nervous? In the middle of an oratorical movement, he can make a diversion from what is tiresome to awaken his hearers.

Informality of Style. The style of extempore speaking is less careful than in a memorized speech, but more natural with freer action. Extempore speaking generally has a conversational base which gives it good speech values. If the preacher builds upon this base to meet the requirements of oratory, he strengthens the elemental modulations of the voice and gains directness, simplicity, animation, and other desirable qualities of action.

The preacher has a better chance to give profit to his listeners who will be more interested in content than manner inasmuch as they have less time to form critical judgments when he is impressing, captivating, and overpowering them. In a memorized speech, many fine expressions must be repeated to gain the same effect as those permeated with the warmth of the improvised speech. Often thoughts come to a preacher during his speech that can be presented to the intelligence of the audience, and which move people vitally.

Inspiration. Sometimes an expression comes to the preacher from Holy Scripture which suggests the finest development. This expression, this image, this reasoning, this thought, strikes him by its novelty, and, with his imagination aroused, he abandons himself to his enthusiasm, and the listeners soon partake of his fervent feeling. According to St. Francis Borgia, the preacher is in a better circumstance in improvisation to react to the mind of God. The inspirations which come in the pulpit are often those which are most suitable to move people and most adapted to the actual dispositions of the hearers.

Skill Required in Extempore Form. Some preachers are perfectly capable of developing a catechetical point, giving an instruction, an exhortation, or even a conference, in simple and familiar language, but lack the skill to apply the extempore method to the more formal kinds of sacred discourse which require facility of conception, prompt judgment, fullness of mind, easy expression, and taste formed by the study of literature and by communion with learned people. To improvise, in a pleasing manner, a sermon according to the rules of formal oratory with a plan, a real sequence, confirmation, argument, development, and the emotional parts calls for experience in speaking.

Difficulties. Among the difficulties which arise in mastering the extempore method are those due to the lack of an active vocabulary and the failure properly to outline material. Language and experience are inextricably interwoven; consequently, when some preachers try to use words to explain common things, to use a vocabulary people can understand, they fail to find words. The first practical need of the preacher is to talk about something he knows from his own experience and express this experience in common terms.

Preachers who may do well with memorized speaking fail in extempore, because their ideas and words are bound together so tightly that they can express themselves only when they find the right words. They have too many thoughts, too many distinctions, and too many means available for expression. Excessive ideas or words may interfere with expression; they take the speaker off the main road and lose him on the branch lines. The solution for the well-educated man who wishes to be a good extempore speaker is to learn how to outline, and then adhere to the outline which he has prepared. He need not give the audience all his knowledge in one sermon. An active vocabulary and a good sense of outlining are therefore very essential to any preacher.

Vocabulary Needed. A preacher who wishes to be a good extempore speaker must, to use the words of Rufus Choate, himself a master in the art of extempore speaking, "tax and torment invention . . . for additional rich and admirably expressive words." But after a good vocabulary has been acquired, it must be used wisely. A fluent but slipshod diction is a common fault in extempore speakers. If a seminarian is to be successful with the extempore method, he must practice speaking and express his ideas exactly, otherwise he may develop volubility and even charm at the expense of sound thinking and wise motivation.

The person who is fluent has a responsibility to use his talent wisely. More than any speech asset, it, if wrongly employed, leads a speaker away from all the fundamentals of good speaking. As a balance for oral expression with its tendencies to loose diction, some speech teachers recommend writing certain speeches when time will allow this procedure. At least the preacher should write something — sermons, articles for the parish paper, current religious publications, and the like — anything in fact to give his style clearness, exactness, and precision.

Value in Outline. Dr. E. D. Shurter, formerly of the University of Texas, who made an extensive study of the methods of speech presentation, felt the key to successful extempore speaking was a well-thought-out plan of action.[3] He suggested that the speaker should first set forth a tentative plan to aid him in the collection of material, then after the collection was completed, revise the plan for his speech. This well-determined plan allows a route to be clearly traced in advance of speaking. It prevents the speaker from stressing the same moral points in his sermons, and aids in maintaining, even under the warmth of emotion, sound theological facts, worthy expressions, exact doctrine, prudence in dealing with the proprieties of pulpit speaking, spontaneity in physical action, and control even in the most emotional movements of a sermon.

Procedure Before Speaking. An outline is practically worthless to the speaker unless it is well memorized. After the plan is well known, the speaker can go over the matter of each subhead until he has the idea of it in mind, and knows how this idea is being developed — by an example, statistical evidence, or some other means. He then can proceed to other subheads in like manner, and relate them to main heads, and these main points to the proposition to be established. Then he can be sure of the manner in which he will introduce his subject matter, and finally he can work over his conclusion until it is strong and effective. After he feels all is in order, that the speech has good proportions, emphasis, unity, and coherence, he can give his discourse two or three times in his room, letting words come as they will to express his ideas. He can observe any particular good expressions he uses in relation to the ideas of the small units of his plan, and can try to employ them to express the same ideas when he repeats this subject matter.

Sermons Must Be Well Planned. A well-written sermon is in general very strong in facts and reasoning, and the action is usually well managed, has variety, and is well sustained. The doctrine is generally treated with theological exactness. But if a preacher gives the same attention to the plan of an extempore speech as he does to writing his discourse, he can develop strong

---

[3] In connection with this topic the student might review to his advantage Chapter III.

conceptions, give depth to his subject, and maintain unity while developing interesting and complete details. No written speech can by nature make as strong impressions as the improvised discourse because it cannot be so animated, yet the strength of its structure impresses people and is a balance for its lack of spontaneity. The better the plan, then, for an extempore speech, the more closely it will approach the written speech, while still maintaining its virtue of animation.

Practice Makes Perfect. Anyone with a talent for improvisation must improve it by repeatedly using the extempore method. In every preparation, he should conceive his thoughts clearly and strongly. "What one conceives well, he will announce well," is an ancient maxim. He must always avoid tendencies which produce obscurity and confusion. He must learn to be concise, as a long-winded speaker brings embarrassment to himself and his listeners. He must be sure to memorize his texts exactly and every thought which requires precise expression.[4] Lastly he should pay particular attention to make the introduction effective and the peroration strong and full of feeling.

In the first year of speech training a student may be given assignments in extempore speech which will in no way interfere with the preparation for memoriter presentation of other speeches. As the student improves in extempore speaking, he will naturally write less, and he will organize his material with this kind of presentation in mind.

4. Impromptu Speaking

Beecher has directed attention to the chief fault in this type of presentation; namely, "slovenly speaking" (*Yale Lectures on Preaching,* p. 216). Slovenliness is brought about when a speaker who has no time for immediate preparation must depend for his content on a more remote source — former speeches, reading, and

---

[4] Father Benno, O.F.M.Cap., realizing that misquotations from the Scripture or exaggerated statements might weaken strong conclusions, would say to his students of sacred oratory, "It may seem strange to you, but no one knows much about Holy Scripture until you misquote it." The remark puts one in mind of a statement by Barrett Wendell in his *English Composition,* "That terrible sanity of the average man is always watching you."

general observation, and either fails to get good material from his past efforts or lacks skill in developing his ideas for an audience.

Impromptu Not Extempore Speaking. Extempore speaking requires adequate preparation, well-thought-out motivation, and a well-ordered outline. Even though the expression is left to the spur of the moment, the development and amplification of ideas have been carefully considered. Impromptu speaking, on the other hand, is not based upon a planned outline or a well-considered confirmation; it is a response to an occasion.

Impromptu Speaking Requires Skill. If a speaker has good conversational ability, a correct use of grammar, a nice sense of diction, he should be able to talk as well to a large group of people as he can to a small group in a living room. Of course, he must have something to talk about, and this "something" must be something definite, or he will wander about saying "nothing." Since impromptu speaking depends for its success upon an ability to think clearly in an audience situation, the speaker must have training as a public speaker before he can hope for success with this method of presentation. He must be able to arrange an outline in a few minutes in relation to some proposition he has well formulated in his mind. He then must rely upon his general preparation and past experiences for examples and facts that may be used to develop his main considerations. The student who feels that he may be required to speak impromptu must acquire from reading, discussions, and the general conversation suitable material for a discourse. Interesting items of information will remain in his memory if he relates them to a possible use in preaching or in general speaking.

Impromptu Not the Usual Method. The discipline of composition is seemingly avoided in impromptu speaking, so this form is often chosen when extempore presentation would be far more acceptable to the audience, and the training in the method would be of great cultural value to the student himself. Some students, however, like the impromptu method. They like to live in a world of words, and become so accustomed to it that they fail to have interest in a world of things or in the operation of things.

To them impromptu speech is fatal, since speech becomes a matter of words, and they are hostile to anyone who suggests the need of content and its organization.

Even some of the older clergymen, who do have time for so many activities, put off preparation of a sermon until the time slips by, and the impromptu presentation is all that can be used. Generally speaking, a preacher on the spur of the moment is not likely to think of better illustrations, or examples, or is not inclined to arrange a better outline, than the ones he could find or plan in preparation for his talk. When the extempore method can be used, it has all the advantages of the impromptu presentation without any of its disadvantages.

Learning the Techniques of the Method. Since, however, impromptu speaking must be done because of circumstances, a student should plan for it. In his practice talks, he must learn to avoid repetition of his pet words and phrases. He must speak without hesitation and without the constant use of *ah* to connect thoughts. He can help himself gain a smoother speech form if he thinks of paragraphing while practicing the impromptu method. If he had dictated a speech, and a typewritten copy were presented to him, he would see wrong use of connectives, repetition of words — in fact, he would catch errors of grammar and rhetoric. He must learn to train his ear to hear what he says. He then can pick out topic sentences, transitions, examples, and connectives.

Some preachers do better in impromptu speaking when they gallop along without regard to gesture or vocal expression. They are better speakers when they use as well as they can the language at hand. They should not try to improve their speaking technique while before an audience. They have ample time in preparation for such training, but if it is neglected, their only direction of interest must be upon what is being said.

The Conversational Mode in Impromptu Speaking. The qualities of conversation must be found in impromptu speaking, yet its style and content must not be the manner and usual substance of conversation. The language of ordinary conversation may be too informal for the subject matter of the pulpit. The content, likewise, may be too trivial, and the proprieties not suitable to sacred oratory. The best element in conversation is often the vocal and bodily expression. Thoughts are often suggested by eye action alone, and emotion is incited by bodily movement. In the pulpit, much of the expression common to informal utterance may be lost. If the preacher carries the faults of conversation to the pulpit, he generally enlarges them. Hesitations, roundabout methods of narration and description, faulty pronunciation, indistinct enunciation, rapid or slow rate, and certain vocal faults perhaps are more or less tolerated in conversation, but cannot be accepted in public speaking.

Some preachers, however, fall into the opposite fault forgetting that impromptu speaking is but a natural development of the art of conversation. They fail to remember that speaking is really a dialogue between speaker and audience. This dialogue is obvious in conversation, but in impromptu speech, the orator talks, and the audience reacts to his thinking and feeling.

The style of presentation generally will force the preacher to become discursive. He can, however, let the warmth of his speech seem to flow from his interests in the needs of the audience; even the logical development will seem to come from the urgent necessities of the situation. The arguments must not seem to have been forged beforehand, although they must be sound. Points may not appear to be held in a rigid sequence, yet they must make good sense. In general, then, the advantages of conversation are sought after in impromptu speaking, while its disadvantages are avoided.

Fluency Not the Only Desired Quality of Impromptu Speaking. Practice in acquiring great facility in impromptu speaking should center chiefly on the quick organization of material and an aptitude for choosing illustrations rather than on fluency of speech. Professor James A. Winans[5] of Cornell University has said that he had no desire to develop the fluency "which many a beginner longs for, but which is rarely lacking

---

[5] *Public Speaking* (New York: The Century Co., 1915), Introduction.

after a little practice." Fluency may not be a virtue in speech, but truly a "grave danger," to quote Professor Winans again, when it is hostile to thought. Swift has said, "The common fluency of speech in many men and most women is owing to the scarcity of matter and scarcity of words; for whoever is a master of language, and with a mind full of ideas will be apt in speaking to hesitate upon the choice of both; whereas common speakers have only one set of ideas and one set of words to clothe them in; and these are always ready at the mouth, so people come faster out of a church when it is almost empty than when a crowd is at the door." Fluency in itself is not the chief objective of training in impromptu speaking. The student should seek to develop his abilities to think well, to feel what he is saying, and to choose from among his thoughts those which will further the purpose of his speaking.

5. *Mixed Method*

Some speakers combine the memoriter method or reading from manuscript with the extempore one. Certain parts of a sermon, particularly those sections dealing with statements of dogma or policy, or passages which have been exceptionally well expressed, are committed to memory. Sometimes evidence has more power to convince when it is read; long quotations also, if necessary to a speech, seem more authoritative when read.

Good Method if Well Used. A preacher who intends to use this mixed method should have a nice sense of proportion so not to burden his speech with obvious changes of styles. The difficulties of making transitions from the memorized parts to the more informal presentation are too great for some preachers to minimize. Practice, however, can make the mixed method a very effective way of presenting instruction. The more formal types of sacred discourse, however, require of the preacher much skill if he is to combine successfully the extempore with the memoriter type.

Techniques That May Be Used With the Mixed Method. Most clergymen lack time to do all the things they would like to do, and in this matter they are no different from many business executives. Some clergymen, however, have learned from business leaders the advantages of organizing work more efficiently, and, in particular, utilizing time while waiting to undertake some duty. Material for sermons, for example, need not be collected at one time. Some well-known preachers employ a recording device and use it when they are reading in order to collect interesting bits of information, important thoughts, and valuable viewpoints. These recorded bits are typed at their convenience. When they come upon valuable articles, they are also filed carefully according to their value as topics for use in a sermon.

When the preacher has time, he prepares a specific outline. He looks over his collected material for possible use, finds additional material, if needs be, and dictates to the machine a rough copy of his talk. After this copy is typed, it can be corrected for all common errors of diction, grammar, and rhetoric; and all quotations, including texts from Holy Scripture, can be verified. This material can be carefully outlined, and the entire speech memorized, or the outline and the quotations can be memorized, and the speech repeated a number of times until the wording is familiar to the preacher. Some preachers then redictate the entire speech to the recording machine about as they intend to deliver it. In spare minutes, this speech can be played back until it makes a definite impression upon the preacher, or the material can be typed so that later it may be read or memorized.

Assignment.

Students will find that subjects from Scripture will offer interesting class exercises in oral reading or public speaking.

The following subjects are suggestive of topics appealing to a speech class: creation (Genesis 1); the flood (Genesis 6–9); the saga of Jacob (Genesis 27–50); stories (Numbers 23–24; 1 Kings 1; 3 Kings 17; Isaias 40); Moses (Exodus 2:11–15; 4; 32; Numbers 11:1–24; 12); Amos (Amos 4–7); the Magnificat (Luke 1:46–55) compared with the Song of Anna (1 Kings 2:1–10); songs (Judges 5:1–31; Exodus 15:20–21; 1 Kings 2); exhortation (1 Machabees 2); a dialogue (Judges 13); speech (Wisdom 7 and 8, Paralipomenon 28); a prayer (Wisdom 9, Lamentation 5); description (Ezechiel 41); Gedeon (Judges 6–8); expressions of the God of war (1 Kings 15); Samson (Judges 13–16); Ruth (Ruth 1–4); Jonas (Jonas 1–4); Jeremias (Jeremias 15–20); David (1 Kings 16 to 3 Kings 2); Saul (1 Kings 9–31); Josue (Josue 6–10:12); Joseph (Genesis 37–50); picture of home (1 Kings 9:22–27); homesickness (Psalm 136); grief (Lamentations).

Other types of speeches or readings that may be assigned concern such subjects as David and Moses, a study in leadership; the story of Esther compared with that of a modern novel; formation of a kingdom from a loose tribal organization; poetic thoughts from Isaias; physical strength (Saul, Samson, Elias, Eliseus, David, Nehemias, Jacob, Amos, Joab); animals in Holy Writ; words in common speech from the Bible; description in the Old Testament compared with the New; comparisons (Osee) and the like.

CHAPTER XVI

VOCAL AND LITERARY INTERPRETATION

Vocal interpretation uses certain modulations of the voice aided by bodily movements which go along with the audible symbols composing verbal expression. Literary interpretation is an evaluation by some person of the content of a selection; it is a proper explanation of the matter, or a construction placed upon the author's language. Since the audience gains some impression from delivery, the question arises whether vocal and bodily expression might not be antagonistic to correct verbal interpretation not only of the preacher's own sermon but of Sacred Scripture. The answer to this question calls for an understanding of the freedom of the preacher in interpreting the Scripture and the content of the pulpit oration.

1. *Consequences of the Relation Between Vocal and Literary Interpretation*

Certain modern texts on sacred oratory point out that the sermon must center in "a personal realization of life." To the authors of these works the best sermon is the most human one. According to them, from life the preacher gains his own interior vitality from which in turn he draws the message that he expresses in words and reveals in bodily and vocal action. The speech product secured by many sectarian preachers is generally highly colored with the personality of the individual speaker. He is a sayer of what he thinks and feels, and his sermon reflects the strength of his convictions. What the preacher conceives to be God's plan is enthusiastically expressed often because he is enthusiastic about his own interpretation of God's plan.

But the Catholic preacher, speaking only as an instrument in revealing Christ, may not explain Scripture as he pleases; his interpretation must conform to the mandates of authority. Yet what he says is mostly in his own words, and what he reveals is through his own bodily and vocal resonances. Even though the spirit of God is speaking through the priest (Matt. 10:20; Rom. 10:8), it is his voice and body that carry the message; it is his pitch, inflection, tone color, volume, gesture, and other incarnated forms that create the signs, symbols, and attitudes for the auditors. Consequently, his delivery becomes good only in proportion as his message is personally realized, and only as it engenders feeling within him.

The vitality in many sectarian sermons often comes from the fact that the preacher thinks less of himself as a channel than as an engineer directing the flow of the water of salvation. He has a personal interest in the operation, and thus his sermon becomes "a personal realization of life." Before the Catholic preacher can get this personal interest, he must assimilate another's interpretation of a plan, and then become enthusiastic in expressing his own personal realization of it. In other words, he is a channel, but first he must be a reservoir. Although he does not have, like many sectarian preachers, complete freedom of interpretation, whatever explanation he does have must be presented to others, and his available means are words and bodily and vocal interpretation.

Dual Aspects of Interpretation. *Creation and elucidation* — Vocal interpretation accompanied with bodily action is a creation of the speaker from his own thinking and feeling. As an art, it is a revelation of a plan worked out by the original author. The interpreter must find this fundamental plan created by himself, or another, when he is examining a sentence, a paragraph, or an entire composition. He must accept also a second principle; namely, that although there is a plan, and a certain unity in all good planning, the variety of plan must be experienced — variety in the structure of sentence, paragraph, composition, and variety in style.

Means Available for the Purpose of Interpretation. Authors, while achieving unity in composition, view their subject matter from different angles, and consequently express their viewpoints in different outward manifestations. The interpreter looks then not only to content, but to its expression. He sees in the subject matter not only someone's apprehension of the beautiful or the useful, but a particular kind of observation expressed by means of the diverse art forms. Seeking the means of interpretation, the speaker finds that there are four ways of manifesting his own or another's creation: (*a*) verbal language; (*b*) bodily language; (*c*) vocal expression; (*d*) bodily expression. But in interpretation he is not free to express any order or any variety of form; he can reveal only the order and variety set forth by the creator of the content.

Vocal and Literary Interpretation of the Bible. In Chapter XV information was given as to a method of reading sermons, and the student was referred to this portion for the general subject of interpreting Holy Scripture. Although composed of various books and different authors, Holy Writ expresses truth in a certain order yet with a certain variety in composition and delivery. To know its content is important but to express it, and to manifest its variety to an audience is of primary importance to a preacher. Holy Scripture employs narration, exposition, description, and argumentation — all art forms which reveal the inner truth. The very spirit of the Bible is expressed in variety: the oratorical spirit, the storytelling spirit, the lyrical spirit, the dramatic spirit — all are present in it, and all must be rightfully interpreted.

2. *The Oratorical Spirit*

Holy Scripture records many examples of speeches. This fact should not surprise us when we realize that oratory abounds when men have convictions and are free to express them. Isaias, Paul, Peter, and others made speeches to convince and persuade men to their views. The speeches of the Bible must then be interpreted as speeches and not as other literary forms.

The first point for the interpreter to consider is the purpose of the original speaker. What was his intention? Instruction? Belief? Action? What was Paul's intention in his speech before Agrippa? The second point deals with the means used to obtain this end. What type of introduction did Paul use at Athens? How did he arouse feelings after his arrest in Jerusalem? What advantage accrued to Nathan by using narration in his rebuke of David? What means did our Lord use in persuasion? Once the end of the oration is determined, and the means of conviction and persuasion analyzed, it is not difficult for the preacher to interpret the speech for his own audience.

He will not make a narration a harangue, or express a persuasive passage as a statement of fact. He will give, once he has digested the plan of another's speech, the thoughts and emotions as his own, or at least the thoughts and emotions of the character he is representing. He will try to catch the mood and feeling of the original speaker, and, in any event, indicate to his own audience the speaking situation in which the original speaker found himself. The preacher, therefore, needs not only to understand the speech itself, but to appreciate as far as possible the circumstances under which the original speech was given. Often these external considerations require more research than the study of the internal evidence of the speech itself.

The following citations refer to speeches in the Old Testament and New Testament: (Luke 13:31–35); (Isa. 5); Peter: choosing of Matthias (Acts 1:15–23), to the Jews at Jerusalem (Acts 2:14–37), at Solomon's porch (Acts 3:12–26), before friends of Cornelius (Acts 10:34–43); Stephen: at the Sanhedrin (Acts 7:2–53); Gamaliel; at the Sanhedrin (Acts 5:34–39); Paul: at Antioch (Acts 13:16–41), at Athens (Acts 17:22–32), at Miletus (Acts 20:18–36), at Jerusalem (Acts 22:3–21), his defense (Acts 24:10–21), before Agrippa (Acts 26:2–23); James: advice about the Gentiles (Acts 15:14–21); Demetrius: defense of Diana (Acts 19:25–28); our Lord: intimate talk of instruction (Matt. 5–7:27), instruction (Matt. 10:5–42), reasoning (Matt. 12:25–37), parable (Matt. 13:3–9), use of dilemma (Matt. 21:21–27), use of a story (Matt. 18:23–35), parable — the story itself (Matt. 13:24–31), explanation of this parable (Matt. 13:36–44), frontal assault (Matt. 18:3–21).

3. *The Narrative Spirit*

When a speaker tells a story, he is representing the impression someone had of a situation, an action, or an event. He is for the time being a storyteller, but he does not become an actor for each character of the story as he would in a dramatic presentation. He is not imitating persons, but is telling a story about them. If he is speaking of Christ, he does not try to assume His character as would an actor; he tells his story with a deep sympathy and understanding as did the one who wrote the story about Christ. He does not interpret the lines of the speaking characters as if he were an impersonator playing many parts. His interest is in the plot, and he keeps the scenes and events of the story moving to its climax.

A story may have many dramatic incidents and characters, but they should be portrayed by suggestion rather than by direct representation. Even when the dramatic spirit prevails, and characters have something to say, they speak as the author of the story remembers them speaking. He is telling the story. He is not giving an impersonation.

In storytelling the story is the first concern. It gives a clear picture of incidents with the people in a situation, in some mood, and at some place. The reader talks directly to the audience. He is the storyteller suggesting by voice and body action the deep sympathy of one who originally viewed some scene or some episode as it was unfolded before his view.

The following citations relate to narrative matter. Old Testament: Genesis 1 to 2:3; 2:4 to 4; 6:5 to 9:17; 18:16–33; 19:12–29; 22:1–19; 37; 39:1–6; 39:20 to 46:7; 46:28 to 47:12; Exodus 5 to 6:13; 19 to 20:21; Josue 23 to 24:31; Judges 7; 13:24 to 17; 1 Kings 14:1–23; 15; 17 to 18:16; 28:3–25; 31:1–6; 3 Kings 3:5–28; 4 Kings 5; Daniel 2; 4. New Testament: Luke 16:19–31; 4:1–15; 7:6–10; Matt. 2:19–23; 8:28–34; 20:29–34; 26:20–25; Mark 8:1–8; 14:32–42; John 9:1–41.

4. *The Lyric Spirit*

Many selections in the Bible indicate the deep realization that someone had of a truth, and the feeling it incited in him. These passages, lyrical in nature, cannot be read as statements of fact or mere sequences of events. Often this lyrical element is found wedged in between parts of narration, but as the spirit is lyrical, it must be interpreted carefully by proper rhythm and tone color. The depth of feeling and the sublimity of conception must be made apparent to the listeners, but not directly communicated as in oratory and storytelling. The listeners in an audience feel the presence of one communing with himself, or see and hear him in a devotional moment with his God. Many selections, lyric in content, will be found among the Psalms, and must be read with a deep realization of their nature.

The lyrical nature of prayer must be understood before one can interpret it effectively. Although prayer expresses a relationship with God, and the factor of petition in public prayer may be present, it is not expressed as a rapid enumeration of facts. Prayer is less objective, has less of the oratorical spirit with its expression by direct communication, and is more lyrical in nature, therefore more subjective. The prayers for the dead, prayers after Mass, and prayers for special purposes are in the main highly manifestive of attitudes. This realization is clearly shown in vocal expression — pause, change of pitch, reflection, tone color, and particularly rate. Rapid rate is not characteristic of prayer, or of any lyric. The recitation of words is not the only characteristic of this form of communion of man with God, for the vocal modulations of the prayer are as quickly interpreted by the audience as the words themselves. The strength of the speaker's realization of the prayer accompanies its verbal expression.

5. *The Dramatic Spirit*

Some parts of the Bible can hardly be correctly interpreted orally without a sense of the dramatic spirit. Many excerpts are dramatic dialogues; as, for example, when a prophet talks to God or to the people. These compositions are essentially dramatic, and not oratorical. The Eighty-ninth Psalm is not a direct communication to the audience. Presumably, Moses is the speaker, and the hearer is God. "Our years shall be considered as a spider!" Whose years? The audience? Or the people who were with

Moses? How is the selection universally applied? In interpreting this or any other dramatic composition, the speaker must create the characters, the situation, the mood, and the place, and reveal them to his audience. Some speakers impersonate only a few external mannerisms of a character, and may even fail to suggest by expression the elements of mood, place, time, situation, and circumstances. The dramatic spirit must arouse in the audience a realization of a total drama being portrayed, just as if it were being unfolded on a stage.

Dramatic Interpretation Is Not Imitation. Dramatic interpretation is always more than mere imitation of one character, and then another. The speaker must suggest hearer-speaker relation in some dramatic situation. His art is suggestive rather than imitative. He must try to express the viewpoint of each character, while maintaining audience interest in the circumstances. He may practice the selections in dramatic composition referred to in the following citations: Canticle of Canticles; The Prophecy of Micheas; Osee 11; Mark 10:17–31; Luke 23:39–43.

Interpreting Scenes and Characters. Sometimes a speaker is not supposed to be speaking directly to his own audience. He becomes a person talking to another person, and this situation must be clear to his listeners. He will locate somewhere to his side a hearer or hearers, and he becomes Peter or Paul talking to a person or a group. His live audience can participate in the scene as it will imaginatively feel the relation between speakers and hearers as well as be observers of the situations.

Value in Dramatic Interpretation. Dramatic action in reading has more power to depict the motives of persons, the working of emotion, and the operations of the mind than the products of the fine arts spread about the church. An audience will appreciate a speaker who can show it by expression where to direct its attention. Where are the people Christ is talking to? Is He on a hillside looking down at a group of people? The suggestive factors of dramatic reading give an audience a true appreciation of mood, scene, place, and the people who are discussing some event or circumstance. What people object to, and what many preachers instinctively feel is wrong, is an impersonation of a person that gives only a few of his outward characteristics with little of his thinking or feeling.

The Technique of Dramatic Art Must Be Learned. If the technique of dramatic art is required in interpretation, no other form of the speech arts can be substituted for it. When a speaker reads so that his voice and body indicate he has obtained the viewpoint of some person he represents, he gives his listeners an insight into some situation, and they become not mere sightseers, but dynamically interested participants. He keeps characters distinct, giving vocal characteristics to each of his imagined persons. One may have a high voice, for example, one a lower, one a quick speech, another a slow one, one a pompous expression, another a choppy light tone, according to the characteristics of things or persons. He can also by the very pivotal action of the body give life to his characters.

Expression, then, supplies language with what it cannot express itself. But such action cannot be a turning to one side, and then to the other. It is the same pivotal action one sees in a group talking at a street corner. There is a range of actions for each person. The speaker turns to his imaginary group as he feels the person he represents would turn. He pivots toward a character he addresses as he would in life. He places buildings, deserts, lakes, objects in general so that the audience may visualize the background of a situation. In other words, he completes a picture for his hearers.

A picture has width as well as depth. It has a foreground and a background. If the preacher desires to give pictorial values to his interpretation of some Gospel scene, he arranges his objects in some order. He places the units in his picture where the audience can in its mind's eye see them, and see them in a foreground or a background, and in proper relation to the persons talking. He suggests objects and people not only by positions of his feet or by an arm gesture, but by eye movements. The turn of the head, the direction of the eyes, the pivotal action of the feet — all indicate reactions of a person to some stimuli. Persons are not only located for the audience, but every movement of the speaker indicates the thinking and the feeling of some character.

The expansive gestures of oratory seldom belong to a dramatic reading unless, of course, they are part of the character being interpreted. But even when representative expression is employed, other actions of the body, particularly in the face, should show the experiences the character is undergoing. In most interpretation, motion can be cut to the minimum unless the character is being portrayed as chaotic or out of control. Whatever action is used for a character, it must be used consistently, and it must constantly give the listeners a true relation of speaker to his background; a fine sense of the mood which is an outgrowth of a situation; and a place, otherwise, the audience may see people talking, yet have a vague notion of the place, mood, and situation. Dramatic interpretation must give a complete dynamic picture before it can be a means to incite an audience to accept the author's purpose.

CHAPTER XVII

MICROPHONE TECHNIQUE

As many churches today are equipped with public-address systems, the preacher will benefit by knowing how to use the different types of microphones in service. He should understand too, something of radio speech since he may at any time be called upon to broadcast.

1. *Microphone Positions*

Voice varies over a loud-speaker system according to the position taken by the speaker, the amount of volume used, and the acoustical properties of the place in which the voice is being heard.

If the speaker comes too close to some types of microphones, some of his consonants will appear to be frayed, and the fricatives in particular may become excessively noisy. If he moves too far out of the sensitive zone, his voice will fade out of the loud-speakers. If he stands too far away from the microphone, the volume must be amplified to make his voice heard, and the increased amplification may then give his voice certain qualities not generally associated with it. If he allows his voice to hit the top of some microphones, he may secure only a series of blasts. In other words, the speaker must first know the peculiarities of the microphone; then he must find out whether his best voice is secured by speaking very close to it in a confidential conversational tone, or whether it is gained by speaking more loudly from a position a foot and half or so away from the instrument presumably to persons some ten feet away.

Amplification. The amount of volume that should be set by the amplifying system is determined not only by the size of a church but by the quality of sound. A preacher's best voice is secured by speaking in an above-average conversational tone, with an average amplification of the instrument, from a position about twenty inches from the microphone but well within its sensitivity area. Volume is important to right reception of sound. If the speaker talks without sufficient force, the amplification must be raised. If he talks too loudly, the volume must be lowered. If he speaks with sudden stress, the peak in energy at the microphone may produce a blasting sound. If a microphone is overloaded with vibrations, discords will result. If a speaker realizes that over the public-address system or radio the properties of his voice are magnified, he will sense that his bad qualities as well as his good ones will be emphasized. He simply must experiment to find the position for his best voice.

Voice Factors. The microphone favors certain pitches, and each person must discover his best pitch and volume level. This level of pitch cannot be radically changed or the level of volume greatly upset. If the volume or pitch must be modified, the speaker should move back and forth in relation to the microphone to obtain the right levels, otherwise the modulations must be controlled by mechanical means, generally with the impairment of tone qualities. If a speaker under the influence of emotion weaves in and out of the area of great sensitivity, his voice will change according to position, presuming, of course, that the amplification has been set at a determinate level.

Maintaining Correct Levels. The preacher should maintain approximately the same distance from the microphone throughout his talk, except in climactic utterance when he should move away from the instrument. However, the preacher using a modern, first-class instrument is allowed much leeway in the distance he stands from the microphone. As an interpreter, he takes a position consistent with the voices of his characters and their situations. To be heard with a consistent volume, a speaker must talk directly into a microphone or at an appropriate angle across its face. The volume control must be set for the speaker and for the acoustical nature of the church. Many persons instinctively raise their voices when speaking over a telephone or a microphone, forgetting that volume can be mechanically controlled.

The psychological factor behind this conduct is a lack of confidence in the instrument.

2. *Reading From Manuscript*

Skill. Reading from manuscript creates many psychological obstacles for speakers as we have seen in the section devoted to reading:

In the first place, the right presentation of the manuscript for reading is a necessity. The copy should be double-spaced on paper that will not crackle when handled. Before a microphone, the rattling of the paper suggests the noise of a fire. All pages should be numbered, but not clipped together. No page should have the last line end in an isolated syllable. The normal reading time of each page might be recorded in its margin. This procedure is helpful when the speaker must keep within certain limits as, for instance, in radio speech.

Secondly, during the reading itself, the speaker must keep his spontaneity, and indicate this by a variety of vocal modulations. His physical action is particularly important to the preacher speaking over the radio or public-address system. There is, as we have previously seen, a close correlation between bodily tensions and mental actions. Right mental attitudes toward the audience will be shown in the voice. Good eye habits in reading from a manuscript will likewise be manifested in the voice of the speakers. The copy, whether in a book or on typewritten sheets, must be held so that the arm positions do not cramp the throat muscles.

Rate of Reading. The rate of reading is greatly affected by emotional attitudes. In general a speed of from 120 to 140 words a minute is satisfactory for longer speeches. A fast rate, accompanied by certain symptoms of nervousness, makes meaning difficult to get. It usually creates faults of enunciation, such as slurring and jumbling of sound. The chief consideration of rate, however, should be its relation to the importance of the subject matter of the smaller units of the composition — the sentence and the paragraph. There will then be a certain variety of rate, yet a consistent one for the speech considered as a whole.

3. Faults

Faults of Speech Affect Radio Delivery. Barriers to good speech are created by wrong habits of delivery. Over a public-address system, poor phrasing, faulty stress, improper pauses, and wrong use of vocal modulations are generally emphasized. Excessive stress upon enunciation will bring about a puffing sound for the overemphasized plosives, and a whistling effect for the overfrictionized sibilants.

The preacher should realize the value of vocal modulations (Chapter XIII). He must stress the vowel of a word only as to its importance and natural rhythm required. Right touch on a vowel is most important to radio speech. Tone color is a consequence of interpreting a state of mind or feeling. Unless mood is expressed, the microphone voice will appear to be even colder than when the voice is not amplified. Inflections in particular should be used correctly over any amplifying system. The mechanical sliding up and down of the voice, irrespective of right thinking and feeling, is annoying to an audience. A little experimentation will show how greatly the faults of vocal expression are magnified by mechanical amplification.

Faults of Articulation. Ordinarily, since a speaker does not need to strain himself to be heard, a microphone should help him with his enunciation. Nevertheless, tensions from the circumstances of talking over a microphone, and from a desire to articulate well, may create difficulties of enunciation. The best articulation, we have seen, comes from good vocal condition, a skill in formulating vowels and consonants, and a co-ordination of movements to assure meaningful symbols.

Faults of Breathing. A most notable fault in a radio talk is the constant interruption of the speech by a wheezing noise made by the speaker in his attempt to get breath. The preacher should not breathe directly into the microphone. He should avoid neck tensions arising from cramped positions of his body. He must learn to phrase well and, in particular, learn how to initiate tone correctly. When a speaker inhales through a tense oral channel, the friction caused by the air striking the tensed surfaces creates a sound. This tensity in the texture of the body can be diminished when he learns how to stand in poise, and how to maintain parts of the body relaxed when other parts must be brought into use. It is also a fatal mistake to exhaust the breath or to secure an inhalation any place in a speech. This sound of breathing will be greatly accentuated in either circumstance.

Mannerisms Create Bad Vocal Conditions. Not only are faults of breathing created by the lack of good posture, but they and mannerisms affect breath control as well as vocal modulations. Speaking from a cramped position before the microphone, bending over the rail of the pulpit, leaning first on one elbow and then on the other, and twisting the head into different positions — all establish improper vocal conditions. What has been said in previous chapters about the conditions of good voice and speech and correct methods of reading can be applied also to radio presentation.

4. *Recording Devices*

In an earlier chapter we have seen that the norm of a good voice took into consideration vocal qualities that were agreeable to people of good taste. As no one hears his own voice as others hear it, a difficulty arises for anyone to gain a good idea of what people like or dislike about it. Today the high-fidelity recording devices can help anyone secure a fine appreciation of the properties of his voice — force, pitch, and quality.

In addition to those instruments used to preserve dictation are types of equipment used for more accurate recording of the voice. We have observed before that many preachers use dictating machines in connection with the preparation of their sermons. Many also make it a habit of recording their discourses for the study of their delivery on equipment especially designed for accurate sound reproduction. This type of recording is a process of impressing or cutting in sound on wire, film, tape, aluminum or acetate disks or on wax devices. If the recordings are upon a sound track and used in connection with motion pictures, the speaker can see his posture, facial actions, and vocal preparation as well as hear his speech and voice. If his utterance is recorded on tape or wire coil the sounds can be played many times for study, and then the mechanism can be demagnetized thereby erasing the sounds and leaving the equipment free for other recordings. Most of the recordings, however, are upon metal or specially prepared composition disks.

A recording system is composed of a microphone, an amplifier, a turntable, a cutting head, a playback arm, and a loudspeaker. For good results, an effective microphone must be used. It must convert the many nuances and variations of the voice into electrical vibrations, and do this work with great fidelity. The amplifying system must work without introducing vibrations other than those from the microphone. These sounds must be increased to the extent of producing action on the cutting needle. The turntable must have a reliable and constant drive, otherwise distortion of sound will take place. The cutting needles, made of several different kinds of material, must be capable of cutting a record without excessive scratching. The cutting head itself which transforms electrical energy into mechanical energy must be capable of recording the lowest sounds of the voice and its highest sounds. In short, a recording machine must have the capacity to record the voice with fidelity. If cheap equipment is used, generally some part or parts cannot perform completely or effectively, for example, they cannot accurately record the total range of the speaker without distortion of some vocal property.

What to Hear in a Recording. When listening to a record, a person can seldom focus his attention on more than a few things. Hence it is well to confine the interest and attention in a playing to one subject. He may, for instance, play a record and listen to his transitions of thought, or replay it and observe the emotional values of his material. Likewise he may at another playback center his attention on his use of one property of sound, perhaps inflections. Another recording may concern itself with his capacity for good enunciation or for correct pronunciation. The speaker may at another time find interest in observing his breathing techniques. After all, if a good recording machine is being used, the bad qualities of voice and the errors of speech belong to the speaker and not the record. He should be interested in making a specific analysis of his speech and voice so that he can correct his faults or modify his delivery to meet the needs of radio speech. Much that has been written in this textbook on voice and vocal modulations should be of help in determining standards of vocal efficiency and in giving the student remedial aid for his faults and difficulties.

5. The Acoustic Problem in Churches

As a final consideration for this chapter, a few thoughts are presented regarding acoustics or the science of sound relating to the sum of the qualities that determines the value of a place as to distinct hearing. The sounds generated in a church that reach the listeners come from different places. Some are from the ceiling, some from the choir loft, some from the pews, some from the pulpit, and some, of course, from the preacher. When sounds from various places are reflected for a few seconds after their initiation, the product, a total fusion, reaching the ear of the hearers is bad; consequently a microphone should be placed where the reverberation rate is correct, not so low as to indicate a "dead" room nor so high as to be "live." About 1 to 1.5 seconds, as a general rule is a satisfactory period of reverberation.

If this condition cannot be met, as it cannot in many churches without acoustical treatment of their walls, the speaker is forced to experiment with his speaking rate and the amplification of his voice before he can secure good speech results. Moreover, the sounds in an empty church are not those when the church is partially filled. And neither are the acoustical conditions of a partially filled church those of a filled church. The speaker must come to know the peculiarity of the place of broadcast unless he is certain that it has been acoustically treated in relation to the position of the microphone.

APPENDIX

Exercises for the Appreciation of Posture[1]

1. Experiment with proper position for poise while sitting. Head erect. Place feet squarely on floor. Do not tense leg muscles. Arms relaxed in the lap. Chest easily expanded. Do not hollow the back. Move easily forward or backward, or sidewise until a position of erectness is discovered and can easily be retained. The correct position is maintained with the slightest effort.

2. Stand easily erect, not overtensed or limp, chin neither thrust forward or clutched backward. Heels together. Hands by the side. Weight well over the balls of the feet. Center attention on breastbone. Imagine an upward pull starting from this point. Do not hollow the back. Rise slowly on toes. Lift arms at same time to a lateral horizontal position. You can imagine a sensation of lightness which one senses when up to the armpits in water. Return to former position.

Do not upset the control of body by a backward movement of hips or by keeping the body weight back on the heels. The hips may be slightly drawn back when the body is erect, but if weight is shifted to the heels, the knees will be in a strained position. Sense the oneness or unity of the body, and its elevation.

When one can feel his chest easily held up by muscular action which does not interfere with the rhythm of breathing, he will have a live center around which he can imagine the parts — arms, legs, head are free to move. If the muscular tension in the chest collapses with each exhalation, and if the chest in inhalation is lifted upward and forward with the shoulders raising with it as in collarbone breathing, good posture is unlikely.

---

[1] Many of the exercises which are in this text for poise, visible speech, breath control, and voice were originally demonstrated to the author by teachers of the Curry School of Expression, Boston, particularly by Anna B. Curry or Edward Abner Thompson. Some are based on Delsarte and Ling. The author's textbook, *Voice and Delivery* (St. Louis: Herder, 1941), contains a number of exercises for physical expression and vocal development. This book also has an extensive bibliography of texts on gesture.

If the body is in good posture, the ear, shoulder, hip, and ankle joint, as viewed from the side, make a vertical line. The shoulders are back and down. The knees should be held straight, but not in a stiff position. The straight line of posture should not be broken by bending at the knees or by slumping at the hips.

The student can check his control of posture by bending his knees, lowering his body slowly until the thighs touch the heels. The shoulders are back, the head is erect, and the chin correctly held in. He keeps the line of erectness, coming back to normal position. Then he may rise and lower on the toes, keeping erectness without putting the weight on the heels.

3. Position of body as in Exercise 2. Place weight over one foot. Viewed from the side which is carrying the weight, the body keeps its same vertical line as in Exercise 2. Let the free foot swing forward, toe to floor, then to the back, then to original position. Place weight over other foot. Repeat exercise. Position. Place weight now on right foot. Viewed from the side which is carrying the weight, the body keeps its vertical line. Place this free foot to the left without disturbing the straight line of the body. Move the body toward free foot. (If you were looking in a mirror, your waistline would move parallel to the lower line of the frame.) Let weight come over left foot. The left hip falls into position. Place free foot forward. Weight brought over it — slowly. Free foot to the side. Weight over it. Free foot to the back. Transfer the weight. Observe in posture that the hips are directly over the balls of the feet. Sense the location of the hinges of the body; note that the arms, legs, and head can be moved about without upsetting the basic posture.

Three tendencies which prevent the gaining of good posture are (1) the hollowing of the back; (2) the drawing in of the stomach, which action creates an exaggerated high frontal position of the chest; (3) constriction and tenseness of the muscles of the neck and shoulders. The student should feel an all-round muscular expansion of the chest as opposed to a strong frontal elevation.

In poise, the weight can be transferred from one foot to the other without much effort. When the preacher can freely change positions, stepping forward, backward, and sidewise, he will find a chief cause for awkwardness eliminated. If he fastens his feet to the floor, the most natural movements of the body, even of the arms, are restricted.

Relaxing Exercises

4. Stand erect, then let the head sink on the chest. Feel neck relax; give up tension in muscles of the face, particularly around the mouth. Mentally consider each restraining action gradually being eliminated. Let the shoulders droop. Let the arms hang heavily at sides, the hands hanging downward become limp — more limp. Slowly fold the spine from the top downward. Feel a sense of curling up. As you bend forward, let the head lead. Do not bend the knees or strain the leg muscles.

When starting upward, unfold the body. The movement begins at the hips — let the head follow. Gradually bring the arms and shoulders into the normal position. Let the head be the last to come back to position. Feel it easily resting on the neck muscles without creating in them excessive tension.

Avoid in this exercise going down in the folding movement while attempting to hold the back stiff. Imagine each segment of the back is free to enter into the folding movement. On the way back (unfolding) do not cramp the neck or tighten the shoulders.

5. Practice now, after relaxing, a tensing exercise for a study in contrasts. Drop head forward, interlace fingers at the back of the head, elbows parallel in front. Push the head back, but resist the movement by pulling forward with the hands. Observe the muscles involved in this action.

6. Stand erect. Drop jaw to chest, relax it, also facial muscles. Let tongue feel heavy in the mouth. Release as much as possible all muscular tension in the back of the neck. Slowly lift the head to normal position. Let the jaw remain relaxed (the mouth should be opened by the relaxing process to about an inch). Let the head go back as far as possible, then bring it forward to normal erect position.

7. When jaw has been brought to the chest and neck feels relaxed, slowly roll the head around describing a circle. Keep the face forward. Feel the pivotal point at base of the neck. Keep the shoulders relaxed, arms hanging loosely to the side, fingers relaxed.

8. Position of poise. Lift arms straight to front, palms down. Let arms fall. Let them swing freely as if someone was actually pushing them. Place arms in different position. Let them fall lifelessly; relax fingers. Extend the arms to a lateral horizontal position; relax fingers, then forearms bending at the elbow, then upper arms.

9. With arms at the side, forearms lifted at right angles, palms down, shake the forearms. Feel the hands move freely at the wrist joints.

10. Grasp the left hand with the right. Thumb of the right hand is in palm of the left. Fingers of the right hand on the back of the left. Shake the left hand. Give up the tension in the fingers and the thumb.

11. Position of poise. Near edge of a platform. Let one foot hang over the edge. Feel the foot becoming a dead weight. Bring it forward; let it fall; let it swing as if with its own momentum.

As a test of relaxation, lie flat on the floor. Give up feeling of life in your face, feel the muscles about the eyes relax, give up the tightness around the lips, the neck. Feel each section of the backbone becoming heavier and heavier as each part sinks to the floor. Give up all tension in the back. Relax the thigh muscles, the tension in the legs. Observe the easy steady rhythm of breathing. Sense the way you feel when the body is relaxed.

Preparation for Gesture

12. Position of poise, then stand with weight on left foot, right foot to the side, free and relaxed. Place right arm across body, fingers to the left shoulder, then fling arm forward, and to the side. Reverse position. Exercise.

13. Group the four fingers of the hand about the thumb. Make a cup out of the palm. Now slowly unfold the fingers. Feel the energy spread out from the center of the palm. Keep all fingers moving steadily in opposition to the thumb, at about equal distances, until hand is expanded. Do not place the thumb back in a plane with the palm. From this expanded position, slowly close the hand until fingers group about the thumb. Avoid stiffening of fingers or tensing of the wrist.

14. Position of poise. Then weight to right foot. Stretch right arm forward and describe a figure eight. Feel movement start from shoulder. Feel the sway of the body in relation to movement of the arm. Do not exaggerate the movement. Repeat with left arm, then with both arms.

15. Position of poise. Then weight on left foot. Place right foot forward. Relax it. Focus eyes on point to the right. Turn head right. Place right foot slightly behind the left. Place weight upon it. Relax, but not left leg. Eyes, head, body, feet, all face original point on which the eye was focused.

16. Weight on right foot back, turn eyes to the right. Choose a point on which eyes may be focused, then head. Turn the left heel out, pivot on the ball of the foot. Transfer the weight to the left foot. Adjust right foot.

17. Weight on left foot back, then eyes to right, then head, step forward with right foot.

18. Weight on right foot forward, look left, turn head, step forward to left.

19. Palm up. Arms stretched. Eyes closed. Feel energy withdrawing from fingers. Fold fingers into palm. Arms down.

20. Palms in. Arms down. Relax fingers. Arms up to front. Wrist stiff. Energize, then relax fingers. Count 1-2. Count 2 is slow. Relax fingers on Count 2.

21. Raise shoulders. Let them drop because of their weight. Relax head. Front. Position. Relax to the side position. Relax to the back. Feel the weight of head as cause of the relaxing movement.

22. For a contrast exercise, raise shoulders. Roll them strongly far back and down. Keep elbow straight. Let the hands feel heavy as if carrying a weight. Up, Count 1, back and down, Count 2.

23. Sway hips in a circular manner forward, to the side, to the back, to the side, to the front. Hold each position momentarily, then relax, and sense movement of muscles used in rotating the hips.

Exercises for Centering the Breath and for Breath Control

24. Review Exercise 4.

25. Lie on your back flat on the floor. Breathe normally. Feel your body relax. One hand is placed well up on the chest. Place the other hand lightly just below the breastbone. Study your breathing. Regular? Shallow? Fast or slow? Observe now the easy, steady rhythm of centralized breathing. Do not attempt to suck in air in a forceful manner by tightening the belt muscles. Feel the ease in the breathing, in the coming in and going out of breath. Notice the slight rise and fall of the ribs and the outward movement of the upper part of the abdomen. Avoid placing your hand over the low abdomen as the breathing process will tend to be localized there.

26. Inhale a little more breath, then retain it momentarily; now exhale easily. Do not try to lift up the chest with each breath.

Collarbone breathing is labored breathing. Let the lungs be filled, and do not force a strong chest action. There will be a slight expansion of the upper chest on each inhalation. On the inhalation of breath the floating ribs which are tied in back to the spine, and in front to muscles, are pressed forward, upward, and outward, i.e., a lateral, anterior, and posterior expansion aided by the downward pull of the diaphragm.

The lower part of your lungs filling with air gives you a greater all-round distension. In other words, the air has entered the lungs to fill up the partial vacuum created by the chest expansion, and to equalize the pressure within with that from without. Now exhale: the muscles below the breastbone move backward, the ribs drop in relaxation, the diaphragm ascends. This muscle is not the leading muscle in breath control; the abdominal or belt muscles give chief support. The size of the chest cavity is decreased when you exhale.

Avoid flattening out or drawing in the upper abdomen when you inhale. If, before inhalation, you have your chest easily expanded by muscles, and then maintain this normal position of good posture and poise, there will be a natural flattening out of the muscles below the breastbone before inhalation, and slight expansion after the downward movement of the diaphragm.

It is a bad habit to contract the abdominal muscles in inspiration and raise the chest, thereby forcing the abdominal organs upward against the diaphragm. The muscles then cannot help to enlarge the lower area of the chest cavity.

Try in a standing position to develop the same ease of breathing you discovered while lying on the floor.

27. Position of Exercise 25. Breathe slowly; exhale; inhale slowly and deeper; retain. Observe in retention a feeling of slight resistance under lower hand. Observe chest remains practically firm. Keep neck relaxed. In inhalation do not push out the muscles below breastbone. Feel rather the expansion to be gradual. In exhalation, do not let the area below breastbone collapse. Feel muscles gradually relax.

28. Procedure as in Exercise 27. Count mentally. Inhale five counts. Hold breath for three counts. Release breath during five counts. Increase count from day to day, but never to point of discomfort.

29. An Important Exercise. Position of Exercise 25. After a few breaths, place arms in relaxed position at the sides of the torso. Yawn. Feel the openness of this action as if beginning inside the throat, and working downward and outward. Do not force open the mouth, and fix the jaw in its downward position. A yawn does not overtense the muscles attached to it. Get a lazy feeling, and really yawn. You will

soon observe the difference between a relaxed jaw, and a fixed tense one. After a yawn, exhale. Inhale a full breath. Feel expansion in the middle of the body — through and through. Exhale slowly — very slowly, making a sound between a hiss and a whistle. Remember — make little noise, and give up little breath. Keep the escape of the breath stream regular. Avoid a "jumpy" kind of action. No collapse of the chest.

30. Repeat Exercise 29, but use vowel *ah* instead of whistle. After phonation, give up some breath before new inhalation for tone.

31. Stand. Repeat Exercises 29 and 30. Follow direction for inhalation, exhalation, whistling, and singing of *ah*.

Expansion of Chest in Relation to Breathing

32. Position of Exercise 25. After a few breaths, withdraw the one hand from across the body just below the breastbone and place it under the body at the small of the back. Feel you are separating the hands by muscular expansion of the chest, but do not interfere with the rhythm of breathing. Do not hold the breath during the act of expanding. The chest adjustment is a muscular action; the breathing is a free act if the chest is muscularly expanded.

33. Adjust chest. Repeat Exercises 25, 26, 27, and 28.

Preparatory Exercise for Phonation

34. The following exercise may be used to secure co-ordination of the activities of different sets of muscles involved in the initiation of tone.

a) Entertain a desire to call to someone at a distance. Act as if you were calling. Observe while directing your main attention to your act of calling that the jaw relaxes, the tone passage opens simultaneously with the contraction of the muscles in inhalation. Relaxation takes place in getting "the open throat," while contraction is the process in getting the diaphragm to push downward. *Imagine* your person has gone farther away. Imagine you are about to call. Prepare! Did the throat open as a result of the stimulation to call? Do not just open the mouth. Openness comes from relaxation, and from the involuntary response of muscles to the desire to call. Repeat exercise until the co-ordination is understood and finally is established. Do not give utterance to any sound.

b) Imagine someone has suddenly startled you. Take a quick, almost spasmodic, inhalation as if you were about to give some exclamation.

Do not speak, but do observe conditions of response. Repeat exercise, and after inhalation, give different exclamation as a response to feeling.

Exercises for Initiation of Tone

35. Stand easily erect. Relax jaw and facial muscles. Mouth relaxed and slightly opened. Keep neck muscles from overtensing. Place weight well forward on one foot. Keep chest well expanded by muscular action. Inhale easily a full breath while allowing the jaw to drop and the throat muscles to relax. Have a desire to call someone, and immediately and quickly sing *lah;* then speak the same sound before the breath is expended, to someone across the room from you.

Repeat the exercise. Be sure the condition of relaxed jaw, open tone passage, and breath supply is present. If you feel tension, relax the jaw as you say *fah.* Keep it relaxed. Now say *lah* with no tense jaw action. Make the tongue action as independent as possible from a mass action of jaw and tongue. Keep jaw relaxed. Repeat sounds like *la-yo-la,* etc.

36. Stand erect, but not overtensed; roll your head to the front, to the side, to the back, to the side, then to the front. Yawn. Relax your jaw and throat muscles. Maintain a hum for a short time. Keep the mind away from the actions of throat. Feel tone coming from a free and relaxed condition of the body. Do not force the hum into the nose. Keep the tone floating, shift suddenly to the sound *lah,* sustaining it for a few notes, then returning to the hum. Was the *lah* sound pleasing?

Repeat this exercise using different pitches; note the action of the soft palate; alternate going from the hum to the oral vowel, and the open vowel to the hum. Try different vowels after humming. Sing *ahrum-ahrah-alah, ahrum,* etc. Dr. Curry used the *lah-lay-lee-lie-low-loo* combination. Lamperti suggests the best exercise for phonation as five short starts, and then the prolongation of the next sound.

Experiment with different placements; note the tone color. Imagine what a good tone sounds like. Sing from high to low pitch. On the high notes feel a descent to the tone, rather than a sense of reaching for it. Vocalize *oo,* shift to *ng,* return to *oo,* then finish the scale with the hum.

If you are overtensed, your voice may be weak, mainly because the breath stream is lacking; but a weak high-pitched voice may be a sign of a glottis too tightly closed for normal operation. If this condition is present when a strong breath stream is directed against the vocal lips, the resistance of the too tightly closed glottis is overcome, but the tone is harsh and tense, particularly when it is directed against the hard surfaces of the oral and nasal cavities.

37. Repeat Exercise 35. Check following points of procedure: take a new breath for each *ah* you make; release the surplus breath after each tone. You can mentally follow these directions:

Prepare — Observe conditions: jaw relaxed, mouth easily opening, tongue relaxed, throat relaxed, neck not overtensed, then *inhale*. Feel fullness of breath in middle of body. Feel chest is easily expanded by muscular action not particularly by action of breath.

Speak — Use various vowels; employ new breath for each tone. Finally use several tones on one pitch and one breath: *au-au,* etc., *ah-ah,* etc.

Let go — After tone or tones are completed, quickly emit the surplus breath.

Support of Tone

38. Sustain *lah* or *law*. Stop when breath control is lost, or tone color becomes poor. Observe the contrast in action of the jaw in eating and yawning. The eating action closes the tone passage. Sing *lah* on the various pitches of the tonal range. Keep quality while increasing intensity and duration. It will be observed a breathy tone tends to become less breathy as force is applied to a tone. The fact is that there is more tension at the vocal folds. There must be activity to bring the vocal fold together.

39. Establish good conditions for tone. Count on a sustained pitch, and use a single breath for each group of sounds. Prepare; speak *one;* let go. Prepare; speak *one-two;* let go, etc. Be sure you have conditions for preparation. Let the breath go after each group of numbers.

40. Same as Exercise 39 except for the count. Substitute for it the following: prepare; speak any phrase of two or three words; let go; prepare; speak a phrase of four or five words; let go, etc. Stress the vowel of each word. For ear training change pitch with each word. Carefully enunciate each word, and do not speak with a rapid rate.

Sense of Placement

41. Combine each of the vowels in the following words: *me, high, day, put, father, no, food,* and *awl* with a consonantal sound, for example, *see, tie*. Vocalize each combination up and down the scale. Use also each combination successively in a series of scales. Employing different duration, vocalize a combination such as *be - pe - me - be - me* on each note of the scale. Use correlative combinations like *te-de-ne* on each note of the scale and various time combinations, such as four beats to a measure, six beats, and so forth. Change the rate at will. Sing the vowel *ah* to develop an open throat and a free tone. Practice with the vowel in the word *me* for tone placement. Return to the vowel *ah* if the tone becomes sharp or nasal. Practice the vowel in *no* and *food* for flute quality. Avoid a forced placement and an exaggerated tension in the ribs. Remember mental attitudes affect tone; a hardness of tone may come from mental tension. If disagreeable qualities result, check fundamental conditions, and compare the singing quality with the tone color of the speaking voice used in reading lyrics.

42. Contrast the action of the soft palate in the following sentences: *Much knowing makes ninety-nine men more mirthless. The bark of the dog awoke the cook.* The sounds *m, n,* and *ng* should go through the nose. Other sounds go through the mouth. Speak this line: *You have hope.* Close off the nose; repeat the line. If there is much difference in tone when the nose is closed, it is evident that the sounds which should be coming through the mouth are, through faulty palatal action, going into the nose. Sustain a tone, now increase it, then diminish it, holding the final sound. Note the change in quality as partials are removed, modified, or added in different vowels. Vocalize on each of the English vowels; use the same emission of tone.

43. Give a number of exclamations, commands, or statements that will elicit total bodily responses. *Eh? My, My. What are you doing? Get out of here. Wait for me.* Direct your voice, step by step, to the rear of the hall. You must prepare for preaching which calls for transitions and variations and demands good voice.

Vocalize a word or a phrase; do not get a breathy tone; vocalization is a gentle process so let your tone float. The retention of breath should leave no sense of discomfort. If, however, you notice a constriction of throat muscles as you increase the volume of the tone, it is probable that you are expending too much effort in jaw action.

Remember one of the chief causes of bad tone color is the active use of muscles related to chewing and swallowing. They should be passive when the throat is open in inhalation. Work for total bodily response to situation. The total muscular activity is a response. Effective vocal modulation comes from the modulating system only as a consequence of this system itself being stimulated.

Sustain *ah* or *la* on the fullness of breath, then test volume and placement by singing abruptly a number of interjections.

The tongue must form the correct oral cavity without forcing the jaw to act with it in a mass movement. The test of free vocal action is the physical sense of freedom in the production of the vowel and the lack of strain in the muscles having their origin in the chin, hinge of the jaw, the palatine arch, and those muscles ending in the hyoid bone that influence laryngeal action. Focus attention in practicing voice production on proper breathing and initiation of tone. When speaking, manifest mental and emotional life by pitch, intensity, and quality.

44. In your vocal effort have a right conception of projection. The direction of the vocal current is from within out, but the speaker should visualize his muscular resistance to exhalation and tone as flowing from outside in. In other words, sustain and retain the tone; sense it as being imbued with your personality before you project it to your auditors. The tone should be frontal, but do not think of it as being forced out of you. Do not think of a tone as hitting a bull's-eye. Think of a tone as having width to cover a group of persons. Practice singing with open and clear color placed well forward on the hard palate. Get brightness and clearness, but not hardness or harshness.

INDEX

Abelly, on memory, 238; on style, 105
Acoustics, 269
Action, audience view of, 156; nature of, 155; necessity of, 155; qualities of, 157; in sacred oratory, 155 ff; in speaking, aim, 4; training for, 167
Aims, general, 3 f; in preaching, 3 f; specific, 5
Alphonsus Liguori, St., *Exercises of the Missions*, 133; on persuasion, 85; on self-interest in preaching, 106
Amplification, in argumentation, 65; by loud-speaker, 263; need in discussing morality, 66; need in instruction, 56
Ambrose, St., use of topic of doubt, 102
Analysis, use in conviction, 59
Announcements, nature of, 133 f
Apostles, commissioned to preach, x
Argumentation, 57 f
Aristotle, on conclusion, 49; on emotion, 79, 82; on habit, 140; system of divisions, 41
Articulation, art of, 220 f; fault of, 266; nature of, 220
Athanasius, St., authority on the Holy Trinity, 25
Attention, 99
Audience, reaction to proofs, 60
Augustine, St., argument of possibility, 27; authority on grace, 25; on instruction, 54, 56, 123; style in preaching, 110
Authority, use in sacred discourse, 21

Bagehot, Walter, on style, 118
Basil, St., use of material cause, 17
Beecher, Henry W., on impromptu speaking, 247; on persuasion, 216; on speech training, 242
Belief, art of changing, 140 f
Bellefroid, on pause, 212
Benno, Fr., on quotations, 247
Bernard, St., use of Scripture, 238
Body of a speech, 53 f
Bossuet, examples of partition, 35 f; use of comparison, 18
Bourdaloue, art of the eulogy, 148; examples of partition, 35 f; Sermon of All Saints, 34; use of repetition, 103
Breath control, 195 f, 274

Breathing, exercises for, 275; fault of, 266; method of, 195
Brooks, Phillips, on jargon, 217; on style, 117
Brydaine, on announcements, 133; on conference, 130

Canonists, value as authority, 25
Catechism, according to Council of Trent, 24; art of teaching, 122; basis of, 56; benefits, 124; importance of, 121; importance of example, 123 f; suggested method of teaching, 124 f
Cause, use as topic, 17
Change of pitch, 203
Chest, *see* Posture
Choate, Rufus, on extempore speaking, 245
Christ, double mission, ix; nature of His preaching, x; use of examples, 27
Church, the, source of authority, 24
Cicero, on amplification, 66; on conclusion, 49; on emotion, 82; on harmony, 108; on introductions, 41; on motivation, 89; on pantomime, 179; system of divisions, 41; use of repetition, 102
Circumstance, an influence on proof, 61; use as a topic, 20
Coherence, 215; in outline, 31; value in style, 107
Collection of material, 12 f
Comparison, 18 f
Conclusion, Aristotle's views of, 49; Cicero's views of, 49; emotional appeal in, 50; faults of, 51; form of, 49 f; matter in, 49; types of, 49 f
Conference, a form of discourse, 132; method of instruction, 130; parts of, 130
Consonants, explanation of, 224
Contrast, use as a topic, 19
Controversy, errors in, 137; need of, 135; place of exposition, 135; place of persuasion, 140; proper method required, 136; views of authority, 138 f
Conversation, as aid to invention, 12
Conviction, aim in, 4; explanation of, 57; methods in, 58 f; order in, 59 f; relation to persuasion, 58
Correspondence, as aid to invention, 13
Council of Baltimore, on brief sermons, 166; on miracles, 149